Elizabeth Gaskell, Victorian Culture, and the Art of Fiction

Original Essays for the Bicentenary

D1566223

Elizabeth Gaskell, Victorian Culture, and the Art of Fiction

Original Essays for the Bicentenary

Sandro Jung
(Ed.)

ACADEMIA PRESS

© Academia Press
Eekhout 2
9000 Gent
T. (+32) (0)9 233 80 88   F. (+32) (0)9 233 14 09
info@academiapress.be   www.academiapress.be

The publications of Academia Press are distributed by:

Belgium:
J. Story-Scientia nv Wetenschappelijke Boekhandel
Sint-Kwintensberg 87
B-9000 Gent
T. 09 255 57 57   F. 09 233 14 09
info@story.be   www.story.be

The Netherlands:
Ef & Ef
Eind 36
NL-6017 BH Thorn
T. 0475 561501   F. 0475 561660

Rest of the world:
UPNE, Lebanon, New Hampshire, USA (www.upne.com)

Sandro Jung (ed.)
Elizabeth Gaskell, Victorian Culture, and the Art of Fiction – Original Essays for the Bicentenary

Gent, Academia Press, 2010, v + 217 pp.

ISBN 978 90 382 1629 4
D/2010/4804/108
U1438

Layout: proxess.be

Cover: Nevelland.
"A Portrait of Elizabeth Gaskell" (accession number: M73141). Reproduced by permission of
Manchester Archives and Local Studies, Central Library.

Table of Contents

Preface

In September 2006 a group of international scholars gathered in the Victorian Peel Building at Salford University in Greater Manchester to engage in critical dialogue with the works of Elizabeth Gaskell. The setting was fitting, especially as Gaskell spent a large part of her writing life in Manchester, the city whose cultural hybridity and discursive plurality, even in the early Victorian period, inspired and shaped her astute observational and creative powers. Nowadays, significant collections of Gaskelliana are held in special collections at the John Rylands Library, Manchester Central Library, and the Portico Library, and scholars wishing to study the genesis of some of her texts can consult autograph material alongside an extensive range of secondary print sources at these libraries. Equally, important loci associated with Gaskell, 84 Plymouth Grove, her home in Manchester, and Cross Street Chapel, where her husband, William, was the Unitarian minister, can be visited today.

The present collection of scholarly essays on Gaskell's writing was conceived as a contribution to the commemoration, in 2010, of the bicentenary of Gaskell's birth; while some of the essays derived directly, albeit in shorter form, from the proceedings at the conference, others were solicited during the long gestation process of this composite contribution to Gaskell studies. The enthusiastic participation of both national and international scholars in a critical exploration of Gaskell's oeuvre conduced to the success of the event. It is hoped that the expansion of the papers presented and the inclusion of further essays will make this publication an equally successful scholarly endeavour. This assemblage of essays on the contexts, discourses, and cultural milieu of Gaskell and her writings, as well as investigations of the authorial uses of the various "mes" that she fashions throughout her career, takes stock of earlier important scholarship; while consolidating established routes of access, the essays also indicate areas such as the constructions of authorial personae in her letters and the *Life of Charlotte Brontë* that reveal her as a more ambivalent figure. She is eager to negotiate her relationship with Brontë to her advantage, and her performative self-fashioning goes beyond the roles of the benevolent and socially aware writer, mother, and wife – in short, what earlier twentieth-century critics have captured in the unsatisfactory title of "Mrs. Gaskell." Other areas of reassessment include Gaskell's often underrated work for journals, her short stories and tales, while yet others include the revisiting of oft-explored issues such as gender-specific constructions in the Victorian period. Medical discourses are discussed alongside discourses of moral and gendered notions of deviance and representations of female liminality in the form of the coquette. Some of the studies interrogate philosophical questions, especially in *Sylvia's Lovers*, which aim to complement earlier readings and conduce to holistic appreciations of Gaskell's *Weltanschauunng*, while another offers a comparative perspective on the complicated notion of literacy in Gaskell and Dickens. Context-driven research is complemented by textual criticism. In that regard, micro-textual analysis reveals the craft of the author's "fiction" – a term interpreted to comprise all of Gaskell's writings, including her letters, for, as a number of contributions demonstrate, Gaskell constructs even her "private" epistolary voice in ways that invoke her professional strategies of self-fashioning. Yet other essays address questions of masculinity, especially Gaskell's conceptualisation of the Victorian gentleman, her constructions and functionalisation of humour and femininity in *Cranford*, emotional commitment and deceit, class (and Gaskell's personal negotiations of relationships with figures from a different class than her own), or the Wordsworthian presence in the author's early writings. The volume concludes its critical interventions with an insightful Darwinist contextualisation of *Wives and Daughters*. All contributions effectively respond to some of the discursive needs of Gaskell scholarship at the beginning of the twenty-first century that the plenary speaker, Alan Shelston, the President of the Gaskell Society, pointed out in his conference address. The address is the opening piece in this collection and formulates some of the objectives of exploration and critical investigation that the essays following it perform in their assessments of Gaskell's work.

The spirit of collegial exchange that informed the atmosphere at the conference has served the contributors to expand their arguments; the result is a wide-ranging collection that clearly reflects the authors' expertise and the desire to share insights and interrogate formulated positions in Gaskell studies. Ultimately, it is hoped that this critical intervention will encourage further reflection and engagement with Gaskell's works. Three editors of Gaskell's works participated in the conference: Alan Shelston, Joanne Shattock (the general editor of the "standard" modern edition of Gaskell's works published by Pickering and Chatto in 2005-2006), and Angus Easson. The latter, the doyen of Gaskell studies and emeritus professor at Salford University, had kindly agreed to attend the conference and act as a respondent, offering help and guidance to all colleagues, especially in the concluding roundtable discussion. The audience included members of the

Gaskell Society who raised questions, offered comments, and contributed to the lively debate.

The contributions in this volume have made this collection a truly international publication. Essays by scholars from Australia, Belgium, Italy, Turkey, the United Kingdom, and the United States of America stand next to each other and bear testimony to the enduring appeal of Gaskell in all these countries and their academic communities. Without the authors' cooperation this publication would not have been possible, and I am appreciative of their patience while I was seeing the volume through the publishing process. Equally, I gratefully acknowledge the financial support granted by Paul Bellaby, then director of the Institute for Social, Cultural, and Policy Research at Salford University. A personal word of thanks to my former colleagues and students at Salford is in order, too, as it was they who explored with me the literature of the Victorian period and offered new insights. I am especially grateful to Brian Maidment for his support and advice. At Ghent University, I have benefitted from the good cheer of my Victorianist colleague, Marysa Demoor, who encouraged the publication of the volume. Thanks are also due to Pieter Borghart of Academia Press who has been an excellent and enthusiastic editor and who directly expressed his interest in publishing such a fitting tribute to celebrate the art of Elizabeth Gaskell. Lastly, I acknowledge my gratitude to the Manchester City Council – Archives and Local Studies for granting permission to print the image of Gaskell on the cover of this book.

Sandro Jung
Ghent, June 2010

Where next in Gaskell Studies?

Alan Shelston

I shall begin with a little recent history. Had I been introducing this topic in 2000 it would have been a rather easier task.[1] By then Elizabeth Gaskell was fairly well established as a subject for academic study but we were still working in the context of what might be called the first phase of modern Gaskell studies. This takes us back a further forty years, to the 1960s that is, when what Edgar Wright called the "reassessment" of Gaskell began. This saw on the one hand the publication of works like the Chapple and Pollard collection of Gaskell's correspondence, together with Geoffrey Sharps' primarily bibliographical study, and on the other the attention given, in the wake of Raymond Williams's few short pages in *Culture and Society*, to Gaskell's critique of industrial society by critics like, notably, John Lucas.[2] Their readings tended to be confirmed by the editors of the various paperback editions that appeared, and they shifted the ground in Gaskell priorities from provincial to urban preoccupations. The author of *Cranford* was redefined as a novelist of social conscience. Williams's reading of the industrial novels as an expression of exaggerated middle-class anxiety can seem overly simple now (after all the Manchester middle-class, with Peterloo in living memory, had a lot to be anxious about) but it was enormously influential. Furthermore it came at exactly the right moment; for a whole generation of post-war undergraduates – in which I include myself – *Culture and Society* was a seminal work. Gaskell was lined up alongside Dickens and Charlotte Brontë, and admitted to the canonical syllabus. She was no longer the decorous if charming author of a famous minor classic, but a significant contributor to the social conscience literature of the early Victorian period. It is interesting that she took rather longer to establish herself in the United States. When I taught there in the mid-1980s there were no cheap American student editions of her work and it was quite common to find colleagues, let alone students, who knew nothing of her. It was not until my own

1

Norton edition of *North and South* [3] that anything by Gaskell was published in that most influential series of student texts. An issue here I think is the nature of feminist criticism in the '80s – if you look in the index of Sandra Gilbert and Susan Gubar's *Madwoman in the Attic* – then a pioneering work – you will find just five references to Gaskell, all of them to single pages. [4] The "Mrs. Gaskell" tag was the problem of course – if you take Charlotte Brontë as your model, then "Mrs." Gaskell is not going to get much of a look in.

But let me come back to the situation as it was rather less than ten years ago. As I said, the task would have been easier then. Gaskell was well established in the curriculum, and indeed in the academic culture generally. Interest was no longer confined to the industrial novels. Nancy Weyant's up-dated bibliographies of English-language sources of 1991 and 2001 [5] testify to an exponential growth in theses, articles, and full-length studies devoted to her work – and to the full range of her work. In particular, in her 1991 volume, Weyant noticed "more interest in Gaskell's short fiction … comprehensive studies of Gaskell's works by … established, notable Gaskell scholars" and "the emergence of feminist criticism." [6] Here Patsy Stoneman's very subtle feminist reading of 1986, was perhaps the first to make up for previous neglect. [7] Weyant noted too the contribution made by the Gaskell Society, and the possibilities offered by its journal and its newsletter. In her 2001 volume Weyant notes the interest in Gaskell to be found abroad, and above all the contribution made by "her presence on the internet," a presence established by the Japanese scholar Mitsuharu Matsuoka whose work in this respect continues, to the benefit of all of us involved in Gaskell studies.

Things were looking up then by the end of the century – but there still remained a lot to do. Furthermore the priorities were not difficult to identify. There was still not a complete critical edition of Gaskell's work. If you worked on Gaskell then, you still had to struggle with the not entirely reliable Knutsford edition – if you could find one that is – or with the numerous paperback editions that seemed to increase and multiply. [8] There remained a further body of uncollected Gaskell correspondence, which had accumulated since the Pollard and Chapple edition, and which had to be tracked down in libraries, in private collections, and in secondary sources. And while it is true that the range and variety – qualitative and quantitative – of Gaskell's work was becoming increasingly acknowledged, it was still the case that the full complexity of what she offers – in genre terms, but also biographically and culturally – was not being fully considered. Furthermore much of the commentary on Gaskell continued to be of a somewhat self-enclosed kind. Where theoretical perspectives were concerned, Gaskell critics tended to operate like the "sane people" of *Middlemarch*, who "did what their neighbours did, so that if any lunatics were at large, one might know and avoid them." [9] Exceptions to this generalization might be two critical studies by Hilary Schor and Felicia Buonaparte that came out in the early 1990s, but it is fair to say that for the most part the theoretical debates of that time passed Gaskell studies by.[10] And for the most part, while it was true that the old industrial-provincial polarity that has dogged Gaskell criticism was breaking down; especially with reference to the shorter fiction, it tended to be the same short stories that were coming to the fore. Finally it seems to me that little work had been done that really considered Gaskell in all of her dimensions – not just as writer, as working mother, and as social observer, but as someone working within the specific contexts of cultural influence and production.

Until comparatively recently then it would not have been difficult to say what was needed in Gaskell studies. And why I say it is more difficult now is that in the last few years many of our wants have been supplied. The new Pickering and Chatto edition of the complete works, under Joanne Shattock's general editorship, gives us the entire Gaskell canon in ten volumes, with thoroughly edited and collated texts, and extensive annotation.[11] This is the first time this has been done, and not the least of the features of the edition is the way it has achieved a practical sense of order over such a varied range of material. One of the distinctive features of Gaskell's life and her work is its range and variety: this seems to me one of the most important things to keep in mind about her, but it can make editorial work on the scale of a collected edition very difficult. Then, as well as the edition, we have the supplementary collection of correspondence – *Further Letters of Mrs. Gaskell* – which has added quite considerably to our knowledge of her cultural and literary affiliations.[12] The "further" letters were not simply an add-on, they contained major holdings extending our understanding of the multi-faceted life that Gaskell led. Not only do we have whole sequences on Gaskell's relationships with publishers, we have additions to our knowledge of her overseas acquaintance, and from the names of her correspondents alone we can chart her movement into the heart of the period's social and cultural movements. Her acquaintance with Pre-Raphaelitisim, for example, is revealed via letters to Rossetti and to others, and her acquaintance with Oxford dons and clergymen, and with military families drawn into the Crimean war and on the subcontinent, shows her to be heavily involved in the leading issues of her day. Walter E. Smith's "Bibliographical Guide," with its comprehensive details about matters of format, presentation, and the like, and with its superb illustrations of early editions, both British and American, set new standards in the bibliography of Gaskell's publishing history.[13] A comparison of the elegantly bound first edition of *Wives and Daughters* with those of her earliest works shows just how far, in the less than two decades of her writing life, she had travelled. Furthermore we have Weyant's bibliographies – now promising to be a regular feature – while on the web Mitsuharu Matsuoka's initiatives continue to provide an invaluable scholarly source. So, where to next? The possibilities proliferate, but that only makes them more difficult to define.

What I have just been talking about are largely what might be called the scholarly resources. This kind of work can never be called complete. Determined to include only what could be authenticated, Joanne Shattock deliberately excluded from the Pickering edition a number of unattributed items, some of which might yet be proved to be Gaskell's. Unpublished letters continue to come to light, even additions to that famous correspondence between Gaskell and Charles Eliot Norton – we thought we had tidied all that up long ago. But Gaskell is now as well established in these terms as any of her contemporaries, I think, and better than some of them. There are still gaps in the primary Dickens and George Eliot sources, for example. The question now concerns the use we are to make of them, and while the papers in our programme testify to the extent of interest in Gaskell, and to the range of Gaskell studies at this point in time, it seems to me that there are still areas where more can be done, and there are indeed some yet uncharted territories. Let me first return to my point about the range and variety actually offered by Gaskell.

The persistent image of Gaskell is that she led a life under the constraints of an ordered Victorian marriage, and that her fiction reflects her basically bourgeois Victorian values. It is an image that all of us working on her have struggled to dispel. By contrast, and without exaggeration, I would go so far as to say that she lived a more varied life, and produced more varied work than most of her contemporaries. That may seem a large claim, but consider the life alone. The circumstances of her childhood were themselves destabilizing: orphaned before she was two years old, she spent her early years with an aunt no longer living with her husband from whose care she moved to boarding school and then to a sequence of her Unitarian relatives.[14] She thus had a more varied, and indeed traumatic, formative experience, at least in geographical terms, than most of her contemporaries. Whereas George Eliot, for example, might idealise the landscapes of her childhood – "These are the things that make the gamut of joy in landscape to midland-bred souls" (67), she says in an early chapter of *Middlemarch* – Gaskell had no such stability in which to root her memories. We talk about her as a Manchester novelist, but on her own testimony she would "fain be in the country" – as indeed she often was.[15] These are elementary biographical points but they made her, I think, far more restless and far more experimental as a writer.

If we stay with the life for a moment, the shifts and changes are fascinating. Central to it all is Gaskell's position as a married woman with four children, and this raises all sorts of questions not only of motherhood, but of class status. And what is true geographically is also true socially. The complexities here can be considerable. What we might call "Knutsford Gaskell" may have been an orphan

brought up by an aunt with her own family difficulties but she had socially pres-
tigious connections in pre-Victorian terms. Looking at it in one way, she might,
I think, have seen herself as socially superior to her husband in spite of his professional status.[16] Her responsibility for her daughters – about whose upbringing she
was watchful in the extreme – reinforces a process of social self-establishment that
provides a remarkable index of the possibilities of the Victorian social strata.
Working on her letters, as I have done, nothing is more fascinating than observing
the way in which she networks her way into various social groups: educators public and private, wives with titles, or at least with husbands with titles, prominent
lawyers and philanthropic young men, Oxford deans and dons, the London literary elite, continental notables, the American exiles in Rome. Just as she moves in
her professional capacity from the lower-middle-class literary culture of *Household Words* to George Smith and the *Cornhill* magazine, so she moves from Cross
Street Chapel – in its own terms an elite community, but a restricted one – to the
worlds of the English cosmopolitan upper middle class. "Dear Duke" she writes
to the Duke of Devonshire,[17] and we feel that for once she has overstepped the
mark.

That has been something of a detour, but what I am suggesting is that even in
simple biographical terms we have not entirely got to the complexity of Gaskell.
Jenny Uglow's major biography has been justly praised, and Chapple's *Early Years*
is a masterpiece of detail on the formative years of Gaskell's life.[18] But I have
always felt that Gaskell biography still hasn't defined the reality of the adult
woman, not least perhaps because it is inevitably prejudiced by its affection for its
subject. In particular it has not really got to that side of her that can be related to
the Victorian susceptibility to shifts of social class, and of cultural self-definition
– what perhaps we need, following Chapple, is a "middle years," or a "later years"
– even a "final years." There is work then still to be done on biography, and here
could I make one further plea. Gaskell's relationships with her daughters, each of
them different and traceable through correspondence, have always seemed to me
a potential field for feminist biography. Through each of those relationships we
can see not only the detail of how a Victorian mother related to her female children but what the consequences were. Gaskell's own account of them should provide a stimulus: Meta, we are told "looks at nothing from an intellectual point of
view; & will never care for reading," while Marianne "gets so absorbed in her own
thoughts that she forgets everything." Florence "has no talents under the sun …
Julia is witty, & wild, & clever and droll."[19] Two daughters married and two did
not.[20] Meta, after surviving her broken engagement to an Indian army engineer,
became very much the guardian of her mother's reputation, while Julia would be
active in the movement for the higher education of women. There is a wonderful
opportunity for a composite biography here, and one that would reveal the variety

of lives lived by women of the Gaskell daughters' social position in the latter part of the nineteenth century and beyond.

I have spent too long on biography, but it gives us a context. The next area where I would suggest there is work to be done is that of publishing history. Here we are fortunate, we have the two books by Linda Hughes and Michael Lund, *The Victorian Serial* (1991) and *Mrs. Gaskell and Victorian Publishing* (1999).[21] As I was saying, amongst the "further" letters that John Chapple and I brought together there was much more material than had previously been the case in this area. As well as individual letters relating to specific issues there was the whole sequence of letters to her French publisher, Louis Hachette, not only about the translation and publication of her work, but that of a number of her contemporaries as well. Translation studies, incidentally, offer up a rich field where the Victorian novel is concerned. More centrally Gaskell's personal publishing history is an interesting index to her wider social development; furthermore, many of her experiments in genre can be directly related to the publishing and indeed consumer context. Going beyond her death we have the case-history of *Cranford* in the later nineteenth and early twentieth centuries, with the sequence of illustrated editions initiated by the work of Hugh Thompson in the Dent edition of 1891 which, with the Knutsford edition of the complete works, elegantly bound and with decorative frontispieces, bears witness to the way the novelist has been packaged according to consumer demand. If my basic theme is the need to reveal Gaskell's variety, publishing history can, I think, provide a useful way in. In particular publishing history can throw considerable light on the short fiction, now coming very much into its own, because of all the formats Gaskell attempted it was most exposed to questions of commission and readership demand. It is in the shorter fiction in particular that we see Gaskell devising her various stratagems – the chain stories of *Cranford* and the interpolated story in *My Lady Ludlow*, for example, or the altered endings of several of the stories – and it is here that we are perhaps most conscious of her awareness of her readership.

There is a lot still to be done, then, with Gaskell, in the fields of biography and of literary history. But since my starting point in the 1960s much has changed in the world of literary studies, most notably through developments in first literary and then cultural theory. It is important here to observe a distinction. What I term "literary theory" is really a development from critical positions held over the last fifty years and more; in that sense it retained for the most part the notion of the priority of the canonical tradition. In the forms of deconstruction, reader response, death of the author, anxiety of influence, etc., it was another form of text-based criticism, traceable fairly easily back to the founding fathers of New Criticism. But cultural theory, of the kind now practiced in many English departments has had a more radical agenda. As Terry Eagleton puts it in his conclusion to *Literary Theory: An Introduction* (1983), "Discourses, sign-systems and signifying practices of all kinds, from film and television to fiction and the languages of natural science."[22] It sounds a bit like Darwin in the final paragraph of the *Origin*.

As it happens, discussion of Gaskell's work has remained relatively untouched by these developments. There are, of course exceptions: I have already mentioned the work of Hilary Schor: her *Scheherezade in the Market Place* shows how publishing history can reinforce the insights of theoretical criticism. Patricia Ingham, in *The Language of Gender and Class*, offers a reading of *North and South* that is more strenuously theoretical than most feminist interpretations, while Margaret Homans' chapter on Gaskell in *Bearing the Word* similarly draws on feminist theories of language and formative experience. Deidre D'Albertis, by contrast, in her *Dissembling Fictions* argues that Gaskell "has fared … poorly in feminist accounts of women's literary culture in the Victorian period," a problem which she confronts by approaching the full range of the work through a consideration of its generic complexity.[23] This identifies Gaskell's diversity, and it shows, too, how much the work has to gain from theoretical criticism with a wider cultural dimension. Furthermore, the disestablishment of the canon which has been one of the consequences certainly of cultural theory, has opened up the possibilities, since in traditional terms Gaskell's diversity has sometimes been seen as a matter of literary value as much as of content. Where traditional critical studies are concerned they have given us much in the way of thoughtful reading, but by concentrating on the rival categories of "urban" or "provincial," they have not always done justice to the range of the wider contexts of Gaskell's life and work. And even within those categories, vision has been restricted. Think about the Manchester fiction for a moment – we accept axiomatically that Gaskell knew all about the living conditions of the Manchester working class. But did she? Intimately, that is? She surely knew far more about the lifestyles of the Carsons than she did about the Bartons, but her middle-class affiliations have received far less attention. So here is where more specifically cultural frameworks have their opportunity – the very variety of Gaskell's life and work should surely make her an ideal subject for the application of commentary that might be culturally informed, as much as one concerned with exclusively literary priorities. I will close with two examples of how I think this might be done, one from a book recently published, and one a suggestion of my own.

My published example is a new book by Allan Christensen, *Nineteenth-Century Narratives of Contagion*.[24] Christensen's book examines the "discourse of contagion," both within the texts selected for discussion, and within Victorian culture more generally, showing how it interacts with other prominent discourse patterns of the period – those of imperialism, religion class, etc. – to identify specific Victorian anxieties. Christensen considers a sequence of eight nineteenth-century novels, so he still focuses primarily on literary texts, but he prefaces his discussion of them with an introduction in which he identifies his predominantly Foucauldian framework. Given his subject-matter, Foucault is the obvious point of departure, but in fact Christensen's study has a fairly traditional methodology. It is primarily text-based, but it might have done more, I think, to draw upon non-literary discourses of medicine and disease. On *Ruth*, the Gaskell text in question for example, there might perhaps have been more on its author's well-documented involvement in individual medical histories. Gaskell would have had as much to contribute to the discourse of illness and its treatment in mid-Victorian England as any of her contemporaries.[25] It is noticeable too that as with many books of this kind, the theoretical authorities make their appearance at the beginning to provide a framework and at the end to confirm a conclusion. In the chapters between, the theoretical input is as much implied as stated. But what this book does is show how the pragmatic application of theory can interact with critical analysis of a text-focused kind in a mutually beneficial way.

My own suggestions can be illustrated primarily from *North and South*, which is certainly a novel which might repay a wider investigation of its various "discourses" than it has usually received. Whereas most Victorian realist novels close with a wedding, *North and South* opens with one. Not the wedding of the heroine – attention to her is deflected until we realize that the wedding will mark a greater change in her life than it will in that of the bride. Narrative is inverted then, and the central character emerges through a process of deferral. As the novel develops, her ultimate marriage will act as a reflection on that first very conventional marriage, and on the nature of gender relationships in general. We learn also in that opening chapter that the happy couple are to move to Corfu, the husband being an army officer and stationed in the garrison there. But *North and South* was begun in late 1854, just as the war in the Crimea was about to begin. The honeymoon will thus be horribly overtaken by the realities of the Crimean war, since we know from history that that was the fate of the men stationed at Corfu. Did Gaskell know this? If she did, there was no chance of revising her opening, since the weekly publication demanded by *Household Words* precluded such a possibility.[26] Furthermore Gaskell finished writing the novel while staying alone in the home of Florence Nightingale, who had left it to take up her role at Scutari. These coincidences have tended to be disregarded by accounts of *North and South*; it is almost always discussed exclusively with reference to its industrial subject-matter. But if we pick up these references and look beyond the novel to its cultural context it begins to take on a rather different shape. Consider the role of Frederick Hale, the absent brother. He is excluded from the novel's action, but he is an ever-present ghost at the family table. His exclusion – he is on the run for a supposed offence when he was a midshipman in the Navy – has the effect of taking him among other places to Central America and then to Spain, where he finds a wife. His absence, then, allows Gaskell to explore her sense of the foreign – something we find often in her novels. From the discourses of marriage and family then, and from the discourse of institutional power, we move to those of travel and the connotations of the foreign. However "local" a Gaskell novel may be, the sense of the wider world is always there. In *Cranford*, so often misrepresented by its reputation as the most localized of all the fiction, we have the detailed references to the experiences in India of poor Mrs. Brown, the wife of Samuel Brown, aka Signor Brunoni, the Cranford conjurer, and then the narrator sending her letter summoning the long-absent Peter from "the strange wild countries beyond the Ganges." In chapter 12, Peter "was 'surveying mankind from China to Peru,' which everyone thought very grand, and rather appropriate, because India was between China and Peru, if you took care to turn the globe to the left instead of to the right." In *Mary Barton* Will Wilson's travels take him to the Pacific Ocean, while the novel concludes with the emigration of the major characters to Canada; Manchester is never just Manchester in the Manchester fiction.[27] Returning to *North and South* we have the discourse of high culture, as in the very Arnoldian debate between Mr. Bell, the Oxford don, and Mr. Hale; the discourse of religious belief and affiliation embodied in Hale's crisis of conscience, and the competing discourses of education when Margaret returns to the village school, and what we have is not just an industrial novel – and according to Raymond Williams an inferior one at that – but a full-scale condition-of-England novel.[28] I'm conscious that what I have said about it has been very much in terms of a critical reading, and not a specifically theoretical one, but as I say, these are issues that cultural theory is surely well placed to address. In larger terms, though, I have wanted to suggest that if it is time we had some theoretical Gaskell, the traditional and the theoretical need not be opposed to each other. For if the sheer range of Gaskell's cultural vision has much to offer to the new movements in English studies those movements have much to offer to our reading of Gaskell.

Notes

1.   In that this paper originated as a spoken lecture I have largely retained its informal mode of expression, and notably my use of the first person where it could not be easily adjusted.

2.   Edgar Wright, *Mrs. Gaskell: A Basis for Reassessment* (London: Oxford Univ. Press, 1963); J. A. V.Chapple and Arthur Pollard, eds., *The Letters of Mrs. Gaskell* (Manchester: Manchester Univ. Press, 1966), hereafter *Letters* (all references in the text to page numbers); J. G. Sharps, *Mrs. Gaskell's Observation and Invention* (Fontwell, Sussex: The Linden Press, 1970); Raymond Williams, *Culture and Society* (London: The Hogarth Press, 1958, 1987); John Lucas, "Mrs. Gaskell and Brotherhood," *Tradition and Tolerance in Nineteenth Century Fiction*, ed. J. Goode, D. Howard and J. Lucas (London: Routledge and Kegan Paul, 1966), 141-205.

3.   Elizabeth Gaskell, *North and South*, ed. Alan Shelston (New York: W. W. Norton, 2005).

4.   Sandra M. Gilbert and Susan Gubar, *The Madwoman in the Attic* (London: Yale Univ. Press, 1979).

5.   Nancy S. Weyant, *Elizabeth Gaskell: An Annotated Bibliography of English-Language Sources, 1976-1991* (Metuchen, New Jersey: The Scarecrow Press, 1994); *Elizabeth Gaskell: An Annotated Guide to English Language Sources, 1992-2001* (Lanham, Maryland, Toronto, Oxford, 2004).

6.   Weyant, xii.

7.   Patsy Stoneman, *Elizabeth Gaskell* (Brighton, Sussex: The Harvester Press, 1987).

8.   Elizabeth Gaskell, *The Works of Mrs. Gaskell*, ed. A. W. Ward (London: Smith Elder & Co, 1906). The Knutsford edition; it is incomplete; its texts are unedited, and their origins often unspecified.

9.   George Eliot, *Middlemarch*, 1872-3, ed. Bert G. Hornback (New York: W. W. Norton, 2000), 7.

10. Felicia Buonaparte, *The Gypsy-Bachelor of Manchester: The Life of Mrs. Gaskell's Demon* (Charlottesville: Univ. Press of Virginia, 1992); Hilary M. Schor, *Scheherezade in the Marketplace: Elizabeth Gaskell and the Victorian Novel* (New York: Oxford Univ. Press, 1992).

11. Joanne Shattock, ed., *The Works of Elizabeth Gaskell,* 10 vols. (London: Pickering and Chatto, 2005-2006).

12. John Chapple and Alan Shelston, eds., *Further Letters of Mrs. Gaskell* (Manchester: Manchester Univ. Press, 2000, 2003), hereafter *Further Letters.*

13. Walter E. Smith, *Elizabeth Gaskell: A Bibliographical Catalogue* (Los Angeles: Heritage Book Shop, 1998).

14. See John Chapple, *Elizabeth Gaskell: The Early Years* (Manchester: Manchester Univ. Press, 1997), for details of Gaskell's aunt, Hannah Lumb, and her unfortunate marriage.

15. *Letters*, 139.

16. As ever, discussions of Victorian class are compromised by limitations of terminology. In discussion Professor Chapple has queried this point, and certainly the extended Gaskell family into which she married were by no means socially or financially insignificant. But the Holland family, into whose ambit Gaskell's Knutsford childhood brought her, were indeed socially significant, both locally and ultimately nationally.

17. *Further Letters*, 172.

18. Jenny Uglow, *Elizabeth Gaskell: a Habit of Stories* (London: Faber and Faber, 1993).

19.   *Letters*, 160-61.

20.   Despite her lack of talent, Florence married a successful lawyer whose usefulness Gaskell was to appreciate: she died childless at a comparatively early age. Marianne, the oldest daughter, outlived all her sisters; she was the only one of them all to have children of her own.

21.   Linda K. Hughes and Michael Lund, *The Victoria Serial* (Charlottesville: Univ. Press of Virginia, 1991); Linda K. Hughes and Michael Lund, *Victorian Publishing and Mrs. Gaskell's Work* (Charlottesville: Univ. Press of Virginia, 1999).

22.   Terry Eagleton, *Literary Theory: An Introduction* (Oxford: Basil Blackwell, 1983), 210.

23.   Patricia Ingham, *The Language of Gender and Class* (London: Routledge, 1996), 55-77; Margaret Homans, *Bearing the Word: Language and Female Experience in Nineteenth-Century Women's Writing* (Chicago: The Univ. of Chicago Press, 1986); Deidre D'Albertis, *Dissembling Fiction: Elizabeth Gaskell and the Victorian Social Text* (New York: St Martin's, 1997).

24.   Allan Christensen, *Nineteenth Century Narratives of Contagion: 'Our feverish contact'* (Abingdon: Routledge, 2005).

25.   One thinks for example of her fear of the "fearsome Dr. Protheroe Smith," the pioneering gynaecologist and proponent of the Hospital for Diseases of Women whose enthusiasm for invasive surgery, according to Gaskell "amounted to absolute cruelty" – so much so that she investigated mesmerism as an alternative (*Further Letters*, 95).

26.   She did, of course, revise the novel for volume publication, and in some instances quite significantly. But it would have been very difficult to alter such a matter of substance without embarrassment.

27.   Here I should acknowledge my debt to the work of Dr. Shu-chuan Yan of the National University of Kaohsiung, Taiwan, whose PhD thesis on the significance of the foreign in Gaskell's work, *'Spinning Around the Word': Imagined Geographies in Elizabeth Gaskell's Major Fiction* (2002), was completed under my supervision at the University of Manchester.

28.   Williams, 91.

11

The Presence of Wordsworth
in Elizabeth Gaskell's Early Writing

Irene Wiltshire

One of the most unequivocal opinions Elizabeth Gaskell expressed about another writer may be found in a letter to her sister-in-law in 1836. Writing from her uncle's farm at Sandlebridge, she said, of Wordsworth, "my heart feels so full of him I only don't know how to express my fullness without being too diffuse."[1] At this stage of her life Gaskell was a young wife with an infant daughter and this letter describes her contentment in the flower-filled garden deep in the Cheshire countryside. She shared with her husband an interest in poetry but she had not yet written for publication. The purpose of this essay is to consider the reasons why Gaskell admired Wordsworth's poetry so much and how it informed her own writing.

Gaskell's own early reading had consisted of her aunts' and uncles' old books, which included prose and poetry of sensibility, which itself pointed the way to the poetry of the Romantic period.[2] Gaskell was receptive to poetry that elevated human feeling and imagination partly as an antidote to the dry reasoning of her Unitarian heritage. She was not alone in her religious reservations, for her Newcastle mentor, the Reverend William Turner, had also valued the feeling heart as well as the enlightened mind.[3] Life in Manchester, following her marriage in 1832, brought her into contact with urban poverty and hardship. As her husband tried to raise the aspirations of working men in the city, she and William turned to the poetry of humble life. For William, this was George Crabbe as well as Wordsworth. But while William appreciated Crabbe's challenge to the myth of the rural idyll, Gaskell found his representations of poverty and immorality in the countryside too bleak. She showed a preference for the greater optimism of the Lakeland poet. It was in the poetry of Wordsworth that she found the seeing-beauty spirit; a belief in the quiet heroism of ordinary people and the valuing of those on the very margins of society.

In 1800 Wordsworth stated his intentions in his Preface to *Lyrical Ballads*: "The principal object then which I proposed to myself in these Poems was to make the incidents of common life interesting." He claimed that "low and rustic life" would be the subject of his poetry and that feeling would give importance to the action and situation, and not action and situation to the feeling.[4] Much of his early poetry takes an unremarkable place, for example a heap of stones or a muddy pool, and then suggests the emotional experience that is associated with that location.

In 1838, two years after she expressed her admiration for Wordsworth so fulsomely at Sandlebridge, Gaskell wrote a letter to another admirer of Wordsworth, Mary Howitt, in which she described her husband's lectures to the poorest weavers in Manchester quoting from Wordsworth's "Old Cumberland Beggar." This poem, written in 1797, was Wordsworth's statement of belief in the value of every human life, however lowly, and the capacity of even the poorest people to contribute to the care of the poorest members of their community. "In short," Gaskell says, "the beauty and poetry of many of the common things and daily events of life in its humblest aspect does not seem to me sufficiently appreciated."[5] This suggests that she was by this time taking something very specific from Wordsworth, something more than a counterweight to the dry reasoning of her Unitarian upbringing; it was a desire to show what lies behind the ordinary, to portray human emotion at least as much as dramatic incident, and to focus on characters who were socially insignificant. Gaskell was not the only mid-nineteenth-century writer to focus on the ordinary: Charles Dickens and George Eliot were also heirs to this aspect of Romanticism. Introducing the first number of *Household Words* in 1850, Dickens declared that one of the aims of his new paper was "To show to all, that in all familiar things, even in those which are repellent on the surface, there is Romance enough, if we will find it out."[6] George Eliot, at the early age of 21, owned a six-volume set of Wordsworth's poetry and claimed to have worked through the first three.[7] Nonetheless, each of these writers showed a debt to Wordsworth in a different way. As far as Gaskell is concerned, Stephen Gill makes the case most clearly when he says that Gaskell's finest tales and novels are adventures of the heart.[8]

Gaskell's first published short story was *Libbie Marsh's Three Eras*, published in 1847 by Mary and William Howitt in their *Journal of Literature and Popular Progress*.[9] This early text is too often regarded as a simple tale of working-class life in nineteenth-century Manchester, but a closer look suggests a strong Wordsworthian influence. There are allusions to *The Excursion* and to "Ode: Intimations of Immortality": "the sweet hour of prime" which delineates the ambience of the bank holiday outing carries echoes of "the prime hour of sweetest scents and airs" in *The Excursion*; and the sick child's approaching death is heralded with the reference to the "cloud of glory from heaven, 'which is our home,'" recalling "Intimations." But there is more than mere allusion or quotation for, as Stephen Gill has observed, Gaskell was one of the few Victorian writers whose work was actually shaped by Wordsworth.[10]

Where the Lakeland poet took rural situations that were off the beaten track to reveal the human drama associated with obscure places, Gaskell did something similar in *Libbie Marsh's Three Eras*, for to reach the narrow city court where much of the action takes place you must, like the reader of *Michael*, turn your steps from the public way. The public way here is a busy urban thoroughfare, behind which lies a complex of mills, factories, and narrow courts consisting of tightly packed, cheaply built domestic dwellings.[11] It is an obscure city location of which most people would be unaware. The opening scenes appear to be commonplace: a young poor single woman changing her lodgings, but the author goes behind this ordinariness to reveal the inner lives of the main protagonists. This is achieved by foregrounding states of mind and feelings; and by showing rather than telling.

Libbie's feeling of desolation is demonstrated by the slowness and heaviness of her movements. Her inner loneliness is so deep that she cannot respond to the kindness of those who welcome her. As the reader is introduced to more of the characters who inhabit the court, we see that the two main protagonists, Libbie Marsh and Margaret Hall, like many of Wordsworth's characters, occupy the lowest possible status within their community, for they are not even tenants, but merely lodgers, each occupying one room only.

In economic terms Mrs. Hall and Libbie do not occupy quite the lowest rung of the social ladder, for Franky Hall, as an invalid, is confined to his bed and cannot earn his keep in any material way. He can be viewed as a useless individual, in the same way as Wordsworth's child in "The Idiot Boy," except that Franky is more advanced mentally than Johnny Foy. As with Johnny, Franky needs looking after, making him dependent on others, but, again, like Johnny, he is loved, gives purpose to his mother's life, and significantly, he shapes the plot of this tale. Given her sense of alienation in the court, Franky is the one human being to whom Libbie can relate; he is the only person to whom she can make any overtures without fear of rejection, and St. Valentine's day makes it possible for her to test the water by giving him, anonymously, the gift of a caged bird. His participation in the Whitsuntide outing will make him the agent of moral and spiritual growth in the community of the court.

As the story unfolds, we as readers, see how Gaskell is drawing on lines from "The Old Cumberland Beggar" to shape the plot of her story. As a mere lodger, Libbie is one of the poorest poor, but through personal sacrifice and frugality, she too becomes a dealer out of gladness, in her purchase of the bird and cage for Franky, who in his suffering needed a kindness more than anyone in this little community.

Libbie's second era focuses on the Whitsuntide excursion which she arranges to benefit both Franky Hall and his mother. From the time this journey commences the story could have developed into a tragedy or even a tragicomedy with elements of melodrama. The fact that the weather remains ideal and the journey is altogether uneventful is evidence of Gaskell's intention to portray the inner journey of the heart, rather than the outward adventure of a physical journey. The Whitsuntide excursion is a vehicle for the development of the inner lives of its participants, whose thoughts and feelings will give importance to this event. The focus of goodwill during this outing is Franky, but he also acts as an agent of reconciliation between Mrs. Dixon and Mrs. Hall. For Gaskell, it is through Franky that "the soul grew much on this day" (*DNW*, 183).

Era three moves on to the inevitable death and funeral of Franky. The funeral of a child in nineteenth-century Manchester would be a regular event, unremarked on except when described by an imaginative writer. The personal sorrow and grief of the occasion is evident from the way in which "slowly, slowly, along the streets, elbowed by life at every turn, a little funeral wound its quiet way" (*DNW*, 185). The insignificance of the event to passers-by, who were principally occupied with shopping and social calls, is emphasized by the way in which the cortege is "elbowed by life at every turn." Gaskell is going behind an ordinary everyday event to reveal the inner lives of the people involved and, in this instance, to contrast the personal experience of an event with the way in which the world at large sees it. Libbie's involvement with the invalid child has for her been an adventure of the heart. She and Mrs. Hall have undergone a profound change to their inner lives, even though their external circumstances remain the same.

William and Mary Howitt did more than just admire Wordsworth's poetry, they met the poet and his wife on a number of occasions, welcoming them to their own home and visiting them at Rydal Mount, Grasmere.[12] Gaskell had found in the Howitts publishers who were sympathetic to her own intentions. Just three months after the publication of *Libbie Marsh*, the Howitts published a very different kind of story, *The Sexton's Hero*.[13] The location of this tale, Morecambe Bay, links it to Wordsworth immediately: it was when crossing these sands that the poet learnt of the death of Robespierre, an event that promoted renewed hope for the principles of the French Revolution.[14]

This, however, is not the only link between the two compositions, for the narrative structure of *The Sexton's Hero* shows the influence of Book 1 of *The Excursion*. In addition to the common narrative framework emphasized by Stephen Gill, in both compositions the primary narrator relates a tale told to him by a much older person.[15] In *The Excursion*, the older person is "a Man of reverend age," and in *The Sexton's Hero* he is one to whom the narrator's companion, Jeremy, "bowed in deference to his white, uncovered head" (*MC*, 102). The social inferiority of the Sexton is made clear when he addresses the two young men: "If I might be so bold sir," while he waits "leave to speak." This is not, however, a crude social class relationship since the young man is willing to bow in deference to the Sexton. Old age here is to be associated with wisdom and will, like the friend of "reverend age" in *The Excursion*, command respect. It is because of this respect that the two young men are willing to sit under the shade of a yew-tree and listen to the Sexton's account of events that took place 45 years earlier. Stephen Gill rightly points us again to Wordsworth and the beginning of *The Excursion*, Book 1, for a likely influence on Gaskell's descriptive writing in this story. For Wordsworth, "'Twas summer, and the sun had mounted high"; for Gaskell, "The afternoon sun shed down his glorious rays" (*MC*, 101).

The yew tree becomes the backdrop and wings of the stage on which the Sexton's narrative unfolds, drawing the reader into the action, and bringing to mind another of Wordsworth's poems: "Lines left upon a Seat in a Yew-tree which stands near the Lake of Esthwaite" (*LB*, 38-40). In this poem the traveller is invited to rest and hear about "one who own'd / No common soul." Like *The Sexton's Hero*, this poem deals with notions of solitude and isolation. The concluding lines would have appealed to Gaskell: "True dignity abides with him alone / Who, in the silent hour of inward thought, / Can still suspect, and still revere himself, / In lowliness of heart" (*LB*, 40. 57-60).

The *Sexton's* hero is Gilbert Dawson, a carpenter, whose actions were governed by inward thought and reason, and who, as a consequence, was rejected by a society which subscribed to different ideals. Through his rejection of contemporary values, and social pressures, Dawson retreats from society and becomes a solitary figure rather like one of Wordsworth's solitaries, socially isolated, yet with a strong personal history. The indications are that loss of human company caused him great unhappiness, for he "fell into a sad, careless way" (*MC*, 105). Just as Libbie Marsh's inner loneliness and despair had been demonstrated by her slow movements, so Dawson's inner pain and anguish are shown by the way in which his gait changes from a brisk walk to a lingering step.

Having taken a moral position that separates him from the majority of members of the community, Dawson is forced to rely more and more on his own inner resources. But while this position allows freedom of thought and action, it also invites danger because it increases his social isolation. Unimpeded by public opinion, which might have included warnings for his own safety, he prepares to embark on his final act of heroism, at the very time that the Sexton was setting out, with his young wife, on the final crossing.

The crossing of Morecambe Bay involves serious risk, for it must be completed before the tide comes in. It is, therefore, a physical adventure and one in which Dawson demonstrates his capacity for physical heroism without the use of violence. But this episode is part of a wider experience that changes the Sexton's opinion of Dawson, making it for the Sexton and his listeners, an adventure of the heart. The Sexton and his young wife survive the menace of the incoming tidal waves, but only at the cost of Dawson's life. The pacifist has enacted the ultimate heroic sacrifice: he has laid down his life for others. The Sexton is a sadder and wiser man.

The story could have been a simple didactic moral tale, about the importance of the individual conscience, and the true nature of heroism. One factor which makes it more than this is the use of multiple narrative, common also to *The Excursion*. Here we have three voices: Jeremy's friend, the Sexton, and Jonas, the parish clerk. The Sexton had told the story to the two strangers because their conversation had reminded him of events which had taken place 45 years earlier. Those events had shaped his life and continued to haunt him. His experience of the fatal crossing is recollected in a mood of extreme tranquility, in a situation that stands in sharp contrast to the circumstances of the event that he is recalling. When the two young men leave the churchyard what they have learnt is the way in which events, which took place many years earlier, have shaped the heart and mind of the wise old gentleman to whom they had been listening. *The Sexton's Hero* has revealed the journey of the Sexton's heart.

Gaskell's first full-length novel features another hero, though of a different kind from the Sexton's: an honest weaver turned murderer. For Gaskell, John Barton was, in spite of his crime, her hero in *Mary Barton*.[16] This novel has not been well served by its designation as a "social problem" or "industrial" novel. Many readers were introduced to it through Raymond Williams's *Culture and Society*, an influential book in which Williams discusses *Mary Barton* alongside Gaskell's *North and South*, Dickens's *Hard Times*, Disraeli's *Sybil*, Kingsley's *Alton Locke*, and Eliot's *Felix Holt*.[17] But while recognizing the shared subject matter I do not feel that *Mary Barton* sits comfortably with these companions. The reason for this is the sheer emotional force, less marked in *North and South*, and absent from the other novels in this group. This quality was recognized early on by John Forster when he said of *Mary Barton*, "The internal passions and emotions are its materials of interest."[18] Stephen Gill points in the same direction when he discusses Barton as a Wordsworthian bewildered figure.[19] Gaskell's own emotional condition at the time of writing this novel is well known, and many readers do find it a presence, notably her handling of parental grief following the death of a son. Given her personal circumstances at this time, coupled with her receptivity to the Romantic valorization of human emotion, it is likely that she did take her cue from Wordsworth, not only for his representations of humble life, central to *Mary Barton*, but for his representations of loss and elevation of human feeling above reason.

When we look at Wordsworth's Preface to *Lyrical Ballads* and to the ballads themselves we see many of his intentions fulfilled in *Mary Barton*. The essential passions of the human heart are all here: the husband's grief and anger following the death of his wife; the daughter's unwavering love for her father, and his for her; the love and anxiety for the sister who has gone astray; the anger and bitterness that leads to the murder. The one human heart is signified by the experience of loss and sorrow shared by rich and poor alike.

John Barton's actions are precipitated by emotional states, illustrating Wordsworth's dictum that "men who do not wear fine cloaths can feel deeply."[20] Barton's emotional journey is carefully charted from his first appearance in the novel to his last gasp of breath. When we first meet him, the good predominates over the bad, but his heart begins to harden after the death of his wife. One of the ties that had bound him to humanity is loosened and he becomes a changed man. The second downward step in his emotional journey is the death of his young son, who dies from scarlet fever. Unable to buy the food that would aid the child's recovery, he sees the mill-owning class buying luxury goods. It is at this point that vengeance enters his heart. The third step is the failure of the petition taken to parliament. Barton returns home a broken man who has tried all legitimate means to improve his situation. His willingness to step outside the law follows the masters' callous refusal to increase wages; insult added to injury by the caricature drawn by young Carson of the starving men. It is this that makes Barton's heart burn and leads him down the path to murder. Yet even then, shortly before he commits this terrible act, his humanity is shown by his affection for his daughter and by the way in which he stops to soothe a lost child and restore him to his mother.

The essential meaning of "The Old Cumberland Beggar" may be recognized in *Mary Barton*. The poorest of the poor do help each other in times of need. Even when John Barton is hungry himself he still takes his dinner to the Davenports who are in even worse straights, at the point of death. He pawns what few possessions he has to buy essential items for them. Following the death of Mr. Davenport, Mrs. Davenport's neighbours pay her rent arrears and make a collection. In return for these kindnesses, Mrs. Davenport manages to find a decent shirt collar for Barton to wear when he takes the petition to parliament. Alice, who earns a meagre living as a washerwoman, is willing to sit with a sick child even after a day's work and makes herbal remedies for anyone who is ill. As a poor woman she can feel for the poor.

Acts of violence are rare even under the intense pressure of want and anxiety.

Barton strikes his daughter only once, and even then because she has provoked him. One of the strikers throws vitriol at one of the strike breakers but this act is followed by intense remorse. Barton visits Jonas, the thrower of the vitriol, in gaol and visits the victim in hospital. Members of this community accept responsibility for each other and this is in contrast to the mill-owning class who are portrayed as thinking only of themselves, sloughing off any feelings of obligation to their workforce who are starving because of low wages, short time, or no work at all. This lack of social responsibility on the part of the masters is the root cause of the ultimate tragedy that engulfs John Barton, the weaver, and Mary Barton, the dressmaker's apprentice; humble life caught up in a tragedy of epic proportions. Yet when Carson finally confronts Barton, as the killer of his son, he is forced to accept the one human heart, the grief and loss experienced by both men following the death of a child. It falls on Job Legh, the naturalist, to cut across all the narrative complexities and contradictions when he makes that most Wordsworthian observation that God gave men feelings and passions which cannot always be worked into a problem.

While the action of *Mary Barton* does not share the rustic environment of Wordsworth's poetry, many of the characters have a rural background; Alice Wilson and Job Legh, for example. Wordsworth's social outcasts include a beggar, a leach-gatherer, a mad mother, and an idiot boy, but Gaskell goes one step further in her creation of Esther, the prostitute. Esther is the ultimate social outcast, but she is more than a cipher; she is presented as a human being with an inner dignity and a personal history. She also helps to shape the plot. Her disappearance is such a source of anxiety to her sister, Mrs. Barton, that she is seen as a cause of Mrs. Barton's death. It is Esther who alerts Jem Wilson to the relationship that is developing between Harry Carson and Mary. It is because of this information that Jem confronts Carson; the ensuing fight witnessed by a policeman is a factor in his conviction for murder. It is Esther who finds the scrap of paper that points to John Barton's guilt. Esther provides a thread of continuity for she is present in the narrative from the opening pages when her disappearance is discussed to the end when she is buried next to John Barton. The plot is dependent on Esther; she is the outcast who still has value.

Following the publication of *Mary Barton*, there were no more opportunities for Gaskell to submit work to Howitt's journal, for the final number appeared in June 1848. This was not, however, to be a problem. Dickens was so impressed by *Mary Barton* that he invited Gaskell to contribute to his new journal *Household Words* in the following terms:

'I do not know what your literary vows of temperance or abstinence may be, but as I do honestly know that there is no living English writer whose aid I would desire to enlist, in preference to the authoress of *Mary Barton* (a book that most profoundly affected and impressed me) I venture to ask you whether you can give me any hope that you will write a short tale, or any number of tales, for the projected pages.'[21]

Gaskell had again found an editor who was sympathetic to her aims. It is not possible to discuss here all the work by Gaskell that Dickens published, but there is a cluster of short stories, all published in 1850, that deserve special mention.

The first of Gaskell's stories to appear in *Household Words* was *Lizzie Leigh* which reflected a preoccupation shared by Gaskell and Dickens at that time: the rehabilitation of young women who had fallen into a life of sin.[22] The title was Dickens's idea and it directs the reader to Lizzie's trajectory, but we do not meet her until near the end of the story. If Lizzie is perceived as a plot convenience, necessary for Mrs. Leigh's trajectory, the story can be read as a family power struggle; one in which the older son tries to preserve the patriarchal power exercised by his late father, while his mother tries to assert her own free will. This interpretation, the basis of this discussion, reveals the inner conflict of Mrs. Leigh and illustrates ways in which Gaskell engaged with some of the ideas and images that figure in Wordsworth's writings.

Lizzie's circumstances can be traced, not only to observation of real life in a city such as Manchester, but to fictional counterparts in the poetry of Crabbe and Wordsworth, though it was Wordsworth who handled the subject of loss most powerfully. Lizzie pays for her transgression through the death of her child, but, unlike Gaskell's Ruth or Oliver Twist's mother, her own life is spared. She must then come to terms, not so much with her transgression, but with her sense of loss following the death of her beloved child. Lizzie's survival also completes the matriarchal resolution of the story in which Mrs. Leigh sets up home with her daughter.

Lizzie's illegitimate child must be buried in the hills, some distance away from the grave of the family patriarch. The child's burial place, in a Quaker graveyard noted for its simplicity and isolation, is in contrast with Mr. Leigh's grave; for he had been buried in the parish churchyard at Milnrow. The choice of burial place for the child is significant on two counts. Firstly, while a minister of the parish church might have been unwilling to inter an illegitimate child in his churchyard, there is no suggestion in the story that this was the case. There is, instead, the implication that the "stern grandfather" would not have welcomed such an arrangement, although this seems contradictory, since his last words before dying had been those of forgiveness towards his daughter. If the author of *Lizzie Leigh* had wanted to complete the cycle of forgiveness and reconciliation, the interment of the illegitimate child next to her pious grandfather would have been entirely appropriate, adding substance to Mr. Leigh's words of forgiveness. But Gaskell has reasons of her own for choosing a more modest site for the burial of Mrs. Leigh's granddaughter. Our search for these reasons takes us again to Wordsworth and, in particular, to *The Thorn* (*LB*, 70-78).

In this poem Wordsworth takes an unremarkable location, one that is furnished only with dreary natural features: an "aged thorn" and a "little muddy pond ... three feet long, and two feet wide."[23] Here the poet reveals an intense personal drama that is associated with this spot. First of all, we learn of a "beauteous heap, a hill of moss / Just half a foot in height" (*LB*, 71. 36), which suggests an infant's grave, and which is close to the muddy pond, beside which the woman often sits weeping. Secondly, as the narrative unfolds we learn that the woman, Martha Ray, was, as a young girl, deserted by the young man to whom she was betrothed, and whose child she was carrying. The circumstances surrounding Lizzie Leigh's betrayal are not explained, but Lizzie's trajectory concludes in the same way as Martha Ray's, for both women bury their child on a lonely hillside and both make tearful visits to the burial place. Martha Ray's rather stylized lamentation: "Oh misery! Oh misery! / O woe is me!" finds a softer echo in Lizzie's expression of grief and remorse, for she, more modestly, "sits by a little grave and weeps bitterly" (*CP*, 32). Martha Ray's behaviour disconcerts the reader because it is witnessed "High on a mountain's highest ridge, / Where oft the stormy winter gale / Cuts like a scythe" (*LB*, 70. 23-26). The solitariness and mental derangement of this woman underpins the sublimity which may be experienced by the reader of the poem.

This sublimity does not, however, represent the "seeing-beauty spirit" sought by Gaskell, and neither will it do for her as a resolution to her story of maternal suffering. The final scene, in which Lizzie takes a child to the sunny burial place in the uplands, where the youngster makes daisy chains, and Lizzie weeps at the grave side, is not one of sublimity, but one of beauty.[24] Although this scene is suffused with tears of regret, it is also lightened by the actions of Lizzie's young companion. Moreover, unlike Martha Ray, Lizzie has been restored, not merely to human society, but to her family, for she is reunited with her mother.

This restoration, however, would not have been possible if Mrs. Leigh had not asserted her own free will in the face of opposition from her son. The story begins with Mrs. Leigh's emotional turmoil, but it ends with her peace of mind. Upclose Farm, with its memories of patriarchal rule remains sublime in its moorland situation, but the secluded cottage in the hollow is now home to Mrs. Leigh and her daughter. The beauty, as opposed to sublimity, of this new situation symbolizes the new landmark of independent thought, which Mrs. Leigh has constructed for herself, in place of those old landmarks of submission and duty. In this story we have seen Gaskell draw on a powerful Wordsworthian image and transform it to underpin her ideas about the potential for matriarchal strength and solidarity.[25]

For her second contribution to *Household Words*, *The Well of Pen-Morfa*, Gaskell again chose the subject of betrayal and loss, and an obscure location.[26] Once again we must turn our steps from the public way, for "Of a hundred travellers who spend a night at Trê-Madoc, in North Wales, there is not one, perhaps, who goes to the neighbouring village of Pen-Morfa" (*MC*, 123). This particular part of North Wales had strong emotional associations for Gaskell herself, for she had spent youthful carefree holidays at her uncle's home near Portmadoc; her honeymoon had included a visit to this area; and later on she suffered the loss of her infant son while staying at Portmadoc.[27]

Nest Gwynn, the heroine of *The Well of Pen-Morfa*, also experiences three distinct emotional phases: the joy of courtship, the excitement of betrothal to one who is socially above her and, ultimately, the misery and loss that followed his rejection as a result of her physical injury. Edward Williams's reasons for breaking off the engagement are based on sound reason: he needs a strong and able-bodied wife to help him run his farm. His is the voice of Enlightenment thinking, but Nest and her mother Eleanor are governed by feeling. Reason alone had governed Williams's decision, but for Nest, cold reason was inadequate; it could only make her bitter, for she "turned away from cold reason; she revolted from her mother; she revolted from the world. She bound her sorrow tight up in her breast, to corrode and fester there" (*MC*, 134). Gaskell set up a dichotomy between the sound practical reasoning of Williams on the one hand, and the human emotion and sensitivity of Nest and her mother on the other. When Williams, without delay, finds a more suitable wife, Nest's sense of betrayal deepens and she turns away from all consolation, including her mother's love. The emotional lives of Nest and Eleanor reach a nadir before human help can touch them. When help does come, it is in the form of an itinerant Methodist preacher, David Hughes, whose travels and wide experience of human suffering link him to the Wanderer in *The Excursion*, Book 2. Of David Hughes, Gaskell remarks: "His rambles and travels were of use to him. They extended his knowledge of the circumstances in which men are sometimes placed, and enlarged his sympathy with the tried and tempted" (*MC*, 136). Of the Wanderer, Wordsworth says "He wandered far; much did he see of men, / Their manners, their enjoyments, and pursuits, / Their passions and their feelings; chiefly those / Essential and eternal in the heart."[28] The creation of David Hughes is significant on two counts. Firstly, we see Gaskell drawing on a Wordsworthian idea: a man using his personal experience of life to help someone who is facing an emotional and spiritual crisis. But we also see her, as we often do, not only drawing on, but adapting such an idea to bring it closer to her own personal vision. Her own emotional experiences associated with this part of Wales find a parallel in the story of Nest Gwyn: extremes of both happiness and sadness, the latter as a result of loss. While Gaskell's Unitarian religion stressed the value of reason, there are indications that she sometimes found this inadequate. In chapter 14 of *Cranford*, Miss Matty's servant, who insists on staying with her employer even without pay, says: "I'll not listen to reason. … Reason always means what some one else has got to say." Cold reason does not inspire Miss Matty's selfless servant, and nor does it bring comfort to Nest Gwynn. David Hughes reaches Nest and her mother through his understanding of the human heart. Through his teaching Nest finds a way forward by caring for one more troubled than herself. Her restoration is made complete when she feels able to revisit the well, where Williams plighted his troth and where she sustained the injury that set in motion all the subsequent changes in her life.

Williams has not been presented as a villain, so he is not punished within the context of the story, but neither does he invoke in the reader feelings of admiration. He is blessed with business acumen and the faculty of reason, but denied the quality of moral strength. In this story moral strength is aligned with the capacity to feel deeply, and in particular with the deep feelings of Nest. This alignment of moral strength with feeling legitimizes the supremacy of feeling associated with Romanticism. For Wordsworth, men who did not wear fine clothes could feel deeply; for Gaskell, those who did feel deeply were also capable of moral superiority.

The third story by Gaskell to appear in *Household Words* in 1850 was *The Heart of John Middleton* and, as the title suggests, this is an account of a man's inner life.[29] Of this contribution Dickens said: "I think The Heart of John Middleton – that's the name I have given it – a story of extraordinary power, worked out with a vigour and truthfulness that very very few people could reach."[30] The qualities that impressed Dickens so much are aspects of Gaskell's Romantic inheritance: the foregrounding of feeling and a man's relationship with the natural world. Some elements of this Romanticism are specifically Wordsworthian: low and rustic life; emotional turmoil recollected in tranquility; and the innocent child figure who has powers of redemption.

John Middleton, like John Barton, is another Wordsworthian bewildered figure. As a rural factory worker he is of low social status but his second occupation as a poacher makes him a social outcast. Unloved as a child, and full of hate towards his adult enemy Dick Jackson, he is an unregenerate character, though he seeks spiritual betterment. His search for redemption and peace of mind is the focus of the story and it is achieved by two principal means: the innocence of a child and an unconventional means of communion with God.

God's mercy first manifests itself in the form of the child whom he meets when she is crossing a simple rustic bridge. This first meeting with young Nelly

Hadfield is overtly symbolic, as the child crosses the bridge over the brook, she symbolizes John Middleton's attempts to make a transfer from evil to goodness in his life. But there is more than religious symbolism here, for Nelly's isolated life with her grandmother, and her affinity with nature, links her to the Wordsworthian child in the *Lucy* poems:

'She dwelt among th'untrodden ways
Beside the springs of Dove,
A Maid whom there were none to praise
And very few to love.' (*LB*, 154. 1-4)

John Middleton's desire to emulate the innocent child's goodness, and to be worthy of her regard is the first catalyst for the spiritual change that he longs for. Without this motivation he would not have learnt to read the Bible, nor would he have acquired the self-knowledge necessary for moral progress.

As a man who is outside the community of regular church-goers, John Middleton must find an alternative form of prayer, one that is more pantheistic.[31] His only attempt at church worship, at the behest of Nelly when she has grown up and become his wife, fails because of the presence of his old enemy Dick Jackson. He feels closer to God praying in the open air. His first attempt, outside the old abbey walls, is doomed to failure because he is asking God to give him the power of revenge. He is more successful when he joins in communal worship on a hillside where he listens with fellow workmen and social outcasts to an itinerant preacher, whose passion and earnestness reaches his heart. At this point his redemption seems complete but when he meets his former enemy again his instinct is still for revenge, rather than forgiveness. Once again it is a child figure who saves him, this time his young daughter sent by her dying mother to prevent her father from fetching a constable to arrest Dick Jackson. The ensuing act of forgiveness completes John's moral rehabilitation.

The death of Nelly keeps her image true to Wordsworth's Lucy in two ways. Firstly, in the short poem entitled "Song," Lucy is not well known, but when she dies she leaves one person bereft: "But she is in her Grave, and Oh! / The difference to me" (*LB*, 154. 11-12). Secondly, in "Three years she grew in sun and shower," Lucy's spirit, like Nelly's, survives inextricably bound up with nature:

'She died and left to me
This heath, this calm and quiet scene,
The memory of what has been,
And never more will be.' (*LB*, 199. 39-42)

Gaskell drew heavily on Wordsworth for this story: the choice of low and rustic life; the recollection in tranquility of strong youthful emotions; the innocent child, redolent of Lucy, a vital force in the life of the narrator; and the power of nature as a means of spiritual communion. All of this, together with her delineation of human feeling, is what give this story the power and vigour praised by Dickens.

In her later works Gaskell engaged with a wider range of writers from the Romantic period, but through it all she retained an interest in what lies behind the ordinary; her final novel *Wives and Daughters* even carrying the sub-title, "An Every-Day Story," suggesting a rejection of the sensational, popular at that time. The Wordsworth of Gaskell's early writing retains a presence, one way or another, throughout her work. This places her very firmly in that line of English writers including Dickens, Eliot, Hardy, and Lawrence; all of whom acknowledged a debt to Wordsworth.[32]

Notes

1. J. A. V. Chapple and Arthur Pollard, eds., *The Letters of Mrs. Gaskell* (Manchester: Manchester Univ. Press, 1966, 1997), 7; hereafter *Gaskell Letters*.

2. For Gaskell's account of her own early reading see *Gaskell Letters*, 562.

3. William Turner, *The Goodness of God Illustrated in the Appointment of Private and National Adversity: A Sermon Preached to the Congregation of Protestant Dissenters, Assembling in Hanover Square, Newcastle-upon-Tyne, on New-Year's Day 1817* (York: Thomas Wilson, 1817), 22-24.

4. R. L. Brett and A. R. Jones, eds., *Wordsworth and Coleridge, Lyrical Ballads* (London: Methuen, 1968, 1984), 244-48; hereafter *LB*.

5. *Gaskell Letters*, 33.

6. Charles Dickens "A Preliminary Word," *Household Words: A Weekly Journal*, 1 (1850): 1.

7. Stephen Gill, *Wordsworth and the Victorians* (Oxford: Clarendon Press, 1998), 146; hereafter Gill.

8. Gill, 128.

9. The text referred to here is in Elizabeth Gaskell, *A Dark Night's Work and Other Stories*, ed. by Suzanne Lewis (Oxford: Oxford Univ. Press, 1992), 67-193; hereafter *DNW*.

10. Gill, 116-117.

11. See *Old Ordnance Survey Maps: Manchester (Piccadilly), 1849, (Manchester Sheet 29)* (Gateshead: Alan Godfrey Maps).

12. Margaret Howitt, ed., *Mary Howitt: An Autobiography* (London: Isbister, 1891), 121-122; 135; 184.

13. The text discussed here is in Elizabeth Gaskell, *The Moorland Cottage and Other Stories*, ed. Suzanne Lewis (Oxford: Oxford Univ. Press, 1995), 101-110; hereafter *MC*.

14. For an account of the impact of Robespierre's death on Wordsworth see Kenneth R. Johnston, *The Hidden Wordsworth: Poet, Lover, Rebel, Spy* (New York: Norton, 1998), 418-420.

15. For Gill's discussion of the relationship between Wordsworth and *The Sexton's Hero*, see Gill, 130-132.

16. *Mary Barton* was first published, with encouragement from the Howitts, by Chapman and Hall in October 1848.

17. Raymond Wiliams, *Culture and Society: Coleridge to Orwell* (London: Hogarth Press, 1987), 87.

18. John Forster, an unsigned review in the *Examiner* (4 November 1848): 708-709; reproduced in Angus Easson, ed., *Elizabeth Gaskell: The Critical Heritage* (London: Routledge, 1991), 69.

19. Gill, 139.

20. Ernest de Selincourt, ed., "Wordsworth to Charles James Fox, 14 January, 1801," *The Letters of William and Dorothy Wordsworth: The Early Years, 1787-1805* (Oxford: Clarendon Press, 1967, second edn.), 315.

21. Graham Storey and others eds. *The Letters of Charles Dickens*, 1850-52 (Oxford: Clarendon Press, 1988), 6: 22.

22. *Lizzie Leigh* was serialized in three parts, commencing 30 March and concluding 13 April. The text discussed here is in Angus Easson, ed., *Elizabeth Gaskell, Cousin Phillis and Other Tales* (Oxford: Oxford Univ. Press, 1981), 1-32; hereafter *CP*.

23. *LB*, 70, l.6; 7, ll.30 and 33.

24. The relationship between the Sublime and the Beautiful is discussed by Edmund Burke in Adam Phillips, ed., *Philosophical Enquiry into the Origin of our Ideas of the Sublime and Beautiful* (Oxford: Oxford Univ. Press, 1998).

25. Gaskell returned to the image of Wordsworth's *Thorn* for *The Moorland Cottage*, published in 1850 by Chapman and Hall. It is not possible to include a discussion of this tale here but see Alan Shelston "'The Moorland Cottage': Elizabeth Gaskell and Myles Birket Foster," *The Gaskell Society Journal*, 2 (1988): 41-58, for the influence of Wordsworth.

26. This story first appeared in *Household Words* on 16 and 23 November; the text referred to here is in *MC*, 123-143.

27. Winifred Gérin, *Elizabeth Gaskell: An Autobiography* (Oxford: Oxford Univ. Press, 1976; 1990), 29-30; 49; 73.

28. Wordsworth, *Poems*, 2: 50, 341-44.

29. *The Heart of John Middleton* was first published in *Household Words* 28 December 1850; the text discussed here is in *MC*, 145-165.

30. *Dickens Letters*, 6: 238.

31. For a discussion of Wordsworth's Pantheism, especially as suggested in *Tintern Abbey*, see Gill, 67-69.

32. For further reading on Wordsworth's legacy see John Powell Ward, *The English Line: Poetry of the Unpoetic from Wordsworth to Larkin* (Basingstoke: Macmillan, 1991).

Gaskell the Journalist: Letters, Diaries, Stories

Joanne Shattock

At the end of a long, and characteristically news-filled letter to her friend Catherine Winkworth, written in October 1854 while in the midst of writing *North and South*, Elizabeth Gaskell concluded by saying: "I must go to my *real* writing now; but I hope I have earned a letter from you."[1] In this paper I want firstly to reflect on what constitutes Gaskell's "real" writing, in the eyes of her contemporaries and in ours, in other words what kind of writer she is perceived to be. I want then to focus on one of her shorter works which I think might help to answer this question.

It is as a novelist that Gaskell's reputation was established in her lifetime and solidified in the four decades following her death. The architect of her twentieth-century reputation was A. W. Ward, in his capacity as the editor of the Knutsford edition published in 1906. Each of the eight volumes of the edition was devoted to a major text or collection which provided the title of the volume: *Mary Barton*, volume 1, *Cranford*, volume 2, *Ruth*, volume 3, *North and South*, volume 4, *My Lady Ludlow*, volume 5, *Sylvia's Lovers*, volume 6, *Cousin Phillis*, volume 7 and *Wives and Daughters*, volume 8, the suffix "and other tales" acknowledging the shorter works, stories, essays, and poems, which were fitted in, out of chronological order and without any obvious rationale, according to available space. *The Life of Charlotte Brontë* was not included in the Knutsford edition because it had been recently republished by Smith Elder as part of the Haworth edition of the *Life and Works of Charlotte Brontë and her Sisters* in 1900.

In response to the projector of one of the many biographical directories in circulation towards the end of her life, and having refused, as was her custom, to submit biographical details, Gaskell included the sentence "I do not see why the public have any more to do with me than to buy or reject the wares I supply to them."[2] It might have been deliberately arch, but the image of a writer who was aware of the literary marketplace has been picked up by a number of her more recent critics, among them Hilary Schor, in *Scheherezade in the Marketplace* (1992), and Linda K. Hughes and Michael Lund in their book *Victorian Publishing and Mrs. Gaskell's Work* (1999). Linda Peterson has shown how Harriet Martineau redefined authorship away from Romantic notions of originality, genius, and inspiration towards a more pragmatic and "Victorian" engagement with the market, with editors and book publishers, often with the help of a male mentor.[3] Martineau could have been described accurately as a "woman of letters." I want to suggest that "woman of letters" is an appropriate title for Gaskell too, but one which her readers and critics have been reluctant to bestow.

More recently Peterson has noted how infrequently modern critics as well as nineteenth-century commentators have used the term "woman of letters" in contrast to the frequency with which the term "man of letters" was and still is used.[4] Taking a cue from Carlyle's essay "The Hero as Man of Letters" (1841) the masculine version initially was seen to be imbued with some of the characteristics of Romantic genius, above the negotiations of the marketplace, unconcerned with contracts, fees, the requirements of editors and the demands of readers. But as the century progressed, the term "man of letters" came to denote more straightforwardly a professional author, one who earned his living from writing. G. H. Lewes's essay "The Condition of Authors in England, Germany and France" in *Fraser's Magazine* (volume 35, March 1847, pp. 285-95) is directed to and written about such mid-century professionals. In the essay Lewes argued that as a result of the burgeoning periodical press in England it was now possible to earn one's living by writing, something that was less likely on the continent due to the comparatively poor rates of pay in France and Germany. Lewes's article is implicitly directed towards and concentrates on male writers. Their female counterparts were dealt with in his July 1852 article in the *Westminster Review*, "The Lady Novelists" (volume 58, pp. 129-41) which included a review of Charlotte Brontë's *Jane Eyre* and Gaskell's *Mary Barton*. Lewes was the prototype Victorian "man of letters." In his eyes professional authors were men; "the ladies" were novelists, and presumably, although he doesn't mention them, poets or poetesses.

Linda Peterson also notes that women writers like Harriet Martineau and Anna Jameson, essayists, critics and prolific contributors to the periodical press were designated as "miscellaneous writers" by the original *Dictionary of National Biography*. Their male counterparts were described as "men of letters." These descriptions were adopted, not coincidentally, by *The Wellesley Index to Victorian Periodicals* (1968-89). Does this matter? I think it does. By refusing to designate them "women of letters" the professionalism, the scholarship and the sheer range of writers like Martineau, Jameson, Eliza Lynn Linton, Margaret Oliphant and Alice Meynell, among others, were implicitly undervalued.

There is another factor in this discussion, what Elisabeth Jay in her book *Mrs. Oliphant: a Literary Life* has termed the "Eliot paradigm" or the Eliot model, in which Marian Evans's career is taken as the norm, and the ideal. Evans first engaged with literary London in the 1840s when she became a contributor to and later assistant editor of the *Westminster Review*, writing also for the *Leader* and *Fraser's Magazine*. Once her career as a writer of fiction was established, she very consciously put reviewing and essay writing aside in order to concentrate on her novels, the assumption being that novel writing was a "higher" calling.[5] It is worth reminding ourselves that Eliot also wrote a journal and travel dairies, although she regarded these modes as essentially private writing and definitely not for publication.

Gaskell's posthumous reputation (and particularly her reputation in the twentieth century) has been influenced by the "Eliot model" in which the fiction, her full-length novels, has been privileged over her short stories, her essays, book reviews, and "miscellaneous writing." Her journalism has been regarded as journeyman work, part of her literary apprenticeship, even though, unlike Eliot, she continued to write essays, short fiction, book reviews, prefaces and at least one biography, until the end of her life. And so we have biographers like E. S. Haldane in *Mrs. Gaskell and her Friends* (1930), influenced, I believe, by the structure of the Knutsford edition, regarding Gaskell's "journalistic strain" (her phrase) as sub-standard, and suggesting that it had been a pity that she had continued to produce essays and stories for the periodical press, at the expense of the full-length realist novels which had crowned her career. Haldane does admit that as well as earning her welcome extra money Gaskell's "journalism" was a source of enjoyment, some of it enabling her to experiment with sensational elements denied to her in her realist fiction.[6]

Biographers, critics and readers alike are conscious of the impact on Gaskell's reputation of the publication of her collected letters in 1966, reinforced by the *Further Letters* in 2000.[7] Earlier biographers and critics made use of her published letters to Charles Eliot Norton (1932) and some had access to typescript copies of others,[8] but there is no doubt of the transforming power of the collected letters on the way in which her work as a whole has come to be regarded.

The impact of the letters has been twofold. Firstly they reinforce the point made by Winifred Gérin, the first biographer to have access to all the letters, – the close links between the letters and the published work. Gérin used the example of *Cranford* to demonstrate how much of the Gaskell revealed by the letters is reflected in her writing, particularly her writing in the first person: "Strangely enough," she wrote, "the style of *Cranford* resembles far more the style of her letters than any of her other fictions; because in her letters she was herself – and it must be remembered that she was an educated woman expressing herself with ease and humour when writing to her friends – and not concerned with pleasing the public."[9]

I agree with Gérin about the links between the voice of the letters and very often the voice in her articles, essays and stories, but I am sceptical of her easy assumption that in her letters Gaskell was "herself" and never self-consciously concerned about her readers.

The similarities between the voice of the narrator of many of her stories and the voice of the letters *are* striking. "You can hardly live in Manchester without having some idea of your personal appearance. … The factory lads and lasses take good care of that, and if you meet them at the hours when they are pouring out of the mills, you are sure to hear a good number of truths." That is the opening of *Libbie Marsh's Three Eras* (*Howitt's Journal*, volume 1 [5 June 1847, p. 310]). The story ends, again with a question from the narrator: "Do you ever read the moral, concluding sentence of a story? I never do, but I once (in the year 1811, I think), heard of a deaf old lady, living by herself who did" (volume 1, p. 347). The early story, "Martha Preston," published in *Sartain's Union Magazine* in February 1850 begins, "Within the last few years I have been twice at the Lakes. There is a road leading to Grasmere, on the least known side of Loughrigg" (volume 6, p. 133) which can be compared with the opening of "Cumberland Sheep-Shearers" in *Household Words* 22 January 1853), "Three or four years ago we spent part of a summer in one of the dales in the neighbourhood of Keswick. We lodged at the house of a small Statesman" (volume 6, p. 445). The extracts could be from Gaskell's letters, or from a travel diary. "I do not know if you have ever noticed it," the narrator of "Martha Preston" interjects at one point, "but it strikes me that a very active mother does not always make a very active daughter." It could be an extract from one of her letters. And there are other passages, for example in "Company Manners" (*Household Words*, 22 May 1854), her review of Victor Cousin's 1854 book on Madame de Sablé in which she regales her readers with stories of dinner parties gone wrong, or overly elaborate suppers prepared by anxious hosts. "No wonder I am old before my time" she muses at the end of one such anecdote in "Company Manners," which is recognizable from an event described in one of her letters.

The argument about how much the "I" of the letters is or was transparently "Elizabeth Gaskell," in contrast to the consciously constructed narrator's voice of the story, takes us to some of the theoretical issues raised by the letter as a literary genre. For whom is a letter written – is it an intimate document, intended for one recipient, part of an exchange, "written speech," a long distance conversation? How candid and natural can the letter writer be assumed to be? How much is the self as presented in a letter a construct, a fiction? As Charles Porter, a scholar of the letter as genre has suggested, "Like the diary and the autobiography ... the 'I' of the letter is to some extent a fabrication or 'fiction', not necessarily identical to its author." There is, he suggests, "an internal contradiction between the letter's implied spontaneity, naturalness and originality, and the inevitable artifice of its form."[10]

"For writer and recipient" as Mireille Bossis has observed, the letter is above all an extension of daily life. As such, an author's correspondence is treated as "a gold mine of biographical information, taking on a fixed and univocal value." The documents are used, she points out, without having passed through any critical filter; as such they are taken literally, "by the letter." It is assumed that they "tell the truth" – unlike novels, which weave fictions. Biographers of writers in particular regard letters unproblematically as revelatory of the "real" person behind the books.[11] But in the case of Elizabeth Gaskell, is this wise?

Rosemarie Bodenheimer, in her book *The Real Life of Mary Anne Evans* (1994) was one of the first to question this assumption, and to argue in George Eliot's case that the representations of the self in her letters were as much of a construct as her fictional heroines. Bodenheimer goes on to argue that Eliot's letters should be read in tandem with her novels and that together they are revelatory of the author's "real life." The reading of Gaskell's letters critically, and in tandem with her published work, particularly what I have loosely been calling her journalism, also poses new possibilities for interpretation.

One of Gaskell's first "publications" was a letter, an account of a schoolgirl visit to Clopton Hall in Warwickshire, which she wrote to William Howitt, and which he published verbatim in his *Visits to Remarkable Places* (1840). Other letters were extracted by Howitt in a subsequent book. Jenny Uglow has compared the carefully composed, measured prose of the Howitt letter, written as if consciously practising her writing, to the "slapdash tumble of news" and the breathless versatility of her letters to her sister-in-law, written at the same time.[12] In all of her writing, I would argue, Gaskell was conscious of the audience for whom she was writing, whether in her letters, in *Household Words*, the *Athenaeum*, or in her later pieces in *Fraser's*, the *Reader*, *Macmillan's*, in the 1860s.

In a frequently quoted letter to her friend Tottie Fox in 1850 Gaskell commented that she had a great number of "Mes": "One of my mes is, I do believe, a true Christian – (only people call her socialist and communist), another of my mes is a wife and mother. ... Now that's my 'social' self I suppose. Then again

I've another self with a full taste for beauty and convenience whh [sic] is pleased on its own account. How am I to reconcile all these warring members?"[13] Readers of Gaskell's published letters, on the other hand, have sometimes seen only a "social," rather carefully constructed self reflected in them. They note the busyness, the self-mockery, the irritations, the depressions, and occasionally the anger. But they note, too, the absence of any glimpses of an interior intellectual life, or of the impact of her reading. And they note the absence of any revelation of her deeper and more private relationships, with her husband and children, of the kind exhibited in her diary, written when her daughter Marianne was a baby. This is explicable, perhaps, because so few of the family letters survive, but not entirely. The "me" presented by the surviving Gaskell letters is, to many readers, a self-consciously constructed, social persona.

As well as the links between the "I" of the letters, which I am arguing was a carefully constructed "self" whether directed to Catherine Winkworth, Tottie Fox, and others, and the "I" of her shorter fiction, or her essays and reviews, as directed to readers of *Howitt's Journal, Sartain's Union Magazine, Household Words, All the Year Round, Fraser's Magazine, Macmillan's,* the *Athenaeum,* the *Reader,* etc. the other major impact of her published letters has been to put her work into context, and to show how professionally busy she was. The letters show her in receipt of a steady stream of invitations from journal editors and proprietors after the publication of *Mary Barton.* Eliza Cook invited her to contribute to her forthcoming *Journal* in 1849. The editors of *Chambers' Edinburgh Journal* were in pursuit in the 1840s. The flattering invitation from Dickens to contribute to *Household Words* in 1850 is well known. Less so is her polite refusal of Fanny Mayne's invitation to write for the evangelical penny magazine the *True Briton* in 1853.[14] No matter how pressed she was with her novels, she still had energy to organize another collection of her works: *Lizzie Leigh and other Tales* (1855), *Round the Sofa* (1859), *Cousin Phillis and other Tales* (1865), *The Grey Woman and other Tales* (1865), *Lizzie Leigh and other Tales* (1865), the last two compiled in the months before her sudden death in November 1865. Even in the midst of the storm surrounding the publication of *The Life of Charlotte Brontë* she had time to write a preface and notes to Maria S. Cummins's *Mabel Vaughan,* a writer and a text with which she seems to have had no obvious connection. While in the middle of writing *Sylvia's Lovers* she set off for Paris with Meta and Meta's friend Isabel Thompson, for a holiday, but also to undertake research for a projected biography of the seventeenth-century French salon hostess and letter writer Madame de Sévigné, a project which unfortunately she never completed.

In my introduction to the collected journalism I argued that throughout her career Gaskell was an astute judge of the literary marketplace, one who was not overly concerned about the status of the periodicals in which her work was published, but who regarded the press as a key element in her writing life.[15] The picture of the working life of this woman of letters, as presented in her own letters, demonstrates that the various strands of her writing, essays, short stories, reviews, prefaces, poems, diaries, letters, and novels are much more integrated than has been previously thought, that her writing life was much more seamless and coherent than has been recognized. What Haldane termed her "journalism," by which she meant everything other than the full length novels and a few novellas, was not the waste of time and energy she suggested it was, but an essential part of Elizabeth Gaskell: woman of letters.

To illustrate my point I want to turn briefly to a three-part series of articles, with the title "French Life," which Gaskell published in *Fraser's Magazine* between April and June 1864. It was connected indirectly with the unfinished biography of Madame de Sévigné, which she told her publisher George Smith she was working on in the spring of 1862. She made a special trip to Paris in May to locate manuscript collections, identify portraits, and to discuss her project with the French publisher Hachette, who was bringing out a collection of De Sévigné's letters. Together with her daughter Meta and her friend Isabel Thompson they went on to Chartres, and then toured the area around Vitré, near Madame de Sévigné's country estate Les Rochers.

More than a year later, in September 1863 she again wrote to George Smith about the book on de Sévigné, "more in my head than out of it, but I think it will be good," she told him. In the same letter she mentioned another half-finished work, "'Notes of a Wanderer' all sorts of odd bits, scenes, conversations \with rather famous people in Paris/, small adventures, descriptions &c &c met with during our two last journeys abroad in Brittany, Paris, Rome, Florence – 50 pages written – \I thought of sending this to Mr. Froude."[16]

It is an accurate description of the articles. The first part begins very much in the style of one of her letters: "We went to-day along the Boulevard Sévastopol, Rive Gauche, to pay a call. I knew the district well about six years ago, when it was a network of narrow tortuous streets. I used to have much difficulty in winding my way to certain points in the Quartier Latin from the Faubourg St. Germain, where I was staying."[17] It then turns into a diary of two of her journeys, the May 1862 expedition in search of Madame de Sévigné, part travelogue, part autobiography, part fiction, and a second trip, made to Avignon and the south of France en route to Rome in the spring of 1863. Uglow suggests that the articles draw on memories or even lost diaries from early trips in 1855 and 1857.

Gaskell disrupts the chronology of the two journeys, deliberately altering the dates of the fictional diary across the three parts of the article. Meta and Isabel become the Mary and Irene of her narrative. And she writes amusingly about herself – fearing circus lions that might enter her hotel window from a nearby square, improvising lunches from a local charcuterie, dealing timorously with churlish hotel servants, wondering whether to tip a supposed aristocrat fallen on hard times. The opening descriptions of Paris recall the area around her friend the salon hostess Mary Clarke Mohl's apartment at 120 Rue du Bac. Descriptions of individual rooms and of the domestic life of "a French family of the middle class" draw on the Mohl establishment, and those of some of their more exotic friends, like the ancient grand dame who tells the story of the *levée* of Voltaire's adopted daughter. Parts of the travel narrative can be mapped against her letters, which describe the scenes in less detail – the visit to Madame de Sévigné's country house, the food and daily routine of life with Mary and Julius Mohl.[18]

The third part of "French Life" is based on a journey made with Julia and Meta to Paris and Rome in the spring of 1863, following the completion of *Sylvia's Lovers*. The dates in this fictionalized travel diary are closer to the original journey, which was planned on the advice of the French historian Montalembert, whom Gaskell had met at the Mohls. Following his suggested route they arrived in Avignon to see the Palace of the Popes, but then found themselves detained by a seasonal mistral or wind. Their hostess, according to the narrative, provided them with a selection of books, some of which contained local history and legends, among them the "authorized report" of the trial for the murder of the Marquise de Ganges.

In the third part of "French Life" Gaskell proceeds to retell the real life story of a famous crime, the murder of a beautiful Provençal heiress by her husband and his two brothers. J. G. Sharps suggests an eighteenth century French collection *Causes Célèbres et Intéressantes* by François Gayot de Pitaval (1734-43) as a possible sources for her story. He also notes that Alexandre Dumas the elder included the story in his *Crimes Célèbres* (1839-40), which were in turn translated as *Celebrated Crimes* for Chapman and Hall's Foreign Library series in 1843.[19] The precise source for Gaskell's narrative is unclear. As part of the fictionalized diary in part three the narrator relates that she and her party visited a convent in nearby Ville-Neuve to see the Marquise's portrait painted by Mignard, which was in fact true. Gaskell, Meta and Julia visited the convent before embarking for Rome.

Dumas's version of the murder of Madame de Ganges was continuously reprinted in the second half of the nineteenth century and into the twentieth. Earlier the Marquis de Sade had also used the story for his 1813 novel *La Marquise de Gange*. Another popular version of the tale was published in *Tait's Edinburgh Magazine* for May 1842, the year before the Dumas translation. "The Story of the Marquise de Gange: a Real Tragedy of the 'Good Old Times' in France" was signed "V," and thought to be by J. R. Chorley, one of the magazine's regular contributors.[20]

Gaskell's version of what must by then have been a familiar tale is less detailed than Chorley's and her omissions are significant. She avoids any reference to the sexual predatoriness of the Marquise's two brothers-in-law, a key feature of Chorley's narrative. She glosses over the attraction of the young Louis XIV to the Marquise during her first marriage and the young woman's possible indiscretion, which Chorley implies is a possible slur on her innocence. Uglow sees in Gaskell's appropriation of the Marquise's story the familiar dark themes of male power, female submission and entrapment, men's physical and mental cruelty, women rendered helpless and denied speech, which are reminiscent of *The Grey Woman*. There is another incidental narrative in the third part of "French Life," the story of an aristocratic family during the Revolution who find themselves in the power of their servants, which is reminiscent of the interpolated tale in *My Lady Ludlow*.

The hybridity of "French Life" renders it unique. It is part autobiography, part travel diary, and part fiction, but fiction in one instance retold, at second hand. Gaskell may have read the Marquise de Gange's story from materials supplied by her Avignon landlady, as the narrative maintains, but she could have been drawing on earlier versions of the story, by Dumas or de Pitaval. Her adaptation and Chorley's, twenty-two years apart, are coincidental.

The mixing of genres in "French Life" was unprecedented and not repeated, at least in the journalism so far identified. The poise, subtlety and vitality of the pieces on the other hand, present no surprises. The voice and the personality which preside are recognizably the Gaskell of the letters, the author of the non-fictional articles in *Household Words*, in *Fraser's*, in *Macmillan's*. She is "herself," as Gérin said of *Cranford* and the letters. That "self," however, is as carefully constructed as the narrators of the major novels and tales.

A student of Elizabeth Gaskell, the novelist would probably ignore or underplay "French Life," and indeed most studies to date have done so. A study of Elizabeth Gaskell, Woman of Letters would give it the prominence in her oeuvre it deserves, connecting it with *The Grey Woman*, *My Lady Ludlow*, and with her letters, and seeing it as part of the seamless writing career which began with "Clopton Hall" and was still going full tilt in her last eighteen months, not only with *Wives and Daughters*, but with articles, a book review, and yet another collection of her essays and stories which this tireless contributor to the literary marketplace had on the stocks.

Notes

1. J.A.V. Chapple and Arthur Pollard, eds., *The Letters of Mrs. Gaskell*, (Manchester: Manchester Univ. Press, 1966, 1997), 310. Hereafter cited as *Letters*.

2. *Letters*, 761.

3. Linda Peterson, "(Re)inventing Authorship: Harriet Martineau in the Literary Marketplace of the 1820s," *Women's Writing*, 9.3 (2002): 337-50.

4. In a plenary session at the Research Society for Victorian Periodicals conference, held at the Graduate Centre, City University of New York, 15 September 2006.

5. See Elisabeth Jay, *Mrs. Oliphant, 'a Fiction to Herself': a Literary Life* (Oxford: Clarendon Press, 1995), especially chapter 7, "A Woman of Letters," 244-45.

6. Elizabeth Haldane, *Mrs. Gaskell and her Friends* (London: Hodder and Stoughton, 1930). See chapter 8, esp. 208-209.

7. John Chapple and Alan Shelston, eds., *Further Letters of Mrs. Gaskell* (Manchester: Manchester Univ. Press, 2000, expanded 2003).

8. Jane Whitehill, ed., *The Letters of Mrs. Gaskell and C. E. Norton* (London: Oxford Univ. Press, 1932). Two volumes of typescript material were deposited in the Brotherton Library, University of Leeds, compiled initially by C. K. Shorter in preparation for his (unpublished) book on Gaskell for the English Men of Letters series, and used by Jane Coolidge, later Whitehill, for an unpublished biography.

9. Winifred Gérin, *Elizabeth Gaskell: a Biography* (Oxford: Clarendon Press, 1976), 124.

10. Charles W. Porter, Foreword to *Yale French Studies*, "Men/Women of Letters," 71 (1986): 1-14.

11. Mirelle Bossis, "Methodological Journeys through Correspondences," *Yale French Studies*, 71 (1986): 64-65.

12. Jenny Uglow, *Elizabeth Gaskell: a Habit of Stories* (London: Faber and Faber, 1993), 121.

13. *Letters*, 108.

14. *Further Letters*, 106-107.

15. Elizabeth Gaskell, *Journalism, Early Fiction and Personal Writings*, The Works of Elizabeth Gaskell, Pickering Masters edition, ed. Joanne Shattock (London: Pickering and Chatto, 2005), 1: ix-xxxiv.

16. *Letters*, 712.

17. "French Life," *Fraser's Magazine*, 69 (April 1864): 435.

18. See *Letters*, 925-28.

19. J.G.Sharps, *Mrs. Gaskell's Observation and Invention* (Fontwell: Linden Press, 1970), 467.

20. *Tait's Edinburgh Magazine*, 13 o.s. / 9 n.s. (May 1842): 293-302. See *Wellesley Index to Victorian Periodicals* vol.4 for identification of 'V'.

Physical and Linguistic Metamorphosis in Gaskell's *The Grey Woman*

Renzo d'Agnillo

Elizabeth Gaskell's *The Grey Woman* is generally acknowledged as one of her finest and most powerful tales.[1] As a story of mystery and terror in which the features of its beautiful young female protagonist are prematurely transformed into those of an old woman, it is an intriguing blend of Gothic sensation and psychological probing. The extent to which this negative physical metamorphosis is reflected in the linguistic transformations of the story is, surprisingly, a factor which criticism has tended to overlook. Yet it is precisely through Gaskell's highlighting of language as the representation of a woman's struggle to come to terms with her altered identity that the story achieves its poignancy and intensity.

The original manuscript of the story contains the writer's brief acknowledgement that it "is true as to its main facts, and as to the consequence of those facts from which this tale takes its title."[2] John Geoffrey Sharps suggests that the realistic description of the opening sequence is derived from one of Gaskell's various holiday visits to the Rhineland in which, to pass the time, the members of her party would exchange "the most frightening & wild stories … all true."[3] This biographical basis serves as a realistic background to a story rife with Gothic elements: an evil, but fascinating, brigand-leader who marries a German miller's daughter before rushing her away to his gloomy castle in which she is held a virtual prisoner; a violent death among the servants; a neighbour murdered for plunder; a case of mistaken identity resulting in murder; the tragic murder of the heroine's friend; the eventual capturing and decapitation of the evil husband; and most importantly of all, a young girl whose attractive features are transformed into those of an old woman almost overnight. Extrapolating the main events of the plot in such a way, however, belies the fact that the surface, textual level of the story is, from the beginning, conditioned by a strategy of prolepsis: the most important information regarding Anna's story is anticipated in a synoptic account by one of the members of the family. As a result, the focus is upon the teller rather than the tale so that the real drama lies not on the story level as such, but in the recesses of the main protagonist's tormented mind. At the same time, however, the incipit itself, rather than preparing the reader for the dramatic events that lie ahead, functions as a sort of temporary foil. For the four neatly counterbalanced clauses of the opening sentence reflect the casual and objective tone of an external, or extra-homodiegetic, first-person narrator (a middle-class female English tourist) who describes a moment during her travels in which she has stopped for a rest and some refreshment at a mill: "There is a mill by the Neckar side, to which many people resort for coffee, – according to the fashion, – which is national in Germany."[4] In the narrator's commonplace observations, in which even the adjectives are markedly neutral, she also does not disdain to insert a teasingly ironic denial of touristy expectations of the picturesque: "There is nothing particularly attractive in the situation of this mill … (the flat and unromantic) side of Heidelberg … a well-kept dusty quadrangle … a garden full of willows, and arbours, and flower-beds not well kept" (GW, 287). This unremarkable scene is enlivened by the good humour and kindness of the old miller whose "loud musical voice," warm hospitality, and "rolling laughter of welcome" (GW, 287) dominate the opening sequence. Although an apparently minor linguistic detail, Gaskell had originally omitted the adjective "loud" and had simply written: "his musical voice," which suggests a more romantic trait that is somewhat at odds with the man's lively, robust character; the change confirms an initial intent to play out the contrast between the rational middle-class narrator and the down-to-earth host who eagerly entertains his guests whilst cheerfully continuing with his own farmyard chores. Yet, in spite of the air of familiarity and reassurance he radiates to all his guests, it is with old Scherer that the first signs of disharmony emerge – specifically in the contrast between the description of his musical voice and the mournful tune he whistles as he passes by: "and, as he went, this great, prosperous, happy-looking man whistled softly one of the most plaintive airs I ever heard" (GW, 288). In her manuscript Gaskell had originally written: "and then left us, softly whistling." The alteration from descriptive past to past tense significantly heightens the dramatic impact to create a disconcerting incongruity.[5] This sudden note of disharmony is immediately followed by a reference to the miller's antipathy for the French, which stretches back to previous generations of his family and, as we shall see, forms the sub-text of Anna Scherer's story:

> His family have held this mill ever since the Old Palatine days; or rather, I should say, have possessed the ground ever since then, for two successive mills of theirs have been burnt down by the French. If you want to see Scherer in a passion, just talk to him of the possibility of a French invasion. (GW, 288)

This sombre revelation is, in turn, reinforced by a violent storm in which "heavy splashes" fall through "the tender leaves of the thick leafy covering" under which the company are sheltered "as if they were tearing them asunder" (*GW*, 288). The storm is of functional importance for, as a result, the guests are allowed shelter in the miller's own house in which the first-person narrator espies the portrait of the beautiful young Anna Scherer. The definite transition from the reassuring, une-ventful reality of the present world of the narration to a past mythical world of terror coincides with the moment the girl's identity and fate are revealed:

> It is the likeness of a great-aunt of her husband's. … See! Here is the name on the open page of this Bible, "Anna Scherer, 1778." Frau Scherer says there is a tradi-tion in the family that this pretty girl, with her complexion of lilies and roses, lost her colour so entirely through fright, that she was known by the name of the Grey Woman. (*GW*, 289)

In the miller's fragmented synopsis of Anna's story the effects of her experiences anticipate the actual events which produced them:

> "Ah!" said he, his face changing, "the aunt Anna had a sad history. It was all owing to one of those hellish Frenchmen; and her daughter suffered for it – the cousin Ursula, as we all called her when I was a child. To be sure, the good cousin Ursula was his child as well. The sins of the fathers are visited on their children. The lady would like to know all about it, would she? Well, there are papers – a kind of apol-ogy the aunt Anna wrote for putting an end to her daughter's engagement – or rather facts which she revealed, that prevented cousin Ursula from marrying the man she loved; and so she would never have any other good fellow, else I have heard say my father would have been thankful to have made her his wife." (*GW*, 290)

By anticipating the outcome of the story without providing all the necessary explanations (for example, the exact meaning of the sinister quotation from the Bible), Gaskell is free to focus exclusively on the subjective perspective of Anna's account to her daughter, Ursula. Although Anna's letters form the narrative from this point onwards, the fact that they are divided into portions (rather than parts) points to a structural incompleteness that has suggestive overtones. For the dis-course situation of the second level of narration (that is, the letters of the intra-homodiegetic first-person narrator Anna Scherer to her daughter) is inscribed within a larger framework in which the external first-person narrator addresses an implied external addressee. Anna Scherer's narrative act is an attempt to put into perspective a series of events of which she was at the centre but over which she had absolutely no control. Whether it is an example of the most strikingly femi-nist aspect of Gaskell's fiction, as Terence Wright suggests, Anna, like so many of her female characters, is "situated where self-discovery and self-creation are essential."[6] In fact, the whole story is nothing less than her attempt to express the difference between the image of her young self in the portrait and the Grey Woman she finally becomes.[7]

The conventional realism of the first extra-homodiegetic 'I'-narrator seems to be set in deliberate contrast to the emotional intensity of the second intra-homodiegetic first-person narrator (Anna Scherer), whose account takes over the rest of the story. In reality, certain discourse and textual features suggest a more disquieting interrelation between the two dimensions represented by the commonplace world of the present, and the past world of deceit and evil than seems initially apparent. First, the extra-homodiegetic first-person narrator, who treads the ambivalent terrain of implicit-internal and real-external narrator, far from being the passive receiver of Anna Scherer's story, is forced to become actively engaged in translating and transcribing the dispersed contents of her letters. Indeed, in re-writing (or re-crafting) the story, she is responsible for its final form. Second, if the central issue of *The Grey Woman* is the recovery of a lost or fading memory (a process already evident with the present members of the Scherer family), it is ironically this narrator, a stranger and foreigner, who is granted the privilege of reviving Anna's 'voice.' The two dimensions of the external, everyday world and the mysterious underworld of menace and terror are also instantly merged on a linguistic level in the opening description of the surrounding landscape: "flowers and luxuriant creepers knotting and looping the arbours together" (*GW*, 287). On a symbolic level, the adjective "luxuriant," and the gerunds "knotting" and "looping" connote a hidden layer of complexity made up of an intricate web of connections and relations that will later characterise the spatial alienation of de la Tourelle's castle in which Anna eventually finds herself imprisoned.

Given Anna's predominant character traits of passivity and submission, it is appropriate that the first portion of her letter begins not with her own words, but those of her distraught daughter: "Thou dost not love thy child, mother. Thou dost not care if her heart is broken" (*GW*, 291). The bitter resentment of the girl's unfair accusation acts as the catalyst for Anna's written justification of her opposition to her marriage to the French artist Le Brun. When she actually begins to set down her own words, they reveal a woman hardened to a relentlessly cruel reality:

> Ah, God! and these words of my heart-beloved Ursula ring in my ears as if the sound of them would fill them when I lie a-dying. And her poor tear-stained face comes between me and everything else. Child! hearts do not break; life is very tough as well as very terrible. But I will not decide for thee. I will tell thee all; and thou shalt bear the burden of choice. (*GW*, 291)

So acute is Anna's distraught state that any direct verbal confrontation with her daughter would only become the cause of her death: "It would kill me to be questioned" (*GW*, 291). Though instigated by her daughter's accusations, Anna's letter-writing necessarily entails a one-way communicative transaction which deliberately avoids dialectics in the search for psychological solace and stability.

The tripartite structure of Anna's story is reflected on as many levels: first, it is divided into three portions; second, Anna is victimised by three people; and third, she marries three times (although the second is the fake marriage to her woman servant, Amante). Her tortuous plight unfolds along the itinerary of this threefold progression, with each stage representing a radical metamorphosis from the previous one.[8] Anna's narration picks up from the moment her ordeal is over and she returns with Ursula to her family who, having believed her dead, are now barely able to recognise the once beautiful girl behind her shockingly aged features. Ironically, the only way Anna is able to prove her identity is to point out the similarities between the portrait of her younger self and her daughter: "I had to lead thee underneath the picture, painted of me long ago, and point out, feature by feature, the likeness between it and thee" (*GW*, 291). Not only does the portrait sanction the spatial and temporal estrangement between her present and former self, but her melancholic recollections of her childhood also reinforce the sense of an irretrievably lost idyll:

> I recalled … the details of the time when it was painted; the merry words that passed between us then … the position of the articles of furniture in the room; our father's habits; the cherry-tree, now cut down, that shaded the window of my bedroom, through which my brother was wont to squeeze himself, in order to spring on to the topmost bough that would bear his weight; and thence would pass me back his cap laden with fruit to where I sat on the window-sill. (*GW*, 291)

Having lived in exile from the protective world of her family home, Anna is now obliged to recall all of the everyday "details" pertaining to her past life there in the desperate attempt to re-affirm her membership. But such, otherwise homely, features are merely enumerated in a static language that is indicative of loss rather than recovery: the "merry words," for example, remain unqualified; the position of the articles of furniture suggests a mathematical precision void of emotion; the father's daily habits are only referred to in a neutral way with no further qualification; and the cherry tree, although such a source of former merriment, no longer exists. Anna's memory of herself sitting on the window-sill is particularly significant. For this liminal position of caution (in contrast with the daring conduct of her brother) is symptomatic of the passivity and weakness that lead to her ruin. This is not to suggest that her fate is completely self-motivated: the two central female figures of Babette Müller, her envious sister-in-law who, desirous to be rid of her rival in beauty, eagerly encourages Anna to accept an invitation to visit her old friend Sophie Rupprecht, and Madame Rupprecht, who practically forces her into marrying the wicked de la Tourelle, both play key roles in the girl's downfall. Yet, whilst Anna lays explicit blame for what happens to her on the former: "That Babette Müller was, as I may say, the cause of all my life's suffering" (*GW*, 292), nowhere does she actually deny Madame Rupprecht's good faith, in spite of her apparently malicious manipulation of her.

Anna's initial delight in her re-acquaintance with her friend Sophie soon yields to dismay when she discovers that the Rupprecht household is the very antithesis of her own home ("just the opposite of what it was at my father's house" [*GW*, 294]). The transition from the natural life of her own home to the affected and artificial manners of the French court becomes an essentially upsetting experience:

> The life in Karlsruhe was very different from what it was at home. The hours were later, the coffee was weaker in the morning, the pottage was weaker, the boiled beef less relieved by other diet, the dresses finer, the evening engagements constant. I did not find these visits pleasant. (*GW*, 294)

In the stifling atmosphere of Madame Rupprecht's house, with its strict rules of social etiquette and severe prohibitions, Anna finds herself obliged to bow to the impersonal pressures of social convention. Her first encounter with Monsieur de la Tourelle occurs precisely during one of these moments of tension verging on boredom:

> I thought I had never seen anyone so handsome or so elegant. His hair was powdered, of course, but one could see from his complexion that it was fair in its natural state. His features were *as delicate as a girl's*, and set off by two little 'mouches', as we called patches in those days, one at the left corner of his mouth, the other prolonging, as it were, the right eye. His dress was blue and silver. I was so lost in admiration of this beautiful young man, that *I was as much surprised as if the angel Gabriel had spoken to me*, when the lady of the house brought him forward to present him to me. (*GW*, 295; italics mine)

Anna is immediately beguiled by what she perceives as de la Tourelle's utter delicacy – a deliberately deceptive trait and one ironically underscored by the explicitly female simile, "like a girl's," and the absurd reference to the guardian angel Gabriel. The naivety of the language and its lingering on exquisite details, such as the "two little 'mouches'" the man has applied to his face to enhance the overall effect of charm and grace, betrays the self-deception that leads to Anna's undoing. Furthermore, beyond the magnetic effect de la Tourelle initially exerts over the girl, emerge other very different elements that expose the falsity of his genteel behaviour (such that her admiration dissipates the moment she perceives his compliments to become exaggeratedly insistent). The deliberate ambivalence of the verb "thought" (ie what she thought at the time or what she believed was the case) already suggests an awareness of the illusion. Likewise, the adjective "lost" appropriately underlines Anna's own helplessness and lack of moral mettle, the latter of which is now made to emerge as her principal negative trait. The terminology employed for the description of de la Tourelle insists on his affectation without for the moment hinting at his underlying brutality. His consequent courtship of Anna is as flattering as it is vacuous, and given the importance Gaskell always attributes in her fiction to the power of dialogue, it is significant that the whole episode is rendered in indirect discourse so as to drive home the point of the couple's complete lack of communication. Thus, the irony of the twice repeated expression: "The conquest I had made," since in no way does Anna directly encourage de la Tourelle; rather she merely succumbs unthinkingly to his devilish traits as if drugged by the mindless conventionality of the whole situation. The uncertainty of Anna's feelings during de la Tourelle's courtship is a reflection of his paradoxical effect on her: "And yet I never quite felt at my ease with him. I was always relieved when his visits were over, although I missed his presence when he did not come" (*GW*, 296). His evil influence necessarily presents itself in a deliberately false guise and is perceived only once it is too late for her to resist it. After protesting against her sudden engagement in matrimony to him, Anna is harshly reprimanded by Madame Rupprecht:

> I learned from Madame Rupprecht that she had written to my father to announce the splendid conquest I had made, and to request his presence at my betrothal. I started with astonishment. I had not realized that affairs had gone so far as this. But when she asked me, in a stern, offended manner, what I had meant by my conduct if I did not intend to marry Monsieur de la Tourelle … what could I do but hang my head, and silently consent to the rapid enunciation of the only course which now remained for me if I would not be esteemed a heartless coquette all the rest of my days? (*GW*, 297)

Indirect discourse again undermines the power of words to reinforce the alienating effects of social conventions for Anna, as she naively allows her destiny to be settled in order to avoid a social condemnation that her own youthful mind exaggerates out of all proportion. On the textual level, the young girl's extremely negative qualification of marriage in the sentence preceding her invitation to the Rupprechts: "I had no notion of being married, and could not bear anyone who talked to me about it" (*GW*, 293), already anticipates her opposition to her betrothal to de la Tourelle which is chillingly conveyed in the extended nounphrase: "the rapid enunciation of the only course which now remained for me."

Once the three central male protagonists (Anna's father, her brother, and de la Tourelle) are eventually united before her, the latter's hostility becomes plainly obvious:

> He was very polite to them; put on all the soft, grand manner, which he had rather dropped with me. ... But he a little scoffed at the old fashioned church ceremonies which my father insisted on; and I fancy Fritz must have taken some of his compliments as satire, for I saw certain signs of manner by which I knew that my future husband, for all his civil words, had irritated and annoyed my brother. (*GW*, 297-98)

This passage deftly articulates the psychological uncertainty of Anna's feelings towards de la Tourelle as well as the ambiguity he evokes in those around him. The first clause registers her objective awareness of his civil behaviour, but the phrasal verb "put on" immediately following unmasks its insincerity, the lexical items "soft" and "grand" being consequently invested with a bitter irony. His mocking reaction to her father's desire for a church ceremony ironically contrasts with Anna's previous comparison of him to the Angel Gabriel, and her brother's detection of the sarcasm behind his words not only exposes the show of pretence de la Tourelle barely manages to conceal but also emphasises his hostility (further marked by the crescendo of increasingly strong modifiers "rather ... a little ... irritated"). The eventual agreement which ensues between the men bears all the cold formality of a business transaction: "But all the money arrangements were liberal in the extreme, and more than satisfied, almost surprised my father. Even Fritz lifted up his eyebrows and whistled" (*GW*, 298). This action also exposes a masculine complicity towards material wealth that transcends any feelings of compassion for Anna as a person and degrades her to an object of possession. It is appropriate that after this encounter Anna fully realises the extent of her loneliness: "I alone did not care about anything. I was bewitched – in a dream, a kind of despair. I had got into a net through my own timidity and weakness and I did not see how I could get out of it" (*GW*, 298). The emphatic "alone" not only expresses her despair more forcibly than its alternative "only I," but the adjective "alone" also points to a psychological as well as physical isolation. Even as the mature (and, as such, presumably wiser) narrator of her own story, Anna's sense of her situation hovers between shifting the blame onto the inexplicable, "I was bewitched," and her own self, "through my own timidity and weakness."

As already noted, de la Tourelle's courtship of Anna is conducted through indirect discourse on the textual level. When he is eventually attributed a speech in direct discourse, it is in the form of a detached and formal admonishment to his newly wedded wife:

"Henceforth, Anna," said he, "you will move in a different sphere of life; and though it is possible that you may have the power of showing favour to your relations from time to time, yet much or familiar intercourse will be undesirable, and is not what I can allow." (*GW*, 299)

The convoluted expressions and passive constructions of de la Tourelle's cold-hearted discourse contrast sharply with the warm and affectionate words of Anna's father: "If my child is unhappy – which God forbid – let her remember that her father's house is ever open to her" (*GW*, 299). Yet, even the miller, in addressing his daughter, disturbingly shifts from the intimate *thou* to the impersonal object pronoun "her," as if to sanction formally their separation on a linguistic level. In fact, in marrying de la Tourelle, Anna loses not only her family but also her nationality; consequently everyone now speaks of her as "being a Frenchwoman" (*GW*, 299). Thus, from the idyllic world of her home at the mill, to the stifling formality and confinement of Madame Rupprecht's urban dwelling, to the dreary isolation of de la Tourelle's castle, where she arrives after a two-day journey, Anna's social exile, which coincides with the first stage of her metamorphosis, is complete. Her exilic state is also extended to the confines of de la Tourelle's castle, the two parts of which – the Chateau, a dreary and "raw new building … hastily run up for some immediate purpose" (*GW*, 299), and the old castle, strong and picturesque but unassuming, are connected by an intricate series of passages and unexpected doors that operate as an objective correlative of his own secretive and devious nature. The spatial and temporal division characterised by the two buildings reinforces the decidedly estranged relationship between husband and wife. Consequently, Anna, forced to occupy the salon which is completely separated from the rest of the building, is strictly forbidden to enter de la Tourelle's chambers in the old part of the castle. As a result, she experiences feelings of mystery and terror which, far from being incited by the supernatural elements of a typical Gothic tale, are, in reality, the products of her own suppressed imagination:

> But when, in the *gloom* of an autumnal evening, I caught my own face and figure reflected in the *mirrors*, which showed only a *mysterious background* in the dim light of the many candles which failed to illuminate the great proportions of the half-finished salon … I trembled in silence at the *fantastic* figures and shapes which my imagination called up as peopling the *background* of those *gloomy mirrors*. (*GW*, 300, italics mine)

The iterative nature of the passage, with its chiasmic link of lexical items, "gloom … mirrors … mysterious … background … background … gloomy mirrors," reflects, in a circular pattern, the obsessive self-absorption of Anna's fear. This state of paralysis is only interrupted on the arrival of Anna's maid and companion Amante.[9]

The importance of Amante's function in the story cannot be overestimated. It is she who organises the escape from de la Tourelle's castle and helps Anna to create a new identity during their hiding, and it is she who first approaches Dr. Voss, the man Anna eventually marries. However, contrary to the writer's intentions, the obvious sexual connotation of her name cannot go unnoticed.[10] Significantly, Amante's positive qualities (which represent the very antithesis of de la Tourelle's deviousness and falsity) compensate for those lacking in Anna's husband: "She was tall and handsome ... and somewhat gaunt ... she was neither rude nor familiar in her manners and had a pleasant look of straightforwardness about her" (*GW*, 302-303). The fact that Amante not only provides the female warmth and companionship Anna desperately lacks, but also, by later assuming a male disguise, literally replaces de la Tourelle as her fantasy husband, may suggest a lesbian attraction (on the subconscious level of play). More importantly, it also underlines the power of female solidarity against male victimisation. Unlike Anna, Amante is fearless in her dealings with de la Tourelle, to the extent of outwardly manifesting her scorn. Thus, for the first time in the story, Anna overcomes her state of isolation to establish a real relationship with another person based on complicity and trust. That she is happy to relinquish all her responsibility to Amante, however (precisely as she does earlier with her sister-in-law), is confirmation of a personality inclined to passivity and apathy. So, after her fatal error in allowing Madame Rupprecht and de la Tourelle to bend her will, she regains her trust in humanity through her reliance on Amante.

Amante's entrance at the beginning of Portion 2 coincides with a metamorphosis on the discourse level, marked by an acceleration in the narrative which, until this point, is characterised by Anna's brooding reflections of self-torment. Naturally, in recounting the terrifying events which involve her witnessing her husband, whom she has discovered to be none other than the leader of a band of brigands called les Chauffeurs, dragging the murdered body of his neighbour, Sieur de Poissy, into their house while she is hiding under a table, Anna (or the external first-person narrator?) alters her style accordingly. There occurs a metamorphosis on the textual level, in parallel to Anna's increasing hysteria, which dramatically contrasts with the relatively controlled phraseology in which approximately the first half of the story is written:

> Now, now was my time, if ever; and yet I could not move. It was not my cramped and stiffened joints that crippled me, it was the sensation of that dead man's close presence. I almost fancied – I almost fancy still – I heard the arm nearest to me move; lift itself up, as if once more imploring, and fall in dead despair. At that fancy – if fancy it were – I screamed aloud in mad terror, and the sound of my own

strange voice broke the spell. … The sound of her [Amante's] voice gave me strength; I walked straight towards it. … Where I was, where that voice was, I knew not; but go to it I must, or die. The door once opened – I know not by which of us – I fell upon her neck,[11] grasping her tight, till my hands ached with the tension of their hold. (*GW*, 315-16)

Parataxis now becomes the dominant clause structure until the end of the story, in marked contrast with the heavy subordination that characterises the first two portions. Such a metamorphosis on a language level appropriately reflects the restless existence of the two women on the run and in hiding from de la Tourelle, and the high frequency of ellipsis and lexical repetition further intensifies the dramatic crescendo of events. The first shelter the women find is, ironically, a storeroom at the house of a miller, whose master is the murdered Sieur de Poissy. In spite of the women's terror at being discovered by de la Tourelle and his gang, who come to the house in search of them, the description of the commonplace objects of this environment have a soothingly therapeutic effect after the terrifying impersonality of de la Tourelle's castle: "There was bedding piled up, boxes and chests, mill sacks, the winter store of apples and nuts, bundles of old clothes, broken furniture, and many other things" (*GW*, 321). It is here that Amante disguises herself as a man by cutting her hair short and "cutting up old corks into pieces such as would go into her cheeks" (*GW*, 323) and that Anna allows her to transform her own features in such a way as to eradicate any sign of beauty: "I let her dye my fair hair and complexion with the decaying shells of the stored-up walnuts, I let her blacken my teeth, and even voluntarily broke a front tooth the better to effect my disguise" (*GW*, 323). This fake metamorphosis is at once a necessary purification process in which Anna is stripped of the beauty which has partly been her undoing and, together with her fake marriage to Amante, prepares the terrain for her real metamorphosis and marriage to Dr. Voss at the end of the story. It is also only through Amante's death that Anna can be completely liberated from de la Tourelle (who is later captured and decapitated) as well as from the exilic dimension of her fictional life, and re-accepted into the world of social convention. Whether it is a final irony or a justified fate, her reconciliation comes in the form of her own social death. For not only do her features undergo such a transformation as to render her completely unrecognisable: "my yellow hair was grey, my complexion was ashen-coloured, no creature could have recognized the fresh-coloured, bright-haired young woman of eighteen months before" (*GW*, 339) but, just as she became a Frenchwoman in marrying de la Tourelle, she finally loses her real identity in marrying Dr. Voss: "The few people whom I saw knew me only as Madame Voss; a widow much older than himself, whom Dr Voss had secretly married. They called me the Grey Woman" (*GW*, 339). The attribute is doubly significant. Not only is the colour grey suggestive of lifelessness and death, but also, as a compound colour in which black and white are both present but neither dominant, it appropriately designates Anna's lack of autonomy and moral direction. Indeed, unlike most of Gaskell's female characters, she desperately requires the powers of self-assertion. It is a final irony, therefore, that at the moment she loses her name she musters the strength, through the power of the written word, to find self-expression. In this sense, her letters represent a desperate attempt to give voice to a personality that until that moment has only been acted upon by others.

If Anna learns any lessons from her experiences it can only be that she has been the main source of her woes. First, her beauty not only rouses the jealousy of her sister-in-law but also attracts an evil-doer like de la Tourelle. Second, her lack of moral judgement renders her easily prone to the negative influence of others. Thus, her dissuasion of her daughter to marry the Frenchman Le Brun, who is none other than Sieur de Poissy's son, is an act of moral cleansing which compensates for her previous lack of courage in failing to report de la Tourelle's crime. Ursula's obedience to her mother's wish offers small consolation, for after her brief initial outburst, her voice is silenced and she remains the innocent victim of her mother's tragedy. If the sins of the fathers fall on their children, it is evidently the latter who pay. Gaskell's inability to provide a final reassuring vision is also extended to the first 'I'-narrator and Anna herself, whose desperate message has only partly been retrieved – its final words being the sudden simple stark sentence revealing Ursula's lover's name: "It is Maurice de Poissy" (*GW*, 340). For just as the reassuring voice of the first 'I'-narrator dissolves into a covert presence behind Anna's letters never to assume control of the narrative again, so is Anna offered no other form of salvation than an obliteration of her natural identity.

Notes

1. Gaskell's *The Grey Woman* was first published in Dickens' periodical *All the Year Round* in 1861, before appearing in book form four years later.

2. I am deeply grateful to Francesco Marroni for allowing me to consult his meticulous notes from the original manuscript of *The Grey Woman* which is now conserved in The John Rylands Library, Manchester.

3. Divisions mine. See John Geoffrey Sharps, *Mrs. Gaskell's Observation and Invention* (Fontwell: Lindon Press, 1970), 335-36. Sharps concludes that the events at the beginning of the story refer to her first visit of 1841.

4. Elizabeth Gaskell, *Gothic Tales*, ed. Laura Kranzler (London: Penguin, 2000), 287. Henceforth *GW*.

5. Terence Wright, *Elizabeth Gaskell: 'No We Are Not Angels'* (London: Macmillan, 1995), 210.

6. Eleven years pass between the portrait of Anna and her marriage to de la Tourelle.

7. This tripartite division is also reflected in the fact that the story itself effectively contains three incipits: the first being the external narrator's opening description, the second the opening phrase of Anna's letter being her daughter's words and the third, the actual beginning of Anna's narration: "My father held, as thou knowest, *the* mill on the Neckar" being precisely the subjective correspondent of "There is *a* mill by the Neckar-side" (emphasis mine). Each incipit is distanced in time so as to increase the estrangement between the two narrative voices.

8. It is worthwhile observing that Gaskell deletes several times in her manuscript the words "my husband" which she substitutes with "Monsieur de la Tourelle."

9. "Amante" is the Italian word for lover.

10. John Fowles, *The French Lieutenant's Woman* (London: Vintage, 1969, 2004), 156. Fowles' sense of the tender relationships existing between women in the Victorian period as being ascribable far more to "the desolating arrogance of contemporary man than to a more suspect motive" may be directly applicable to the particular relationship between the two women in Gaskell's story.

11. Gaskell's original phrase was "I fell into her arms." In the original manuscript "into" and "arms" are deleted and replaced by "upon" and "neck" which convey a decidedly more violent impact.

Liminal Femininity in Gaskell's *Mary Barton* and *Wives and Daughters*

Sandro Jung

In her fiction Elizabeth Gaskell reveals a fascination with marginal figures and the abject and canvases a moral matrix deviation from which constitutes the risk of potential social and moral fall and stigma. Not only is she determined to break down barriers of decorum that protect middle-class readers from disease-ridden, under-nourished, and dying factory workers, as well as the social contagion represented by prostitutes and fallen women, but she also promotes a Christian narrative of inclusion according to which those occupying liminal positions in society should be offered sympathy. In doing so, she contributes to an ongoing debate regarding the need for tolerance towards social outcasts and aims to demolish some widely held prejudices that have traditionally been reinforced by a strict middle-class moral code. Gaskell does not generally assess a character's social fitness through a utilarian consideration of his or her function within society; rather, she concerns herself with the conditions affecting individuals and the reasons preventing liminal figures from being recognised as fit members of Victorian society. And in her treatment of non-normative and transgressive femininity, she does not focus on censuring physical, social, or moral difference, in the terms of the radical, Evangelical rhetoric of the time, as repulsive or depraved. In Gaskell's industrial novel, *Mary Barton* (1848), John Barton, the murderer of Harry Carson, is not categorically rejected as the evil threatening the economic superiority of the capitalist middle classes over the workforce and the balance of the class system; rather, she offers a sympathetic portrayal of his tragedy, reading his suffering in terms of the condition of his class and transforming the grieving mill-owner, Carson senior, into a Christian figure capable of forgiveness. Above all, as a "sympathetic criminal,"[1] Barton is represented through the eyes of his daughter, the eponymous protagonist, whose own experience of social stigma has opened up and refined her understanding, compassion, and tolerance, eventually replacing her shock and horror at her father's crime with her realisation of her enduring love for him and his memory. By learning to interrogate the mechanisms of society, specifically the law, the difference between right and wrong, and realising her own responsibility as a meaningful individual with social and moral duties, she is able to see beyond the verdict of social penalties and, while not trying to diminish his guilt, offer an emotional response that is motivated by her sense of her father's love for her and their past happiness together.

Gaskell's *Mary Barton* is a novel that sketches in a range of characters the difficulty of moral choices and the concomitant consequences that can rarely be calculated. Knowing that Barton must have murdered Carson, Jem Wilson is prepared to be hanged and take Barton's secret to his grave so that Mary will not be tainted by her father's crime; equally, Mary secretly meets the mill-owner's son, Harry, and has to endure the burden of this legacy, even after she realises she loves Jem. Up until her public confession in the Liverpool courtroom, she has to confront secretly the uncanny presence of this clandestine affair and the possible threat of discovery.

While scholars writing on liminal female figures in Gaskell's fiction largely concentrate on the fallen woman, little work has been offered that investigates the practice of coquetry, the deliberate display of female attractiveness, and the moral implications of a careless or calculating publicising of desire in Gaskell's first novel and in *Wives and Daughters* (1865). Ellen Bayuk Roseman argues that the Victorians "demonized" the coquette "because she represents forms of agency and desire that deeply threaten social norms."[2] Morally ambiguous, the coquette is associated with the seduction and controlling of male desire in order to reach "ultimate self-sufficiency."[3] Intent on reversing gender and power relations, she deploys her fetishised beauty and fashion to construct an irresistible femininity for male observers. Roseman observes that: "The coquette raises fears because of her expertise as well as her seductiveness, and for her investment in clothing for its own sake as well as her desire to captivate men."[4] Gaskell puts coquettes to diametrically opposed uses in her fiction. In *Mary Barton*, she relates the "unschooled" (and transient) coquette, Mary, to the moral dangers of the fallen woman, whilst *Wives and Daughters* offers a striking portrait of a "professional" coquette, Cynthia Kirkpatrick. In her persistent use of coquetry and its associated emotional vacuity, Cynthia represents a negative role model of Victorian femininity that will not fulfil its social function of marriage, childrearing, and the proper instruction of housewifely femininity. My discussion of the two types of coquettes as liminal representations of acceptable Victorian femininity will not primarily focus on Hilary Schor's contention that "Mary's romance is a form of class warfare."[5] Rather, this essay explores Schor's argument that female otherness in Gaskell's fiction is represented by means of a woman's deviation from the Christian ideals of virtue and containment but also through a resulting perversion of the Romantic goodness of nature within woman.[6] The coquette, in that respect, treads a fine line between liminality and acceptability; one step out of line can signify the loss of character and reputation, as well as the ruin of her marriage prospects. Her reliance on the public display of her attractiveness and the arousal of men's interest and desire removes her from the traditional domestic context of the unmarried Victorian female to the public sphere in which the male gaze objectifies and commodifies her in sexual terms. The Victorian coquette's principal "crime" is her moral vacuity and superficiality and not her questioning of social strictures, as was the function of the late eighteenth-century, Jacobin coquette.[7] Similarly, she does not use her coquetry to benefit reform and effect change, nor is she defined by a curiosity that characterises the heroines in the novels of Gaskell's biographical subject, Charlotte Brontë.[8] Gaskell recommends the domestic sphere as the appropriate realm for a woman, and cautions against the dangers of leaving the security of the patriarchal home. A female's abandonment of (or, more complicatedly in the case of *Ruth*, the expulsion from) her native community and its protective mechanisms catapults her into a context of desire and violence the language of which she cannot understand and the effects of which are illustrated in Esther, Mary Barton's aunt, who is barred from ever returning to the sanctified hub of the family, the working-class home.

In *Mary Barton* Gaskell outlines the fatal consequences of flirtation for a woman. Meeting Harry Carson clandestinely but with the help of a girl of doubtful morality and reputation, Sally Leadbitter, Mary indulges the fantasy of becoming the wife of the wealthy young man whose fortune would not only enable her to feed her vanity but to secure her father's financial well-being. She relies on the capital qualities of her physical attractiveness, believing Carson's protestations of love sincere and considering herself "as good as engaged to be married" (*MB*, 120) to him; she does not question his motivation, nor does she interrogate whether her lover would willingly draw his equals' censure upon him by allying himself in marriage to the family of one of his father's "hands." Various fantasies converge in Mary's naïve trust in Carson which cloud her little-developed judgment and blind her against the social stigma she is risking were her meetings with Harry Carson known to her class community. While true love represents a motivating force that would (and does in the end) morally redeem her, it is her calculating, financially motivated "ambition" (*MB*, 121) to be a lady that informs her actions and her passive acquiescence to be objectified by Carson so as to represent the absolute symbol of his desire.[9] She regards herself implicitly as taking part in an exchange of commodities, and volunteers her person and its desirable, external

55

qualities in return for the hoped-for elevation to Carson's social status and a fancied life of ease:

> The old leaven, infused years ago by her aunt Esther, fermented in her little bosom, and perhaps all the more, for her father's aversion of the rich and the gentle. ... So Mary dwelt upon and enjoyed the idea of someday becoming a lady, and doing all the elegant nothings appertaining to ladyhood. It was a comfort to her, when scolded by Miss Simmonds, to think of the day when she would drive up to the door in her carriage to order her gowns from the hasty tempered, yet kind dressmaker. But the best of her plans, the holiest, that which in some measure redeemed the vanity of the rest, were those relating to her father; her dear father, now oppressed with care, and always a disheartened, gloomy person. (*MB*, 121)

Some of Mary's wishes, especially "doing all the elegant nothings appertaining to ladyhood," anticipate Mrs. Gibson's desire in *Wives and Daughters* to give up earning her own livelihood, to effect a change of situation, to transform herself from dependent widow into independent wife, to direct others, rather than be directed, and to instruct servants rather than students, thereby exercising authority rather than serving it. The role that Mrs. Gibson fashions for herself is one that runs counter to her social (and natural) role as mother, step-mother, and wife, as she establishes a regime of arbitrarily exerted power from which her pliant husband shrinks and finally detaches himself, once he discovers her unscrupulousness and hard-heartedness. In Mrs. Gibson and Mary, Gaskell delineates two types of women: the one utilising art to achieve her ends and the other the natural, instinct-driven female whose morality is not uncontroversial or steady but is strengthened through engaging with, and overcoming, obstacles; ultimately, the latter type of femininity can be tempted but not corrupted by the lures of art. While Mary's use of dress underscores her natural beauty, she does not seek to use fashion as an emancipatory tool or to conceal blemishes or misrepresent her true surface and the substance of her identity. Her construction and identification as coquette (by Harry Carson) take place externally and are not motivated by the "professional" coquette's "intention" of not "responding to the feelings awakened" ("coquetry," meaning 1, *OED*). Her "ambition" is contained within the boundaries of her inexperience of social mechanisms, strategies of courtship, and the dangers of unlegitimised desire, love, and correspondence with a member of the opposite sex. Having been raised in an environment of benevolent patriarchal authority, she has not imbibed, through explication and example, the model and tenets of obedient, working-class housewifely femininity. Mary's understanding of the boundaries of the public and private spheres is vague; her desire to perform a part in a realm where she can be admired for her beauty is a temptation that she will not resist at this early stage of the novel. Only once she has undergone a severe act of cartharsis, making a very public declaration of her love for Jem at court, does she realise the full extent of her love and the social significance of a female's revealing it to an audience other than her lover. Whereas Mrs. Gibson effectively performed the well-rehearsed role of demure and dependent governess before her second marriage, once the doctor's wife she reveals her true colours, acts out her morally irredeemable character, and demonstrates her failure both as a mother and wife. However, at that point she can fall back upon the contractual security of institutionalised marriage that she coveted from her husband, relying on his means to continue in her new social status.

Mary's initial emphasis on surfaces (the trusting of appearances, but also her marketing herself to Carson in terms of her beauty) and materialistic considerations are transmuted once she internalises Jem's love for her and realises that a life with Jem is what she truly desires. Her coquetry does not represent looseness of morals, abandoned flightiness, and irresponsibility of her social and familial duties, but an ignorance of the rigidity of social conventions and carelessness that are not ingrained and endemic; rather, they are the result of growing up without a mother's guidance. Gaskell's educational approach illustrates the harmful effects that Mary's ignorance of, and unfamiliarity with, class-specific conventions entails. Self-assured that her beauty will secure her a working-class lover such as Jem Wilson, she applies the same expectations to her meetings with Carson, not realising however that she is not an equal in this planned exchange of financial assets and her commodities of physical beauty, reputation, and character. She is unable to comprehend clear demarcation points in social conventions, ceremonies, and the structures regulating female working-class identity in the Victorian period. Unlike a true, "professional" coquette, however, it is this uncertainty – the inability, through ignorance, to decode class- and gender-specific expectations – that endow her character with tragic potential. While coquettes are self-centred and only concerned about their own gratification, Mary never loses sight of her father's future prospects and the wish to return the love with which he sustained her after her mother's death.

The narrator's insistent statement that Mary does not love Harry Carson implies censure nevertheless, as it stresses the potential moral transgression that her actions *could* precipitate. Carson was "a lover, not beloved, but favoured by fancy. A gallant, handsome young man; but not beloved" (*MB*, 80). The transient nature of the protagonist's "fancy" is in clear contrast with Victorian propriety which allowed no such fleeting, unregulated interest in a person who could potentially destroy one's reputation. It reveals her trusting to romance and fantasy and a detachment from the social and moral codes that dominate human relationships at the time Gaskell was writing her novel. Mary's desire to "mak[e] ... an impression" is not only aroused by Carson but also when she meets Job Legh's niece,

Margaret, for the first time. "Margaret could hardly take her eyes off her, and Mary put down her long black lashes with a sort of dislike of the very observation she had taken such pains to secure" (*MB*, 67). Emotionally insecure, Mary seeks to define herself through her brilliant appearance, even in a homosocial context; yet, this brilliancy is merely external and contrasts strikingly with the pseudo-angelic and spirituality-inspiring singing voice of Margaret. At the same time, it is the onset of Mary's illness at the end of the court case that initiates a cataclysmic prostrating of her powers: she is infantilised while ill, helpless, and no longer wilfully assertive; in fact, through an instance of *anagnorisis*, she is transformed into the kind of woman who will find fulfilment once she emigrates to Canada with Jem and Mrs. Wilson senior and turns wife and mother.

Mary's naturally open disposition is constrained by her secrecy about her meetings with Carson and, later in the novel, her knowledge of her father's murder of his employer's son. Initially at least, she relies on womanly intuition and only then develops a more sophisticated perception of her role as a female individual and men's constructions of her as a coquette. Her beauty, in that regard, is an asset but also exposes her to temptations to which the steadfast Margaret is not subjected.[10] A public exposure of Mary's ambiguous intercourse with Carson would tarnish her "character" and, ironically, make her *unattractive* as a future wife to men of her class. The danger that a loss of character entails is exemplified in Mr. Thornton's negative reaction to Margaret Hale's walking with her (then-not-acknowledged) fugitive brother at dusk in *North and South* (1855). Barbara Leah Harman observes aptly: "By protecting Frederick, Margaret traffics with what is dangerous, illicit, even violent, and this fact is reemphasized when she herself commits a 'crime'" by lying in order to shield him.[11] Margaret's clandestine walk with her brother "leads … to the public assumption that Margaret is tainted with desire." She is unable to erase this assumption's "general effect of producing her as a sexual body available to men and of making her ashamed of her beauty."[12] The secret between Mary and Harry Carson, as is shown later in the novel, will haunt Mary, make her both suffer the reproaches of others and feel the sense of abandonment and liminality associated with a transgression of propriety. Then, Esther, an uncanny vision from a happy past, will disrupt Mary's romance by reminding her of her mother. At the same time, Barton's encountering Esther inspires him with anxiety concerning Mary's future. To him, Esther is a haunting phantom, pursuing him and threatening his last link with his past humanity. He blames his sister-in-law for his wife's death and implicitly and unconsciously links this blame with Mary, a conflation of identities that is re-evoked and re-enacted when Mary mistakenly identifies Esther as her dead mother.

In leaving her class (and working-class community) without the sanctioned protection of a husband, Esther made impossible a return as a meaningful member of her family and class. She survives as the relict of her own poor knowledge of patriarchal society and is left to fend for herself in the only profession open to her; on the brink of society, she is no longer an object of desire but fulfils a function only – it is this function that men have assigned to her while at the same time exploiting this function in their own, largely uncensored overstepping of social boundaries and propriety. Esther's life, previously defined by her emotional relationship with the father of her child, is transformed into an existence contributing to an economic process. John Barton's explanation of her physical appearance is couched in economic terms, and he sees this focus on commodity as the root evil of females working in factories. The mechanised work process engrosses the female's attention while in the factory, rewarding her with spendable capital, but this kind of employment also deprives young and inexperienced women of the traditional education – transmitted from one woman to another, from mother to daughter – that instils the values of the family, rather than those of publicised individuality. Barton recalls in chapter 1 that "Esther spent her money in dress, thinking to set off her pretty face" (*MB*, 43);[13] holding her responsible for his wife's death, he notes that her "giddiness, her lightness of conduct, had wrought this woe" (*MB*, 58). Esther's fall not only represents the result of her own wrong choices or anticipates the risk that Mary is running by meeting Carson, but the story of Esther has larger social significance in that, as Elizabeth Gaskell noted in a letter to Mrs. Greg, it "throw[s] light upon their groping search after the causes of suffering."[14]

Esther takes responsibility for her fall by accepting the socially constructed shame that giving birth to an illegitimate child entails. The narrator states that Esther truly loved the father of her child; there is no indication that she calculated – like Mary does – on improving her social position. Her motives are, therefore, pure, which makes her fall all the more terrible. Mary's coquettish acceptance of Carson's attentions, however, is calculated to flatter her own vanity, ensuring that she sees herself in the position of agent to decide whether *she* wants to accept him in marriage and not vice versa. He is seen as a handsome means to an end, but she has no sense of what it means to be a "professional" coquette.

Like Mary, Esther had not adequately been prepared for the duties and the role of a housewife. Identifying parallels in the lives and appearances of his daughter and her aunt, John Barton decides that Mary will not work in a factory; unwilling to "go to service" (*MB*, 62), she is keen to retain the sense of independence that she gained through the absence of a female authority figure in her home. Living in her employer's household, with an implicit control of both her public and private lives as a member of his "family," would run counter to her desire to be admired publicly, at the same time curbing her individuality and integrating her within a clearly organised social and gender framework. The narrator notes:

"Three years of independence of action … had little inclined her to submit to rules as to hours and associates, to regulate her dress by a mistress's ideas of propriety" (*MB*, 62). More importantly, "her mysterious aunt, Esther, had an unacknowledged influence over Mary. She knew she was pretty … [and] had early determined that her beauty should make her a lady" (*MB*, 62). Drawing on the fiction of Esther's success, Mary wants to reach an end (marriage and wealth) by means of her beauty; she thereby functionalises her beauty in the way the coquette does, but her "plan" is not well-thought-through and relies on Carson's undissembling acceptance of her as a valid partner in marriage. The choice of dressmaking as a profession contributes to the realisation of her vision in that she is soon promoted to show-woman, offering a performative display of the clothes and her person (and, of course, but secondarily, her skill). Roseman observes that "'Window-dressers' – young women who modelled the wares of clothing stores – and the shopgirls who sold the merchandise displayed themselves, earned money, and developed a notoriously flirtatious boldness through their work."[15]

Mary contemplates that a "dressmaker's apprentice must (or so Mary thought) be always dressed with a certain regard to appearance; must never soil her hands, and need never redden or dirty her face with hard labour" (*MB*, 62), as servants and factory workers do. The parenthetical tag, "or so Mary thought," introduces the narrator's better knowledge of the ways of the world. Mary's naivety, coupled with her simple desire to improve her lot in life, informs her flirtation and is not fundamentally linked, as in the "professional" coquette, with persistent dishonesty and falsehood. While middle-class women can use coquetry for short periods of their lives, specifically at the time of courtship, and are not reproached for it, the case of a working-class female is decidedly different, as the woman neither has the leisure nor the independence to play the coquette. Working-class coquetry, therefore, is seen as an anomaly in behaviour that indicates moral corruption. Significantly, Harry Carson misunderstands Mary's behaviour in that he judges her in the sense of a "professional" coquette, little imagining that she in fact does not have any idea of his true intentions and that she has been guided by their intermediary, Sally, who appears well-versed in intrigues.

Mary's naivety and intuition are related to what Schor has explored in terms of the Romantic, innate goodness of the female; however, in the secular, industrial world of the Victorian period, a role-specific education for a woman is required. Trusting to her belief in the fiction that Esther made her fortune by marrying outside her sphere and class, Mary shows herself to be ignorant of the differences between the classes that are the basis of John Barton's moroseness, anger, and depression. Barton trusts his daughter and cannot imagine that she would look for a partner outside her own class. Mary's longing for a better life of affluence and security echoes Esther's earlier longing for companionship and a family of her own, independent of John Barton's conservative authority. As an unmarried female member of the working class, Mary relies on the protection of both her father and her community. Her employment at the shop of Miss Simmonds functions as a contact zone between the working and the middle classes. It facilitates an intercourse (if desired by the middle classes) that would otherwise not be possible publicly, but by actively engaging in clandestine intercourse with Carson, Mary becomes subject to the censures of both the middle *and* the working classes; through this act of transgression, she no longer exclusively belongs to either. She is thereby caught up in "the profound moral alienation of [the] classes."[16]

In her analysis of the relations between domestic servants and factory workers, Dorice Williams Elliott argues that, despite the common origin of the two groups, a division existed between them that was inspired by servants' adopting the paternalist view of loyalty to the middle class, that is the Masters, thereby considering themselves superior to their brethren working in factories. Elliott's argument can be applied to the dressmaker, Miss Simmonds, who employs Mary, for Barton's daughter, through her work, is introduced to a new class and its values, and develops aspirations that are in clear contrast with the working-class ethos. According to Elliott, "Mary's language asserts that her class has its own ideas of 'propriety' and its own network of social relations and privileges and that she and her peers do not need to be regulated by middle class employers."[17] Her desire for social mobility indicates that she aspires to the financial security of the middle classes but that she is not aware of the differences in conduct and role of the working and middle-class unmarried female, a contrast that is strikingly borne out in Mary and Cynthia Kirkpatrick. Although *Mary Barton* aims to generate a better reciprocal understanding of the classes, it does not offer alternatives to the system or its social and complex moral codes as such. The pride of the community that John Barton represents is reflected in its members' pronounced identities, whereas the loyalty of domestic servants to their employers commonly results in their "giv[ing] … up their own identities."[18] In that regard, Mary's exploration of the contact zone where working and middle-class individuals meet stimulates her implicit refashioning herself, appropriating her working-class identity to the needs of a new identity as the middle-class wife of Harry Carson.

Mary's assignations with Carson are as much for mutual pleasure and the self-conscious gratification of her vanity as they are escapes from the increasingly depressing environment at home. Keeping her meetings secret, she instinctively feels that they are wrong, as they have not been authorised by her father, a feeling also experienced by the young Ruth when she joins Mr. Bellingham for a walk in the woods. Sally, the low, resourceful female also working at the dressmaker's and employed by Carson to further his cause with Mary, intends to exert her corrupting influence but ultimately shows Mary how morally wrong her secret meetings were. Leadbitter "was vulgar-minded to the last degree," and "in her eyes it was an honour to have had a long list of wooers" (*MB*, 132). She advocates a type of femininity that encourages numerous "wooers," suitors soliciting the female in marriage, but the very encouragement of being approached by numerous suitors runs counter to the working-class female's aspirations to modesty. Judging vulnerable and inexperienced females like Mary by her own intrusive personality, Sally assumes that young women should use an equally intrusive flirtatious persona to attract numerous men. She is oblivious to "[c]onsiderations of modesty or propriety" and is characterised by the narrator as possessing the "talent ... to corrupt others" (*MB*, 132). She represents a disruptive force among the females of *Mary Barton*, and her physical unattractiveness is equalled by her moral callousness.

Lacking the beauty that recommended Esther and Mary to middle-class male figures, Sally, despite her moral perversity, is protected within her community. She has found an occupation for herself by trafficking information between middle-class men and ignorant women from her own class and thereby serves the function of the procuress. Her movement between the classes has given her a degree of mobility and a reputation that make her unattractive to men from her own class community. Unlike Mary's aunt, however, she contains her (sexual) desire.

When Esther and Mary meet, the one represents the potential double of the other. The aunt's non-containment of desire and the impulse to explore the public sphere without John Barton's sanction has resulted in her inability to frame linguistically the experience of her liminality. She "longed to open her wretched, wretched heart, so hopeless, so abandoned by all living things, to one who had loved her once; and yet she refrained, from dread of the averted eye, the alerted voice, the internal loathing, which she feared such disclosure might create" (*MB*, 294-95). Her suffering on the occasion is immense, she craves for love and yet she is an outcast, an alien, doomed by her decision to leave her family and class, to be avoided and shunned by those who once loved her. Inventing a "tale of married respectability" (*MB*, 297), she temporarily fashions a position for herself that she would rightfully have occupied, had the father of her child married her. Yet, this fake return to an innocent, working-class existence only depresses her more deeply, as she knows that she is performing an act of masquerade, wearing a dress that "had a sort of sanctity to the street-walker" (*MB*, 292). Once admired for her "fresh dazzling beauty" (*MB*, 293) and "loving and unselfish disposition" (*MB*, 294), Esther, as a result of her moral fall, has undergone a transformation: she has become a monster whose touch repels John Barton. Gaskell, usually reluctant to visualise physicality, describes in detail Esther's dress, an emblem of her profession:

> It [her profession] was told by her faded finery, all unfit to meet the pelting of that pitiless storm; the gauze bonnet, once pink, now dirty white, the muslin gown, all draggled, and soaking wet up to the very knees; the gay-coloured barège shawl, closely wrapped round the form. … Much was like the gay creature of former years; but the glaring paint, the sharp features, the changed expression of the whole! But most of all, he [John Barton] loathed the dress; and yet the poor thing, out of her little choice of attire had put on the plainest she had, to come on that night's errand. (*MB*, 168-69)

Gaskell's description of Esther's dirty and soaking-wet dress offers a metonymic capturing of the change that she has undergone from a beautiful and innocent girl to a consumed and exhausted prostitute. The very article of dress, previously underscoring her beauty, now serves as a denominator of her functionalised, fallen existence; she has become a grotesque spectacle, rather than the image of the immaculately clean and modest working-class women, Alice Wilson or Mary Barton, senior. The uses of fashion to set off beauty to advantage or the consumption of fashion for its own sake are seen as dangerous. Roseman has noted that in *North and South*, Margaret reveals "self-contained, narcissistic pleasure" in admiring herself wearing a shawl, an action "at once innocent and sensual."[19] Gaskell cautions against vanity and displayed beauty in protagonists such as Ruth, Margaret, Mary, or Cynthia as dangerous in that it can invite temptation, raise male desire, and all too often culminates in a woman's undoing. The transformed Esther no longer possesses "dazzling beauty," but serves as a monument of her personal woe and her profession's condition, being characterised by "sharp features" and "glaring paint." She uses art to attempt a temporary restoration of nature and her former charms, but this art stresses her grotesqueness as much as it highlights her suffering.

Esther understands herself as a monster that would pollute Mary if she allowed herself to be kissed by her niece. The "frantic kind of gesture" (*MB*, 298) with which she pushes Mary from her symbolises the rejection that prostitutes had to endure on a day-to-day basis. It anticipates the rejection that Ruth will be experiencing when she is slapped by a little boy who, having overheard his mother's statements regarding Ruth's sexual impurity, terms her "a bad, naughty girl."[20] Unlike Mary, however, Ruth, at the time of her seduction, was too young and inexperienced to penetrate Bellingham's true motives. Ultimately, one of the main functions of *Ruth* is the recognition of a female's inherent worth, even though she may be fallen. In that regard, Gaskell assures her readers that even the alienating Esther could still love, and that her turning prostitute was not by inclination but out of the necessity to save her child. For Gaskell, her fall was, as Angus Easson has pointed out, "not a psychological perversity but a social responsibility."[21] "Esther is presented as something other than merely a bad girl" and her character bears "more than a facile moral significance in the underlying pattern of the novel."[22] She is an expression of the "disruptive and humanizing energies"[23] of Gaskell's fiction and, through the contrast drawn between her past and present, is re-humanised rather than dehumanised.

Esther's despairing "'Not me. You must never kiss me'" (*MB*, 298) anticipates Mrs. Wilson's rejection of Mary when she learns of her flirtation with Carson. She is then a "dirty hussy" (*MB*, 278) and stands accused of "arts" and "profligacy" (*MB*, 281) with which she is supposed to have ensnared Jem. As Easson notes, Mary is both "the dominant consciousness" of and "the emotional point of growth" in the novel, and as such undergoes a maturing process from a working-class coquette to a loving wife and mother.[24] It is part of this process to *understand* the seriousness of her transgression and to overcome her coquetry, a cultural *habitus* that she possibly copied and emulated from the middle classes. How alienating the charge of flirtation and coquetry was in the Victorian period is reflected in Jem's (painful) reaction to Carson's thoughtless statements about Mary being an "arrant flirt" (*MB*, 227) and "a giddy creature" (*MB*, 227).

Unlike Mary, Cynthia Kirkpatrick in *Wives and Daughters* is an outspoken flirt. Through her mother's neglect, Cynthia taught herself to adopt the appearance of a young lady, without assimilating the values of Victorian middle-class morality and propriety. She negotiates the conflicts between her desires and the legitimacy of these desires by appearing spotless, constructing an image of perfection, which is externally manifested by her striking beauty, her irresistible charm, and the desire to please others. Notwithstanding her engagement with Roger Hamley, the second son of Squire Hamley, in his absence she continues her coquetry, which culminates quickly in an offer of marriage from one of her step-father's former pupils. Mr. Gibson reads her behaviour initially as "thoughtless" (*WD*, 426), rather than as deliberate, but realises that her coquetry is constitutional and that she is unable to be constant.[25] She frequently protests to Molly, her step-sister, that she is not "good," and the secrecy that she adopts to conceal her anxiety at her engagement with Mr. Preston at last brings on depression, a reflection of what Gibson terms the "gloomy things" (*WD*, 326) that occupy her mind.

Cynthia's abject coquetry is made worse by her sophisticated understanding of her own nature and her supposed inability to live a life of truth. Molly, by contrast, is characterised by her "shy modesty" (*WD*, 137), her straightforwardness, and willingness to help Cynthia to free herself from the demands of Mr. Preston. In doing so, she is mistakenly blamed for the transgressions that Cynthia has committed, and is stigmatised temporarily for what is publicly considered her clandestine affair with Mr. Preston. As Barbara Leah Harman has observed, "Molly is initiated by implication into the mysteries of sexual relations through the fiction of her involvement in unsanctioned intimacy."[26] Cynthia, however, is prepared to jeopardise Molly's reputation to save her own.

From her first introduction, Cynthia is a moral alien. When educated in France, she adopts the forms of French coquetry, forms which, to a degree, conceal her inability to love herself or others. When, on her mother's marriage, she is introduced into Mr. Gibson's household, she realises quickly that her coquettish standards are strikingly different from her stepfather's strict notions of propriety. As a role model her mother has failed Cynthia, and it is partly due to this failure that Cynthia cannot enjoy the happiness and fulfilment that Molly will experience in her marriage with Roger Hamley. Easson remarks that Cynthia's

> capacity for self-analysis places … [her] above her mother, yet even this is a source of irritation when she so vexingly will not do what she knows is morally right. Cynthia, it seems, is incapable of being entirely happy, because she can see what is valuable in others and yet always undervalues it until it has passed beyond her grasp. Like her mother she is entangled in mysteries.[27]

In fact, Cynthia, aware of her disposition, anticipates the ensnaring dangers that she will encounter in London, but for pleasure's sake visits her uncle and aunt nevertheless and there meets Mr. Henderson whom she marries at the end of the novel. She acts out her desires spontaneously and does not rationalise them; in that regard, her quick exit from the novel does not allow the reader to develop a sympathetic response to Cynthia. The corrupting influence of coquetry has proven all-pervasive, hardened her into a static figure, unable to change, and will make it impossible for her to be content in marriage.

How alien the flirtatious Cynthia is to Mr. Gibson is evidenced when he learns the truth about her engagement to Mr. Preston. He reprimands his stepdaughter severely, reproaching her for having "been a flirt and a jilt even to the degree of dragging Molly's name down into the same mire" (*WD*, 572). He refers to the "evil constructions [that] are put upon actions ever so slightly beyond the bounds of maidenly propriety" (*WD*, 573) and considers the simultaneous engagement to two lovers as an instance of the duplicity of his stepdaughter's character; rather more drastically, he could have seen it as an act of prefigured adultery. Clearly, the contrast between Molly's high moral standards and Cynthia's imprudence and egotism is echoed in the frictions that exist between Mr. Gibson and his wife.

The striking contrast between Molly and Cynthia is demonstrated when Molly, after one of Cynthia's outbursts of passion, tries to sympathise with her stepsister. Molly's willingness to console Cynthia is immediate and not subject to the forms of Victorian emotional restraint; she tries to soothe her without considering that she has just completed her work in the garden and is consequently covered with soil. The soiled Molly evokes the idea of dirt associated by Natalka Freeland with working-class goodness and integrity, whereas the suffering Cynthia is described as beautiful (and implicitly false); this contrast confirms Freeland's argument that the beauty of the coquette Cynthia is only external and that it conceals effectively her moral perverseness from the public gaze.[28] Molly in due course realises Cynthia's true character, undergoing with regard to her, as Easson observes, "a progression of liking, love, bewilderment, and disappointment."[29]

Cynthia is a victim of her education in that she was neglected by her mother and imbibed the wrong principles regulating femininity in France. She adopted a behavioural code that is unacceptable to Victorian society but that is mitigated by her striking beauty and her public display of decorum. She protests that her coquetry is innate, an even more damning statement as it implies constitutional (moral) corruption and depravity. The Squire of Hamley Hall identifies her as a French woman, in both her manners and coquettish behaviour, whereas Osborne's French widow, Aimée, does not embody the squire's negative notions of French femininity. At the end of the novel, Cynthia, marrying Mr. Henderson, is not held accountable for her actions. As her simultaneous engagement to Roger Hamley was not publicly known, she is saved from the disgrace that it would have been impossible to negotiate as a young woman seeking a marriage-partner. As it is, Cynthia marries a rich barrister and secures herself the independence that she did not enjoy in her mother's household. The open-ended nature of *Wives and Daughters* leaves equally open the fate of Cynthia Kirkpatrick. As a "professional" coquette who consistently declared that she could not reform, she most likely will continue her habits of coquetry even in marriage, not making happy either herself or her husband. The power of the Victorian home, so central to Gaskell's fiction, may be able to transform Cynthia, but in the light of such figures as Mary Barton's aunt, Esther, or the martyr, Ruth, and the suffering both invited through trust in love, this appears unlikely.

Both Mary and Cynthia are liminal females: while Mary's coquetry is the short-lived result of her self-conscious beauty, vanity, and her wish to transcend the class barriers, Cynthia's is supposedly innate. Mary successfully reforms through her love for Jem and his for her, but Cynthia's selfish disposition is not given the chance to reform. Rather, by trying to appear faultless, she seeks to deny male power over her; her beauty, in this regard, serves as the patina concealing her subversive potential and resistance to the model of the obedient female outlined in the character of Molly, who in many ways can be regarded as the sane double of the "mad" Cynthia. To note, as one critic of *Mary Barton* does, that the "cause" of Mary's self-consciousness of her beauty "is not so much natural vanity as cultural reinforcement"[30] is to misread the extreme contrast that Gaskell develops between the fickle, coquettish, and irresponsible Mary from the beginning of the narrative and the disillusioned and loving partner of Jem at the end of the book. She is symbolically "cured" of this vanity when she relives a second infancy on her sick bed. It is through Gaskell's sympathetic presentation of Mary that the morally and sexually transgressive implications of coquetry (also associated with prostitution) are brought to the fore.

While Cynthia is not facing any lasting consequences of her fickleness, Mary through the criticism she encounters from Jenny Wilson is made aware that the working-class moral code appears to be more strict than that of the middle classes. Unlike Mary, Cynthia is not redeemed from her coquetry, but withdraws from the novel through her marriage in what is ultimately an unsatisfactory resolution of her moral ambiguity. Potentially, Mary could have been a fallen woman, especially as at crucial moments positive and negative influences such as Margaret and Sally are striving to guide her. It is necessary that Mary be humbled, and this process of impressing on her the gravity of her guilt is effected through both her illness and the societal illness that kills John Barton. The Victorian rejection of "coquetry as a kind of cover story that conceals deeper fears about gender roles … and above all about female agency, autonomy, and eroticism"[31] is strikingly illustrated in Gaskell's fiction. While *Wives and Daughters* offers the most pessimistic view of the figure, Gaskell's first novel demonstrates that coquettes are redeemable. From her liminal position as beautiful coquette, Mary returns to the centre of a family who love her. Also, the romance of *Mary Barton* inspires hope that tolerance towards social outcasts such as Esther could someday come about as well as that coquetry will no longer be necessary in courtship where two partners truly love each other.

Notes

1. Patricia E. Johnson, "Art and Assassination in Elizabeth Gaskell's *Mary Barton*," *Victorians Institute Journal*, 27 (1999): 156.

2. Ellen Bayuk Roseman, "Fear or Fashion; or, how the Coquette got her bad name," *ANQ*, 15.3 (2002): 13.

3. Roseman, "Fear or Fashion," 17.

4. Roseman, "Fear or Fashion," 13.

5. Hilary Schor, *Scheherezade in the Marketplace: Elizabeth Gaskell and the Victorian Novel* (Oxford: Oxford Univ. Press, 1992), 20.

6. See Schor, *Scheherezade in the Marketplace*, 60-66.

7. See Yaël Schlick and Shelley King eds., *Refiguring the Coquette: Essays on Culture and Coquetry* (Lewisburg, PA: Bucknell Univ. Press, 2008).

8. See Sandro Jung, "Charlotte Brontë's *Jane Eyre*, the Female Detective and the 'Crime' of Selfhood," *Brontë Studies*, 32.1 (2007): 21-30.

9. Elizabeth Gaskell, *Mary Barton*, ed. Stephen Gill (Harmondsworth: Penguin, 1970). All page references are to this edition and are given parenthetically in the text. On the issues of dissimulation and misrepresentation, see Roland Vegso, "*Mary Barton* and the Dissembled Dialogue," *Journal of Narrative Theory*, 33.2 (2003): 163-83.

10. The importance of beauty and the "demoralized sensuality" and "pure aestheticism" that seduce this beauty are elaborately discussed with regard to *Ruth* by Schor, *Scheherezade in the Marketplace*, 61-62.

11. Barbara Leah Harman, *The Feminine Political Novel in Victorian England* (Charlottesville, VA: Univ. Press of Virginia, 1998), 70. Harman also notes that the loss of "moral purity" is inextricably linked with the loss of "sexual purity" (70-71).

12. Roseman, "Fear or Fashion," 18.

13. See Mariana Valverde, "The Love of Finery: Fashion and the Fallen Woman in Nineteenth-Century Social Discourse," *Victorian Studies*, 32.2 (1986): 169-88; Beth Kalikoff, "The Falling Woman in Three Victorian Novels," *Studies in the Novel*, 19.3 (1987): 357-67, and Suzann Bick, "'Take Her Up Tenderly: Elizabeth Gaskell's Treatment of the Fallen Woman," *Essays in Arts and Literature*, 18 (1989): 17-27.

14. Elizabeth Gaskell, *The Letters*, ed. John A. V. Chapple and Arthur Pollard (Manchester: Manchester Univ. Press, 1966), 74.

15. Roseman, "Fear or Fashion," 15.

16. E. P. Thompson, *The Making of the English Working Class* (Harmondsworth: Penguin, 1963, 1980), 376.

17. Dorice Williams Elliott, "Servants and Hands: Representing the Working Classes in Victorian Factory Novels," *Victorian Literature and Culture*, 28.2 (2000): 379.

18. Elliott, "Servants and Hands," 281.

19. Roseman, "Fear or Fashion," 19, 18.

20. Elizabeth Gaskell, *Ruth*, ed. Angus Easson (Harmondsworth: Penguin, 1997), 62.

21. Angus Easson, *Elizabeth Gaskell* (London: Routledge & Kegan Paul, 1979), 114. Also, Melissa Schaub, "Sympathy and Discipline in *Mary Barton*," *Victorian Newsletter*, 106 (2004): 6-21; Kristine Swenson, "Protection or Restriction? Women's Labour in *Mary Barton*," *Gaskell Society Journal*, 7 (1993): 55.

22. Arnold Kettle, "The Early Victorian Social Problem Novel," *From Dickens to Hardy*, The Pelican History of English Literature, ed. Boris Ford (Harmondsworth: Penguin, 1958), 180.

23. Thomas E. Recchio, "A Monstrous Reading of *Mary Barton*: Fiction as Communitas," *College Literature*, 23 (1996): 10.

24. Easson, *Elizabeth Gaskell*, 78, 79. A more traditional view, reading John Barton as the "hero" of *Mary Barton*, is advanced by Arthur Pollard, *Elizabeth Gaskell: Novelist and Biographer* (Manchester: Manchester Univ. Press, 1965), 65.

25. Elizabeth Gaskell, *Wives and Daughters*, ed. Angus Easson (Oxford: Oxford Univ. Press, 1987). All page references are to this edition and are given parenthetically in the text.

26. Harman, *The Feminine Political Novel in Victorian England*, 73.

27. Easson, ed., *Wives and Daughters*, xxii.

28. Natalka Freeland, "The Politics of Dirt in *Mary Barton* and *Ruth*," *Studies in English Literature*, 42.4 (2002): 806. Dirt for Gaskell has an important meaning, for as Natalka Freeland argues, the Victorian "misplaced affinity of cleanliness" that was inspired by both religious and sanitary reform discourse was implicitly criticised by Gaskell. According to Freeland, "[r]ather than signifying innate criminality or moral degeneration, dirt is the expected accessory of respectable, working-class domesticity" (806).

29. Easson, ed., *Wives and Daughters*, xxi-xxii.

30. Swenson, "Protection or Restriction?," 60.

31. Roseman, "Fear or Fashion," 19.

Domestic Humour in Elizabeth Gaskell's *Cranford*

Olivia Malfait

As any reader of Elizabeth Gaskell's *Cranford* will notice, much more than any of the author's other works, this novel is interlaced with humour. For its comedy, the narrative does not resort to the description of unusual adventures, burlesque settings, or blatant jokes. Rather, the humour of *Cranford* emerges from its premise: the novel relates the daily events in the lives of a circle of ladies living in a small hamlet in rural England. It is within the households of these women, with their petty concerns and absurd conventions, that comical situations arise. The ladies themselves are not aware of their being the subject of ridicule, since most of the narrative's comedy becomes apparent only in the portrayal of their actions by the narrator, Mary Smith. She presents the events as a series of memories, situated in a pre-industrial setting that stands in stark contrast to the contemporary, urbanized environment in which she imagines her readers to find themselves. However, the humour that Gaskell constructs in *Cranford* is more than a means to mock the village residents, for the novel has at its heart a serious subject: the portrayal of a group of women who, after their fathers' and husbands' deaths, are left to fend for themselves. The story's comedy functions as a method to negotiate the women's essentially tragic predicament.

Much of the novel's humour derives from the discrepancy between the ladies' belief in their self-sufficiency and their relative ignorance about matters of the world. In the opening paragraphs already, the narrator stresses how the women of Cranford pride themselves on their self-government: they exist in a kind of "huis-clos," detached from the world that lies beyond its borders. A list of tasks is enumerated, for which the village's female residents are "quite sufficient."[1] Immediately, this female oligarchy is set apart from its male counterparts. This band of Victorian spinsters and widows thus constructs for itself an "ethos of community," a social network in which the various members are interdependent.[2] In other words, the village constitutes a society within (or rather outside of) society: a seemingly self-sufficient community with its own established rules of conduct, regulations for human interaction, and prescriptive dress code. The focus lies on plurality, rather than individuality: the various characters are named and described, but Gaskell is interested primarily in how they function as a whole. Additionally, the self-instituted autonomy of the hamlet often entails an increased sense of suspicion towards everything that is alien to the community.

Nevertheless, despite the ladies' assertion of independence, it is apparent that the string of occupations that is recorded in the opening paragraph pertains especially to the private sphere: the list includes traditionally female occupations, such as gardening and performing acts of charity towards the poor. In fact, the absence of men in Cranford's female society entails a seclusion from the public sphere, and all matters (political and economical) that are associated with it. It is this absolute alienation from events out in the industrialized world that causes the women to assign disproportionate significance to the domestic realm they do know. Moreover, this excessive interest in the domestic represents a defence mechanism to conceal the essentially marginal position that these widows and spinsters occupy within Victorian society. Significant in this respect is the sobriquet that the narrator gives the women: she refers to them as a community of "Amazons" (C, 89). This title is relevant to Cranford's residents in more than one way. Most commonly, the term "Amazon" bears reference to a mythological community of female warriors, strong and masculine, who are generally presumed to have remained unmarried. Tradition also describes them as having cut off one of their breasts, so as not to be hindered in their handling of the bow or spear.[3] The Amazonian allusion to the masculine world of warriors gives proof of the narrator's ironic stance. In fact, Cranford is populated with frail, elderly women, whose everyday concerns are very much domestic, and whose secluded town is as far removed as possible from any kind of battlefield. Still, the image of the female warrior is used again by Mary Smith, when she relates how men coming to Cranford are "frightened to death" (C, 89) by the women, and the latter are compared to another group of mythological soldiers, the Spartans (C, 91). The humorous metaphor is continued in the description of Deborah Jenkyns's headgear since her bonnet is claimed to resemble a "helmet" (C, 109). Finally, the image of the breastless Amazon can conveniently be read as a symbol of infertility, as none of the elderly ladies in Cranford have borne any children.

Due to the fact that the Cranfordian Amazons are both unmarried and childless, they cannot contribute to society by reproducing, and increasing the population. To ensure reproduction, the Victorians placed great importance on marriage and the family. Women were indoctrinated with the "marital obligation" from a very young age. Family and social convention expected them to fulfil the task of finding a husband and producing children. Thus, a woman's body was not her private possession, but was seen as having a duty to fulfil towards society.[4]

The same insistence on marriage is reflected in the question of the "surplus woman," which arose with the census that was taken in 1851. When it became apparent that there were 500,000 more women than men in Great Britain, the debate around the "surplus woman" was triggered. In the polemic around the problem of women's superfluity, the unmarried women (of whom there were two and a half million in Britain in 1851) soon became the object of concern.[5] Single women were perceived as "outside of the ideal society," since – as Foucault remarks – they do not belong to the "ideal" group of married couples, who can produce children and thus have a "wholesome" effect on society. Furthermore, the problem of single women was labelled as mainly a "middle-class problem," since women belonging to that class (as opposed to lower-class women) could not work to earn their own income, but were always dependent on their fathers and husbands.[6] The ladies of Cranford are thus all "surplus women": they are neither useful in the nation's economical chain, nor do they replenish the population by producing children. However, one could argue that Gaskell, in creating an alternative society in *Cranford*, translates the performativity that is inherent of marriage to an all-female context. While the women do not act out the traditional roles of wife and mother, they do perform the parts that have been assigned to them within their households and community. Marriage is thus replaced by another kind of union, where priorities shift from a concern for husbands and children to a preoccupation with household matters and proper behaviour. Seen in this light, Gaskell's comedy functions mainly as a means of covering up the ladies' futility by stressing the domestic superficialities that constitute the rare bright spots in their secluded lives. Hence, *Cranford* is characterized by its focus on daily routine, rather than on the dynamics of the plot. The community is described as a static bubble of pre-industrialism, where time does not appear to have much impact on the lives of its inhabitants and where the purchase of a new carpet is a cause of great excitement.

The novel's focus on the private sphere also entails a predilection for the banal: the details of domestic life take centre stage. Most striking is the disproportionate attention that is devoted to caps. Though a seemingly trifling article of dress, it represents an issue of the utmost seriousness in the eyes of the ladies: "The expenditure on dress in Cranford was principally in that one article referred to. If the heads were buried in smart new caps, the ladies were like ostriches, and cared not what became of their bodies" (*C*, 175). Gaskell deftly brings into play the matter of bonnets, endowing them with meaning that surpasses the purely functional. Bonnets are a sign of propriety: ladies are never to venture outdoors without them. Furthermore, the Cranfordian caps often reflect emotions and events that affect their bearers. For instance, a special occasion that necessitates the acquisition of new headgear occurs when Miss Matty is invited by her old suitor, Mr. Holbrook, to dine with him. As a reaction, she "go[es] down to the shop" and chooses "three caps to be sent home and tried on, that the most becoming might be selected" (*C*, 124) for wearing at the dinner. The need for a new cap is felt once more after the sudden death of Mr. Holbrook. As Uglow observes, "Matty's unspoken grief is expressed only by that most Cranfordian object, a new bonnet."[7] Remarkable is the nature of the cap that Miss Matty requests, as Mary Smith relates: "She did not think I heard her when she asked the little milliner of Cranford to make her caps something like the Honourable Mrs. Jamieson's, or that I noticed the reply: 'But she wears widows' caps, ma'am?'" (*C*, 134).

In order to legitimate their peculiar society of single, elderly women, the residents of Cranford conceive of their community in terms of a self-instituted female hierarchy, which is presided over by the Honourable Mrs. Jamieson. In a sense, the women have created an alternative system of aristocracy, modelled on that of the outside world, yet confined within Cranford's borders: outside of Cranford, their claim to authority is non-existent. While they are very serious about their pseudo-aristocratic hierarchy, the validity of their system is repeatedly undercut by the narrator, as is most evident in her ironic treatment of the Honourable Mrs. Jamieson, who – in Mary Smith's portrayal – turns out to be a lot less "honourable" than her friends give her credit for. Consequently, although Mrs. Jamieson is first in line when it comes to Cranfordian aristocracy, she also provides much of the novel's comedy. The lady is characterized as being "fat ... and very much at the mercy of her servants" (*C*, 116), as well as "dull, and inert, and pompous, and tiresome" (*C*, 225). She is "apathetic" (*C*, 170), constantly falling asleep and even snores. Furthermore, she shuns all types of physical exertion, "panting" after taking the stairs (*C*, 165), and is completely averse to walking. Accordingly, she insists on being carried around in a sedan chair "to the very shortest distances" (*C*, 182), "burdening" her servants with her weight:

> It required some skilful manoeuvring on the part of the old chairmen (*shoemakers* by day; but, when summoned to carry the sedan, *dressed up* in a strange old livery – long great-coats, with small capes, coeval with the sedan, and similar to the dress of the class in Hogarth's pictures) to edge, and back, and try at it again, and finally to succeed in carrying their *burden* out of Miss Barker's front door. (*C*, 169, my italics)

Remarkably, Mrs. Jamieson's "lackeys" are actually shoemakers, a fact that challenges the gravity of her status. Moreover, they are forced to "dress up" in "strange old liveries," stressing the fact that Mrs. Jamieson's aristocracy is all an act: they are only playing at being lackeys, so as to uphold the image of their mistress's revered status. The notion of life being enacted in Cranford is not confined to the case of Mrs. Jamieson. Indeed, all the ladies of the village seem to engage in a collective performance of gentility, in which each plays a part. Cranford thus becomes a kind of theatre, where the stage is inhabited by a series of comic character types such as the lazy aristocrat (Mrs. Jamieson), the nervous gossip (Miss Pole), or the childlike naïf (Miss Matty). Gaskell has her characters put on a mask that defines them by exaggerating one of their character traits. This masquerade allows the ladies to hide their poor spinster and widow faces and take up their parts in Cranford's play of feigned aristocracy.

The women's exaggerated valorisation of status is part of their collective performance. The women play up their social significance to blind themselves to the bleakness of their financial situation. For their survival, Cranford's protagonists are all dependent on the means that were left them by their deceased husbands and fathers. Yet, the narrator makes clear in her description of the women's customs and mutual understanding that their pecuniary resources are rather limited. Life without a man to provide an income, one can deduce, is not always as favourable as the women suggest. As Jenny Uglow puts it: "These are the great illusions: that the guide to a person's worth is their social status and that the Amazons can survive perfectly well, indeed better, without that unnecessary and annoying species – men."[8] To conceal their financial troubles, the women have devised what they call, with a typical Cranfordism, "elegant economy" (*C*, 92): the sacrifices they make are presented in such a way that they appear to be serving "aristocratic" ends, rather than being the result of a necessary thriftiness. Moreover, the very mention of money matters is considered "vulgar and ostentatious" (*C*, 92), as becomes apparent when the newly arrived Captain Brown shamelessly flaunts his own poverty.

Instances of elegant economy abound in the novel. The narrator points out how all the women are complicit in keeping up appearances: "If we walked to or from a party, it was because the night was *so* fine, or the air *so* refreshing; not because sedan-chairs were expensive. If we wore prints, instead of summer silks, it was because we preferred a washing material; and so on, till we blinded ourselves to the vulgar fact, that we were, all of us, people of very moderate means" (*C*, 93). One of the precautions that the women take to save money, is their shared subscription to the *St James's Chronicle*, which circulates the town according to social hierarchy, starting its round at Mrs. Jamieson's house. Another strategy of parsimony is the silent agreement to serve only modest refreshments when taking tea or giving a party. Because all the ladies participate in this ploy, the humble servings are never frowned upon. On the contrary, they are accepted as the new standard of propriety, to such an extent that anyone who dares present their friends with more than the usual refreshment – as Betsy Barker unwittingly does – is accused of indulging in improper extravagance. Mrs. Jamieson, likely the most affluent of the group, even goes so far as to limit the size of the sugar lumps she serves at tea to "little minnikin pieces" (C, 179), too small even for the sugar-tongs to grasp. Miss Matty's personal economy is that of saving candles, of which she burns only one at the time, causing complications where visits are concerned: "As we lived in constant preparation for a friend who might come in an evening (but who never did), it required some contrivance to keep our two candles of the same length, ready to be lighted, and to look as if we burnt two always" (C, 137). Once more, in true Cranford fashion, appearance is everything, and the determination with which the ladies devote themselves to it is an inexorable source of humour. Typically Cranfordian is also the attention that is given to the arrival of the Misses Jenkyns' new carpet. This seemingly trivial acquisition is presumably not one that the sisters' budget allows very often. Accordingly, the women are anxious to save the rug from any harmful influences, such as the sunlight. Mary Smith relates:

> We were very busy, … one whole morning, before Miss Jenkyns gave her party, in following her directions, and in cutting out and stitching together pieces of newspaper, so as to form little paths to every chair, set for the expected visitors, lest their shoes might dirty or defile the purity of the carpet. *Do you make paper paths for every guest to walk upon in London?* (C, 104, my italics)

The narrator here directly addresses the reader to stress the absurdity of the women's zeal for economy, saving the carpet even at the cost of their visitors' ease. Moreover, the implied reader is a resident of metropolitan London, the quintessentially modern city marked by capitalism, that functions as the exact opposite to Cranford and its old-fashioned ways. Yet, while the ladies' anxiety about the carpet is described as bordering on the ridiculous, one cannot deny the serious implications of the episode: after all, it is the women's poor circumstances that prompt their necessary thriftiness.

The women of Cranford like to assert their independence from the outside world and the men in it. Nevertheless, the narrator repeatedly calls into question this claim to self-assertion, by pointing out how men do affect the women's lives and opinions. The residents of Cranford, like true Amazons, are keen to stress their hostility towards men – though their spears are made of words rather than wood. Between them, they repeatedly express their "distaste of mankind," persuading themselves that "to be a man was to be 'vulgar'" (C, 96), and engaging in conversations in which they "abuse men in general" (C, 202). A frontrunner in the sceptical discourse about members of the other sex is Miss Pole. Ironically, the only man on whom she can base her claim of "knowing the sex pretty well" is her father, since she herself is a spinster. Still, she strongly asserts her distaste for men in general, and marriage in particular. When Lady Glenmire's engagement to Mr. Hoggins is announced, she indignantly proclaims their engagement to be "madness" (*C*, 222), labelling Mr. Hoggins a "wolf" (*C*, 224) and confirming his presumed coarse nature by revealing that he "sups on bread-and-cheese and beer every night" (*C*, 223). Once again, the lady's indignation serves as a source of humour, since the greatest fault she can find in Mr. Hoggins are his eating habits. Nevertheless, Miss Pole herself is suspected of husband hunting more than once. Not only is she jealous when she imagines that Peter Jenkyns (who has returned to Cranford after a long absence) is developing feelings for Mrs. Jamieson, she is also thought to have once set her sights on the town's rector, as Mary Smith indicates. One cannot help but feel that Miss Pole's disapproval of matrimony is an attitude that she has adopted as a consequence of her spinsterhood, rather than being the reason for it. As Uglow remarks: "Despite their protestations, we gradually learn that none of these single women has deliberately set out to live without men."[9] Indeed, the Cranfordian ladies owe their single status not to their stubbornness, but rather to the fact that their love is unrequited, thwarted, or lost to illness and death.

Quite remarkable is Deborah Jenkyns's attitude towards the other sex: she scorns the idea of women being compared to men, yet aspires to masculinity in her dress: "Miss Jenkyns wore a cravat, and a little bonnet like a jockey-cap, and altogether had the appearance of a strong-minded woman; although she would have despised the modern idea of women being equal to men. Equal, indeed! she knew they were superior" (*C*, 102). Despite her claims of female superiority, however, she lives her life according to the dictates of two men – her father and Dr. Johnson – considering every deviation from their rules an ignominy. However, her rigorous adherence to these codes of conduct, which she also imposes on her fellow Amazons, borders on the absurd. A first example of Cranfordian code is the scene in which the regulations for visiting are explained to Mary Smith. By comparing the recital of the rules to the reading of formal laws, the narrator accords disproportionate importance to the former, stressing the irony with which she relates the whole experience. In their quest for propriety, the ladies give preference to keeping to their rulebook, rather than pursuing in depth their conversation. By forcing themselves to "keep thinking about the time," they cast the talk itself in a secondary role. As a consequence, their topics of conversation are inevitably reduced to those of small talk and banal gossip.

Typical of Cranford's concern with domesticity is the way that food is dependent on codification, which becomes apparent not only during visits, but also in the privacy of the women's homes. A quintessential example is the ritual of eating oranges, as it is performed in the Jenkyns household:

> When oranges came in, a curious proceeding was gone through. Miss Jenkyns did not like to cut her fruit; for, as she observed, the juice all ran out, nobody knew where; sucking (only I think she used some more recondite word) was in fact the only way of enjoying oranges; but then there was the unpleasant association with a ceremony frequently gone through by little babies; and so, after dessert, in orange season, Miss Jenkyns and Miss Matty used to rise up, possess themselves each of an orange in silence, and withdraw to the privacy of their own rooms, to indulge in sucking oranges. (*C*, 118-19)

A seemingly unobjectionable act – eating an orange – is consigned to the realm of the private because of the possible associations it holds. Not only is the very word, "sucking," offensive to Miss Jenkyns, the deed itself, and the possibility of it "being read as a bodily act,"[10] calls for a new ritual in the already highly-ritualized household. The women need to retire to their bedrooms, so as to be able to "indulge" in an action that might be considered distasteful when performed in the company of others.

Another aspect of Cranfordian life where the intrinsic tragedy of the females' situation is redeemed by the comical occasions to which it gives rise, are the instances that refer to the women's lack of children. The absence of children is especially felt by Miss Matty, who continues to experience a "strange yearning" (*C*, 215) whenever she sees a mother with her baby. Her desire for motherhood even manifests itself in her dreams. The fictional nature of Miss Matty's vision of a daughter is stressed by the fact that the little girl never ages: she cannot age, because Matty will never know what it is like to witness a child's evolution the observation of which is a prerogative reserved for its parents, as Gaskell's *Diary* of her own daughter Marianne's development exemplifies.[11] Furthermore, the supernatural quality of the baby is confirmed by the child's being "very noiseless and still," as though she is one of the dolls that little Matty used to play with.

Other Cranfordian women express their need for children in more indirect ways – most notably, in the replacement of their absent offspring with "surrogate children," i.e. animals. For instance, there is Mrs. Forrester's cat, who is still affectionately called "pussy," even after swallowing her mistress's lace, for which she is slapped on the back "just as one slaps a choking child" (*C*, 181). Another striking example is Betsy Barker's cow, who is the protagonist of one of *Cranford*'s quaintest episodes.

> [A]n old lady had an Alderney cow, which she looked upon as a daughter. … The whole town knew and kindly regarded Miss Betsy Barker's Alderney; therefore great was the sympathy and regret when, in an unguarded moment, the poor cow

tumbled into a lime-pit … the poor beast had lost most of her hair and came out looking naked, cold, and miserable, in bare skin. … Miss Betsy Barker absolutely cried with sorrow and dismay; and it was said she thought of trying a bath of oil. This … proposal, if ever it was made, was knocked on the head by Captain Brown's decided "Get her a flannel waistcoat and flannel drawers, ma'am, if you wish to keep her alive. But my advice is, kill the poor creature at once."

Miss Betsy Barker dried her eyes and thanked the captain heartily; she set to work, and by-and-by all the town turned out to see the Alderney meekly going to her pasture, clad in dark grey flannel. I have watched her myself many a time. Do you ever see cows dressed in grey flannel in London? (*C*, 93-94)

Betsy Barker looks upon her cow "as a daughter," not as an animal that one would normally keep for its consumable qualities: its milk and, possibly, its meat. The lady's deep affection for the animal shows in her distress after the cow's accident. The logical procedure to follow when an incident like this occurs, is explained by Captain Brown: the cow cannot survive without the warmth of its hide, so it should be killed. However, Miss Betsy chooses the illogical path. She takes the Captain's jesting remark seriously, and sews a pair of flannel pyjamas for her surrogate daughter. As Eileen Gillooly remarks, traditional roles are reversed, since the Alderney cow is here "receiving nurturance rather than giving it."[12] Gaskell here creates an amusing image for the reader's enjoyment, though she does so at Miss Betsy's expense.

Yet, Betsy Barker's cow is not the only animal in Cranford on whom excessive attention is lavished. She finds a male counterpart in Mrs. Jamieson's spoilt little dog, Carlo. Carlo's owner never accepts an invitation for tea, unless she can bring her "poor ittie doggie" (*C*, 166), regularly offering it pieces of the cake that is destined for the visitors. When the ladies are – exceptionally – invited to Mrs. Jamieson's own house, an even greater exhibition of her indulgence towards the animal is made, when tea is brought in:

In the little silver jug was cream, in the larger one was milk. As soon as Mr. Mulliner came in, Carlo began to beg, which was a thing our manners forbade us to do, though I am sure we were just as hungry; and Mrs. Jamieson said she was certain we would excuse her if she gave the poor dumb Carlo his tea first. She accordingly mixed a saucerful for him, and put it down for him to lap; and then she told us how intelligent and sensible the dear little fellow was; he knew cream quite well, and constantly refused tea with only milk in it: so the milk was left for us; but we silently thought we were quite as intelligent and sensible as Carlo, and felt as if insult were added to injury, when we were called upon to admire the gratitude evinced by his wagging his tail for the cream, which should have been ours. (*C*, 179-80)

Mrs. Jamieson gives preference to her pet over her friends, serving him the cream that was meant for their tea, and is like a proud mother, boasting of her baby's skills. Yet her pride is undercut by Mary's insistence on the impropriety of the dog's manners in begging to be fed in such a shameless way. Not surprisingly, when Carlo suddenly dies, Mrs. Jamieson's grief is acute and sincere, as is apparent from her "loss of appetite and bad nights," which are valid proof of her distress, "for if she had two characteristics in her natural state of health, they were a facility of eating and sleeping" (C, 199). The lady's tragic loss goes hand in hand with the humour with which it is related, since the narrator stresses once more two of Mrs. Jamieson's least elegant character traits.

As a typical English idyll, *Cranford* delights its readership with quaint anecdotes, taken from the everyday lives of the women that inhabit the hamlet. Life in Cranford is guided by an obsolete set of domestic rules (rules for visiting, dressing, serving tea, and even consuming oranges), that are followed with the utmost seriousness by its residents. Yet, the women's overzealous concern with household matters often appears absurdly comical to outsiders. While the narrator gently ridicules her protagonists, the novel's humour conceals the deeper tragedy of the Amazons' fate as poor, childless spinsters and widows. They engage in a collective performance of aristocratic and self-asserted independence from the world outside their village, and the men that inhabit it. However, once the layers of humour that envelope the narrative are peeled away, the women's inevitable exclusion from Victorian society (where family is the greatest good) becomes painfully clear.

Notes

1.   Elizabeth Gaskell, *The Cranford Chronicles* (London: Vintage Books, 2007), 89. Hereafter *C*. All references are to this edition and will be given parenthetically in the text.

2.   Maggie Dunn and Ann Morris, *The Composite Novel. The Short Story Cycle in Transition* (Boston: Twayne, 1995), 23.

3.   The *OED* defines the Amazons as a "race of female warriors alleged by Herodotus, etc. to exist in Scythia" and quotes Trevisa, who described them in 1398 as being "wythout breste," referring to the idea that they "destroyed the right breast so as not to interfere with the use of the bow".

4.   Michel Foucault, *The History of Sexuality: Volume I: An Introduction* (New York: Vintage Books, 1990), 37. As Foucault states: The woman's body "was placed in organic communication with the social body (whose regulated fecundity it was supposed to ensure), the family space (of which it had to be a substantial and functional element), and the life of children (which it produced and had to guarantee, by virtue of a biologico-moral responsibility lasting through the entire period of the children's education)" (104).

5.   Kathrin Levitan, "Redundancy, the 'Surplus Woman' Problem, and the British Census, 1851-1861," *Women's History Review*, 17 (2008): 363.

6.   Levitan, 360, 364.

7.   Jenny Uglow, *Elizabeth Gaskell: A Habit of Stories* (London: Faber and Faber, 1999), 291.

8.   Uglow, 285.

9.   Uglow, 285.

10. Natalie Kapetanios Meir, "'Household Forms and Ceremonies': Narrating Routines in Elizabeth Gaskell's *Cranford*," *Studies in the Novel*, 38 (2006): 1-14.

11. *My Diary: The Early Years of My Daughter Marianne*, begun on 10 March 1835, was Gaskell's first sustained written work, though never intended for publication. In it, she monitored her daughter's development as a baby. See J.A.V. Chapple and Anita Wilson, eds., *Private Voices: The Diaries of Elizabeth Gaskell and Sophia Holland* (Edinburgh: Edinburgh University Press, 1996), 11.

12. Eileen Gillooly, "Humor as Daughterly Defense in *Cranford*," *ELH*, 59 (1992): 901.

"With Arms Entwined":
Deadly Deceit and Romantic Friendship in *Ruth* and *Lois the Witch*

Heather Levy

Although Elizabeth Gaskell was married to a Unitarian minister she declared herself a "sermon hater."[1] The narrators of *Ruth* (1853) and *Lois the Witch* (1859) seem to champion the causes of both earnest orphans and initially grant them generous moral latitude. Ruth's acceptance and embellishment of the lie which covers her teenage pregnancy seems necessary to secure her a comfortable post as a governess in the Bradshaw empire. It almost appears to be a holy and compassionate lie since it is invented by the godly Thurston Benson and sanctioned by his sanctimonious sister, Faith. Ruth later embellishes the lie by appealing to the sympathy of others who pity her loss of the young, successful doctor that she invented as her husband.

Similarly, Lois also tolerates deception when she realizes as a young child viewing the execution with the family maid that the condemned old Hannah is a "poor, helpless, baited creature" (150). She is only four and is unable to stop the stoning and drowning of the suspected witch and her black cat. Old Hannah singles her out from her crowd of accusers as the daughter of the indifferent parson and warns her that "none shall save thee when thou art brought up for a witch" (150). Lois's childhood indifference to truth also follows her to Salem where she is aware that Hota, the Indian servant has been beaten by her white master and tortured by her inquisitors before she confessed to witchcraft. Although Lois insists upon the truth in smaller matters during tales of bewitched horses, prurient gossip between her cousins and Manasseh's graver and violent delusions that they must marry, she merely prays for Hota's happy afterlife. She conveniently convinces herself of Hota's guilt while allowing herself the luxury of "tender moral shuddering" (189).

Ruth and Lois are not initially undone by their own use and tacit acceptance of lies. They both still mourn the loss of their mothers and throw themselves into passionate friendships with younger women. Lois suffers through her single New England winter with the physical affection of her cousin Faith. Jemima and Faith mistakenly believe that Ruth and Lois intend to seduce Mr. Farquhar and Pastor Nolan. Jemima reveals enough of Ruth's prurient past to ignite the gossipy tongue of the village milliner Mrs. Pearson, while Faith accuses Lois of witchcraft in front of the volatile and melodramatic Prudence. This begins a predictable chain of events which leads both women to their graves while ultimately preserving conventional ethical and sexual morality for the reader. Jenny Uglow optimistically argues in her foreword to *Lois the Witch*:

> [Gaskell] always writes brilliantly about the perilous threshold of adulthood. From her first stories to her last novel … she depicts young women coming to terms with their sexual power and their own desires, and finding their own voice and identity. Again and again, her heroines learn to speak out, to tell the truth, even if it hurts them. (x)

This paper offers a more realistic view of the perilous deceit that Lois and Ruth must condone and practice during their aborted thresholds of adulthood. Ruth is seduced when she is an adolescent and this ruins her life. Although she loves Bellingham she never really actively chooses to be with him. She is forced into his wild scheme to accompany him to Wales after her avaricious employer Mrs. Mason fires her after seeing her walking with him. Her own desires are never really clearly formulated and Bellingham capitalizes upon her naiveté. After his seduction and abandonment she must begin a life of deceit to just survive economically. Ruth did not have a meaningful choice after Bradshaw detected her lie. She had to hire herself out as a nurse in order to take care of Leonard and herself. Her angel in the house tendencies with Bellingham lead to her death.

Her lack of agency throughout the novel is striking. She is aware of her dearth of meaningful choices when she sadly observes to Jemima at the onset of her illness that she cannot protect her beloved son: "'I have no plan. … I have no means of planning. All I can do is to try and make him ready for anything'" (435). Lois's moral and economic struggle is not as protracted. She is executed at nineteen. Her love affair with the handsome and wealthy Ralph Lucy is violently curtailed by her parent's sudden deaths and the class snobbery of the Lucy clan. She is marooned in Salem and is forced to throw herself upon the hesitant mercy of her ailing uncle and his incendiary wife. She does find some comfort in the arms of her cousin Faith but this respite is interrupted by Faith's mistaken belief that Lois loves Pastor Nolan.

Ruth's alienation is also briefly salved with a romantic friendship as she gratefully accepts Jemima Bradhaw's ardor: "'Dear Mrs. Denbigh, I will never admire or praise you again. Only let me love you.' 'And let me love you!' said Ruth, with a tender kiss'" (187). The narrator casts a courtly radiance on this romantic friendship: "and no knight-errant of old could consider himself more honoured by his ladye's commands than did Jemima, if Ruth allowed her to do anything for her or her boy" (187). They exchange the most heartfelt and romantic dialogue of any characters in the novel, routinely exchanging "soft and tender looks … fond kisses, tender caresses" (228). Jemima becomes so enraptured by Ruth that she "always want[s] to be in her presence" (328). She spurns Farquhar's attentions and peevishly shoos him away during an early courting scene where she demands that Ruth hold her skein of wool instead (233). Romantic relationships that sour can easily change into a vehemence and Jemima's ardor becomes "almost repugnance" when she discovers that Ruth has agreed with her father's romantic plans for her (315). This second deception, rather than the grandiose lie about her pregnancy and imaginary romantic past with a heroic surgeon, is Ruth's real undoing.

Once again, Ruth tries to take comfort in rationalization. She reassures herself that she is not really serving as Mr. Bradshaw's spy because "if she had seen anything wrong in Jemima … she loved her so much she would have told her in private" (227). She says nothing about Farquhar during her evening tête-à-têtes and allows Mr. Bradshaw to believe that she has counseled his intractable daughter. Mrs. Bradshaw does not recognize such fine shades of ethical rationalization. The very next morning she informs the smitten Jemima that Ruth has betrayed her confidence and love and that she was hired to lecture her and encourage Farquahar's suit. Mrs. Bradshaw reveals her own motives for exposing Ruth's participation in the marital plot: "We neither of us could think what had come over you this last month; but now all seems right" (237). She realizes that Jemima's romantic attachment to Ruth has interfered with more profitable heterosexual pursuits and that Ruth's betrayal will humiliate and anger her.

After this damning exposure, the narrator reveals that one week before the plot, Jemima "had almost considered Ruth as a sister" (239). Gaskell appears to be steering the narrative back to more conventional heterosexual tropes and recasting the relationship as more of a familial, platonic attachment. Just like any spurned lover, Jemima stews and ruminates in regret. She is "amazed by the capability for evil in her heart" (245) and this vengeance leads her to reveal enough salacious details that Ruth's first lie will be trumpeted to all of Eccleston.

Jemima reassumes her knight errant role after Ruth's "detection" (376). She vainly tries to defend Ruth's character in front of her enraged father: "She took the cold, dead hand which hung next to her in her warm convulsive grasp, and holding it so tight, that it was blue and discoloured for days, she spoke out beyond all power of restraint from her father" (338). Her intervention is hopeless. Ruth is dismissed from her governess position and is forced to scrape shillings together as a sick nurse. Jemima and Ruth do not see each for two years. In Ruth's absence, she accepts Farquhar's lukewarm advances. She wins his affections simply by calling him by his Christian name. Their marriage is steady but their exchanges never match the intensity and tenderness that she once shared with Ruth. Once Jemima returns from her honeymoon she finally visits Ruth against her father's wishes. She does not mention Walter's romantic capabilities and instead under-scores his commercial acumen. Ruth spent the two intervening years yearning "all the more in silence to see Jemima" and regretting that she had not thanked her with "word, or tone, or touch" (382). Their reunion is one of the most passionate scenes in the novel: "in the gloom of the apartment she recognized Jemima. In an instant they were in each other's arms – a long, fast embrace" (385).

Jemima once again assumes the mantle of knight errant and protectively cau-tions Ruth against agreeing to assist the parish doctor, Mr. Wynne, as a sick nurse. She tries to convince Ruth that it is beneath her since she is "better educated" (388). Jemima does not seem to be as aware of her class privilege as the indulged wife and daughter. Ruth objects: "At any rate it is work, and as such I am thankful for it. You cannot discourage me – and perhaps you know too little of what my life has been" (389). Perhaps as a sign of jealousy, Ruth refuses to visit Jemima and Walter as a guest but rapturously promises her "Dear Jemima, if you are ill or sorrowful and want me, I will come" (390). This is more than the promise of a sick nurse in training. Ruth rekindles their passionate relationship when she exclaims "But I should come to you, love, in quite a different way; I should go to you with my head full of love – so full that I am afraid I should be too anxious" (390). Jemima reciprocates the romantic intensity when she exclaims "I almost wish I were ill, that I might make you come at once" (390).

Charlotte Brontë (who provided her own fair share of protracted death scenes)[2] once asked of *Ruth,* "Why should she die? Why are we to shut up the book weeping."[3] Ruth's death advances the conventional Victorian moral tone that the novel ultimately endorses. Ruth has lied about her romantic and sexual past as well as her willingness to participate in Jemima's heterosexual indoctrina-tion and she must be punished. The narrator is almost giddy in providing this punishment, describing the "palace of death" (429) that claims many of the vil-lagers, and ultimately Ruth. Typhus fever is the vehicle of castigation.

Gaskell suggests that disease has its own lexicon of morality: "It seemed as if the alarm was proportionate to the previous light-heartedness of fancied security – and indeed it was so: for, since the days of King Belshazzar, the solemn decrees of Doom have ever seemed most terrible when they awe into silence the merry revelers of life" (423). The puritanical impulses of the Salem villagers in *Lois the*

Witch are echoed in the narrator's caveat that the summer merriment of the Eccleston villagers will bring cataclysmic winter suffering. King Belshazzar's foolish largesse is showcased in the fifth chapter of Daniel and is traditionally "invoked as a cautionary tale against the habits of excessively sumptuous feasts."[4] Rembrandt immortalized the doomed Babylonian's king's tardy revelation in his 1635 "The Feast of Belshazzar." Schama's observations about the deathly hand of the serving girl are eerily reminiscent of Ruth's terror stricken, deathly hands when Bradshaw fires her in front of Jemima. Schama aptly describes Belshazzar's feast as "a party with no emergency exit."[5]

Conversely, Ruth's life is never a party and she is reluctant to participate in Bellingham's feasts: "You have been sighing twenty times during the last half hour. Do be a little cheerful" (75). Although she is never offered feasts by Bellingham, rarely eats and only drinks tea throughout their courtship, Old Thomas becomes the equivalent of the ominous hand that writes on the palace walls when he warns her during a bittersweet visit with Bellingham during the first blush of their courtship to her childhood house:

> My dear, remember the devil goeth about as a roaring lion, seeking whom he may devour, remember that, Ruth. The words fell on her ear, but gave no definite idea … She never imagined that the grim warning related to the handsome young man who awaited her with a countenance beaming with love, and tenderly drew her hand within his arm. (51)

Ruth's future, like Belshazzar's, is undone in a single day. After Mrs. Mason forbids Ruth to return to her job and threatens that she will write to her guardian and tell her about seeing her with Bellingham on the country road, he diverts her to a country inn and grandly commands "'Tea, directly for this lady!'" (59). He then upsets her by pressuring her into accompanying him first to London and leaves abruptly when she is indecisive. She cannot even eat a slice of buttered toast that the servant brings her. The narrator then offers the reader a view of Ruth's imperiled health: "Her head ached so much that she could hardly see … Ruth was feverish and thirsty" (59).[6] The fact that she cannot pay for the cup of tea that Bellingham imperiously ordered for her detains her at the inn and precipitates the disastrous ride to London in his carriage. Although she plans on convincing him to take her to Milham Grange, she quickly falls prey to his charisma and subterfuge.

Unlike Belshazzar, Ruth revels only in nature and even if she could afford it she would not be an epicurean. Bellingham indulges her for only a week in Wales. Although he selects an inn that is famous for its lavish, hot breakfasts, Ruth skips all of them and spends her mornings in the pristine mountain air. Bellingham quickly becomes impatient with Ruth but she does not notice his peevishness and tenderly ministers to his infirmities: "'Let me put my cool hands on your forehead,' she begged; 'that used to do mamma good'" (75). Bellingham suddenly becomes enfeebled and suffers from "a bad case" of what the physician Mr. Jones vaguely identifies as "brain fever" (78). Ruth is panicked when she finds Bellingham looking "so strange and wild" (76).

Mr. Jones will not communicate with Ruth about Bellingham's condition and prefers to consult with Mrs. Morgan in Welsh about the patient. Here, Ruth has one of her rare moments of self-possession and decisiveness when she asks the doctor for more information and counsel: "Every direction you give me shall be most carefully attended to. You spoke about leeches – I can put them on, and see about them. Tell me everything, sir, that you wish to have done!" (78). Jones considers using leeches "as a means of bloodletting, a practice common up to the middle of the nineteenth century."[7]

Although Ruth is diligent and loving in her ministrations to the ailing Bellingham, even the kindly but ill informed doctor suggests that she is too young to have to shoulder the burden of nursing him. His mother is summoned and she quickly accuses Ruth: "This was the girl, then, whose profligacy had led her son astray … nay, this was the real cause of his illness, his mortal danger at this present time, and of her bitter, keen anxiety" (85). Although the narrator clearly reveals that Bellingham is the one who really led Ruth astray, the link between illicit sexuality, moral danger and fatal disease has now been firmly established for the Victorian and contemporary reader.[8]

Bellingham, once he escapes from what his mother perceives as the evil temptation of Ruth, recovers from his mysterious brain fever. Margaret Bellingham leaves a scorching letter for Ruth with a bribery of fifty pounds. She has even considered the possibility of Ruth's pregnancy and admonishes her to enter an asylum for unwed mothers. Ruth, in spite of her poverty, is self-possessed enough to return the money. This episode of independence is short-lived however, and she runs after Bellingham's carriage. She becomes both animal and child-like in her grief when she cannot catch up to him: "crouched up like some hunted creature, with a wild, scared look of despair, which almost made her lovely face seem fierce … the poor, lost wanderer" (96). Ruth does not recover from Bellingham's desertion. Even though she distracts herself by tending to another suddenly enfeebled male, this time Thurston Benson, who has stumbled over a stone in a field, Ruth cannot escape from tragedy. Although her sexual indoctrination happens beyond the narrative frame, it is provocatively suggested by her admiration of the water-lily stalks: "the flowers were hardly seen at first, so deep was the green shadow cast by the trees. In the very middle of the pond the sky was mirrored clear and dark, a blue which looked as if a black void lay behind" (74). Bellingham himself ironically intimates about the danger of sexual charisma when he warns her "The ground is spongy all round there" (74). He fashions the symbolic stalks into a watery crown for her[9] and invites her to become a womanly version of Narcissus: "Come and look at yourself in the pond. Here there are no weeds. Come" (74).

Ruth pays heavily for this sensual episode. Bellingham develops his brain fever after the escapade, allows himself to be "rescued" by his caustic class conscious mother and then deserts Ruth again. The narrator prepares the reader for the permanence of Ruth's moral decline and the grave consequences of her brief Belshazzar-like aborted sensual feast with the gothic observation: "Ruth looked as if the shadow of death was upon her" (99).

It is not a vague brain fever that kills Ruth. She is undone by her love for Bellingham and she fatally reverts back to her nurturing self when he becomes enfeebled with typhus fever. This is a perfect plague for a narrator who wishes to allude to moral misconduct while simultaneously critiquing poverty. Typhus fever is coined from the Greek word *typhos*, meaning smoke or cloud.[10] Endemic typhus is "among the most notorious of all bacterial diseases. It is considered one of the most prolific killers of humans ... it has altered the course of history such as when it helped to decimate the Aztec population in the 1500's."[11] Zinseer makes the alarming observation that "epidemic typhus has probably caused more deaths than all the wars in history."[12] Twenty percent of the troops during the Napoleonic wars died of typhus. Twenty-five million people were infected during the Russian Revolution and three million died.[13] The severity of epidemic typhus is "largely determined by the nutritional state of the population infected and in the most extreme situations of malnutrition, such as in Bergen-Belsen in 1945, a mortality rate of fifty percent and upwards may occur."[14] Most recently, in 1996-97, typhus fever killed six thousand displaced refugees from the Hutu-Tutsi ethnic massacres in Burundi.[15] Raoult observes that the refugees were infected by prisoners who were suffering from epidemic typhus in a N'Gozi jail and warns that the "disease could be efficiently and easily treated by antibiotics. This epidemic highlights the appalling conditions in central-African refugee camps and the failure of public-health programmes to serve their inhabitants."[16] Cowan cautions that epidemic louse borne typhus "remains a risk among refugee populations of the world, despite its omission from a recent review of health care in refugee camps."[17]

Typhus is caused by *Rickettsia prowazekii*.[18] Gaskell would not have known that the bacteria are transmitted between individuals by head and body lice of the genus *Pediculus*. This was not discovered until 1928 when Charles Nicolle won the Nobel Prize in Physiology. Gaskell adds a mythical moral dimension to the disease when she observes: "there came creeping, creeping, in hidden, slimy courses, the terrible fever – that fever which is never really utterly banished from the sad haunts of vice and misery, but lives in such darkness, like a wild beast in the recesses of his den" (424). Gaskell creates a moral economy of disease in her description of the social evolution of the plague: "not merely among the loose living and vicious, but among the decently poor – nay, even among the well-to-do and respectable" (424). The louse or mouse borne plague runs rampant in overcrowded, filthy conditions where people are forced to live in close proximity and cannot wash or change clothing: "It had begun in the low Irish lodging houses" (424).

Typhus fever is characterized by fever, mental delirium, necrosis of the skin with gangrene in severe cases. Victims develop a white fur that coats the body and mouth. In severe cases, the fur becomes black and clots the tongue and throat. The tongue may become rolled up like a ball at the back of the throat. The tips of fingers, noses, earlobes, scrotums, penises and vulvas may rot.[19] It is more than symbolic that Ruth, in all likelihood, contracted the disease from Bellingham, given the fact that she fell ill and died within four days of tending her infected ex-lover. Gaskell did not take poetic license with Ruth's incubation period. Clinical illness "begins with fever, headache, and myalgia two-fourteen days after a bite."[20] Ruth begins to present symptoms on the third day of tending Bellingham. Even the predatory and appallingly intimate transmission of the disease seems like a metaphor for Bellingham's treatment of Ruth.

Rickettsial diseases are transmitted in a particularly gothic and vicious way. The infected louse must penetrate the broken skin of its victim. Youman observes that "host defense mechanisms can have little influence on the multiplication of rickettsias within endothelial cells."[21] Rickettsias, like Bellingham, have extraordinarily destructive capacities: "[they] are able to penetrate in some unknown manner the membrane of the host cell and pass directly into the cytoplasm or cell material."[22] Gaskell, of course, would not have been aware of the pathogenesis of typhus fever but the exploitative seduction of Ruth and her incomprehensible love for Bellingham's destructive force over her life is uncannily similar to the violent force of rickettsias. Ruth's personal and economic vulnerabilities prove fatal and she is infected at a spiritual and cellular level.

It is apt that Bellingham becomes the instrument of Ruth's contagion. Ruth patiently nurses villagers who are suffering from the plague and survives. She becomes fatally ill after heroically tending her ex-lover Bellingham. This is a perfect device for the narrator who wishes to artfully conform to Victorian mores surrounding promiscuity, carnal pleasure and the consequences of deceit while offering some sympathy for the vulnerable working class young woman. Neither Mr. Davis or Bellingham's servant who attend him during his sickness at the Queen's Hotel become infected. This is unlikely given that "history shows that they [medical attendants] are at high risk."[23]

Perhaps Charlotte Brontë should have asked why Bellingham survived. Siv

Jansson suggests that Gaskell refuses to "permit Bellingham to escape the consequences of his treatment of Ruth."[24] Gaskell is very lenient with Bellingham and this is a realistic assessment of what usually happens to the unscrupulous. He consummates his passion for Ruth, recovers from his episode of brain fever, his political ambitions are realized and he never loses his fortune or the affection of his mother. He survives his bout with typhus fever, is visited by hallucinations about the sexually provocative water lilies and is nursed tenderly to recovery by the woman he impregnated and abandoned twice. He does not convince Ruth to marry him but he does not have to live with the jealousy of seeing her affections being given to another man or woman. Admittedly, he does not gain the affection of his illegitimate son, Leonard, but this does not cause him much suffering.

Ruth's actions throughout the novel cannot accurately be described as sustained episodes of moral courage. She is always worried about money, employment prospects, food and shelter. The narrator even introduces the inevitability of her succumbing to typhus using mercantile metaphors: "it was but too evident that Ruth 'home must go, and take her wages.' Poor, poor Ruth" (447). She does not even have the two weeks that she said she needed to consider Mr. Davis's offer of obtaining a medical apprenticeship for Leonard. She is a servant until the bitter end, dismissed from her own life as if it was a chore she was commanded by her employer to rapidly complete. She does not have very many meaningful decisions and does her best to survive. She spends her entire life beleaguered by the judgment and carelessness of others. She is not rewarded with life, love, sexual power, her own voice or identity other than a repentant martyr. She loses the love and tenderness that she shared with Jemima and the only man she ever romantically loved betrays her repeatedly and viciously.

The narrator is elegiac and utilitarian during Ruth's death vigil. Generally, during the first three days of illness the victim will experience nausea, vomiting, abdominal pain and tenderness and diarrhea.[25] Ruth instead is a beautiful victim who has experienced no visible physically marring symptoms. She is an aesthetic spectacle for those keeping her death vigil, which is fitting considering that her remarkable good looks first drew the morally contagious Bellingham. There is no description of the black fur coating the tongue or the rotting of fingertips, noses or genitals. Ruth has not experienced the balling up of her tongue at the back of her throat like a castigated instrument of sexual satisfaction since the "watchers" note her continual low and soft singing.

One very interesting symptom of typhus fever involves muscle twitching and compulsive *carphologia* or picking at the bedclothes.[26] The watchers also remark upon the fact that Ruth is "keeping a strange sort of time with her pretty fingers, as they closed and unclosed themselves upon the counterpane" (448). Ruth first manifests symptoms of typhus fever when she is tending Bellingham in the "best

room of the Queen's hotel" (443). She cannot "remember who the sleeper was …
sank into a whirling stupor of sense and feeling" (445). She is running out of
energy and "listlessly obeys the command" (445). She is dizzy and is "suffering
from an oppressive headache" (445). Fever is characteristic of rickettsial disease in
epidemic typhus.[27] The onset is severe and so Ruth's sudden infirmity is realistic
and her severe headache is obviously symptomatic.[28] Gaskell uses poetic license
when she observes that Ruth's pupils are "distended" (445). Victims of typhus
have contracted pupils and injected eye membranes.[29] Prostration is also one of
the symptoms and is demonstrated in Ruth's dizziness: "She held Mr. Davis's
arm. If she had let it go, she would have fallen" (446).

Ruth is even unlucky when the medical odds should be in her favour: "the
mortality rate in uncontrolled acute disease may vary from ten to sixty percent,
the highest mortality rate being found in people over the age of fifty."[30] The
relentlessly fortunate Bellingham survives and he is older than Ruth. Mr. Davis is
even older than Bellingham and he survives in spite of prolonged contact with victims of typhus fever.

During Ruth's final death scenes, Gaskell confines herself to the more decorous symptoms of fever and delirium that degrades into a "sweet child-like insanity" (448). This is the same mental fugue state that characterized Ruth at the
beginning of the novel and Lois in the Hickson household. There is no description of a characteristic rash on Ruth's face or trunk and her watchers praise her
"sweet lips" and the "exquisite peacefulness of her look" (448). She is even
unlucky in having this group holding her death vigil since "recovery requires isolation and absolute rest."[31] The narrator is remarkably cold and utilitarian in the
description of her death:

> There she lay in the attic room in which her baby had been born, her watch over
> him kept, her confession to him made; and now she was stretched on the bed in
> utter helplessness, softly gazing at vacancy with her open, unconscious eyes, from
> which all depth of their meaning had fled, and all they told was of a sweet, child-
> like insanity within. (448)

Ruth is reduced to her reproductive capacity. She becomes a discarded vessel.
Instead of struggling against the pain and infirmity of typhus she ends her life
with "some happy vision" and a rapturous smile. Gaskell adds the improbable
flourish of Ruth being able to rise from her deathbed, however slowly and exclaim
"The light is coming" (448). Even on the threshold of her death she still must wait
for illumination and fulfillment. Victims of typhus fever have lesions, constipated
bowels and hemorrhages.[32] These conditions usually do not inspire rapture in the
victim or spectators; however metaphysical.

Bellingham never regrets his seduction of Ruth and even sexually objectifies her when he sees her laid out on the bed where she gave birth to his child. He is upbraided for his selfishness by the narrator, Sally the maid and Mr. Benson but he survives nicely and even gets to keep the sovereign that he offered as a flippant reward to Sally for her mortuary skills. He also does not suffer from transverse myelitis, peripheral neuropathy, bacterial infection, cardiac failure, peripheral gangrene or venous thromboembolism which are all possible complications suffered by survivors.[33] Good nutrition helps a typhus fever victim fight off the disease. Bellingham, unlike Ruth, has suffered no shortage of nutritious and lavish meals.

Interestingly enough, although Jemima appears at the onset of Ruth's illness with an impractical offer to spirit her and Leonard off to the bittersweet Eagle's Craig, she never appears in the death scene or during the funeral suggesting either that the loss of Ruth is too much to endure or she is now too preoccupied with her roles as mother and wife. Mr. Bradshaw sheepishly offers to erect a tombstone for her and tries to soothe Leonard at his mother's grave. The novel ends with the empowerment of Bradshaw who is invigorated by his remorse. Ruth's grandiose lie about her marriage to a glorious and heroic surgeon is ironically recast when Leonard, in spite of his mother's inability to consent from the grave, is offered a medical apprenticeship. Ruth has paid heavily for this opportunity by fatiguing herself while nursing the contagious typhoid victims and more disastrously, by falling prey to her need to nurse Bellingham a second time.

Uglow observes that in *Lois the Witch* "Gaskell is a realist, almost like a doctor, identifying an infection and watching helplessly, as it spreads."[34] Gaskell has more agency. She is like a physician intent on finding an antidote for moral failings. She identifies the infection of Ruth and Lois's economic and spiritual vulnerabilities, injects a heavy dose of realism, greed and human desire and watches with a coolly rational eye as the infection spreads along its unavoidably lethal moral trajectory.

The same grave and ineluctable consequences for women's deceit are also meted out in the novella *Lois the Witch*. Lois arrives in Salem on the good ship Redemption. She has also participated in the heterosexual economy and fallen in love with Ralph Lucy. Just like Ruth, the sudden death of her parents has left her economically vulnerable. She is also punished for her affection by her lover's jealous, class conscious mother. Lois's own mother was selfish and wished that her only surviving child would die with her but she does take a moment from her indulgent reverie to instruct her to seek shelter with her uncle Ralph Hickson in Salem. Although she does have a contentious relationship with Grace Hickson, like Ruth, she soon establishes herself as an angel in the house ideal which is "based on the notion of women's innate purity coupled with her innate sinfulness."[35] Siv Janson argues that Gaskell stages a "confrontation with the angel in the house."[36] However, for Gaskell it is not just a confrontation, it is reconciliation. Ruth and Lois restrain their anger, tolerate injustice and become industrious Bible reading, hymn singing workers in their surrogate families. Lois, like Ruth, also participates in deceit since she does not tell Pastor Nolan that Hota was tortured into confessing that she was a witch. Faith has told her that the letter that she is supposed to deliver to Nolan concerns "matters pertaining to life and death" (196). Lois promises to deliver it and speak with Nolan after he has read it. Here, like Ruth, she is offering to be a reluctant emissary on a distasteful mission. And just like Ruth who fails to live up to her promise of spying, Lois gets distracted by the morbid details of Nolan's vigil with Hota: "She had not enough urged the pastor to read his letter" (198).

Faith, like Jemima, reacts with furious indignation and takes the letter from the Pastor. Nolan is on his way to Hota's hanging. He also fails his moral obligation and does not read the letter since he is so distracted by Lois. He is punished for this neglect and is hung as a Satanist. Unlike Jemima, Faith is more smitten with Nolan than she is with Lois. Although they work together, share the same bed and many affectionate confidences and embraces, Faith is clearly enraptured with Nolan. However, curiously her heterosexual impulse is also denied since Faith's affection cannot save Nolan from execution. His relationship with the hysterical Hickson household and his unrequited passion for Lois earns him the noose. The subversion of heterosexual and lesbian desire in *Ruth* and *Lois the Witch* is one of Gaskell's most compelling legacies.

Lois sends Faith out to meet Nolan during one of his visits by smoothing her hair and kissing her cheek (175). Although she claims to be happy during this visit she also quizzically sends Nolan on his way with the admonishment "Sir, you must go. My cousin has not been strong for some time, and doubtless she needs more quiet than she has had to-day" (177). This emotional deceit becomes her undoing because it enrages Faith who mistakenly suspects that Lois is angling for Nolan. The narrator observes that Lois notices Nolan's lack of affection and "grieves" over it (180). The cousins manage to briefly mend their conflict and listen to Nolan's sermons during subsequent visits "with arms entwined, as in the days before the former became jealous of the latter" (184). This resembles the ruminating period when Jemima is aware of Ruth's deceit but has not decided how to act upon it. Nattee, the Indian servant of the Hickson's, slowly becomes Faith's confidante.

Nattee does not live up to her metaphysical promises to Faith and is eventually executed on the same day as Lois. They share a prison cell the night before the hanging and Lois spends the night soothing her with hymns and prayers. This compassion is in marked contrast with her indifference to Hota's fate. Faith does not manage to secure Nolan's affections and transforms into a person with a "bad and wicked smile" (201). Lois's final act of moral deceit happens just before Hota is executed. She refuses to loan the wildly unpredictable Prudence her muffles and mantle sternly admonishing her, "I wonder at you, Prudence, seeking to witness such a sight" (200). She forgets her own childhood prurient participation in the execution of Old Hannah and her black cat. Faith has heard Lois's recollection of this deadly event and recognizes the hypocrisy. She stages the first accusation of Lois' witchery. Lois, like Jemima, is stung by this betrayal: "and turning round with passionate reproach in her look and voice, 'what have I done that you should speak of me; you that I have loved as I think one loves a sister?'" (201). Faith will not reconsider her anger and will not even walk with Lois to the meeting house after Hota's hanging. She averts her eyes and remains silent when her sister accuses Lois of being a witch. Grace Hickson is only preoccupied with protecting the reputation of her mentally ill son, Manasseh and decides to encourage the community of Salem to believe that Lois bewitched and enfeebled her son. Here she is like the bitter Margaret Bellingham who is intent upon convincing the world that Ruth has bewitched and enfeebled her beloved son.

Even when Lois finds herself imprisoned in the Salem gaol with an eight pound shackle she is still the angel in the house, "Why even now she could love all the household at home, if they would but let her" (212). Faith, like Jemima during Ruth's illness, does not visit Lois in jail. Grace Hickson appears however, "hooded and cloaked up to her eyes" (219). Lois is once again the angel in the house when she reassures Grace that none of her children did her any harm. She does not mention Manasseh's incessant hectoring to marry him or face death, Faith's jealous machinations or Patience's outright lies to the religious authorities which directly lead to her hanging. She has only visited to try and convince Lois to release what she believes to be her satanic grasp on Manasseh's precarious mental health. Lois blesses her and the Hickson family. Grace responds to this spiritual munificence by spitting on her kneeling form.

Lois goes to the scaffold singing Psalms and spending her last energy trying to comfort Nattee with prayers. She becomes a Christ-like figure who is trying to comfort the thief on the adjoining cross. She cries out to her dead, selfish mother. Faith, like Bellingham, never repents. Prudence lives up to her mercurial nature (which she shares with her mentally damaged brother Manasseh) and repents in front of the congregation long after when repentance was in season. Manasseh, who spent the final portions of Lois's trial drugged with poppy seed and tied to his iron bed railing by his mother, rejects society completely and becomes a hermit in the woods. Here Gaskell's narrators suggest that all human intimacy is predatory and damaging. Faith, like Jemima, never reappears in the narrative and becomes another female character that has not come to terms with her sexual power. She happily allows Lois to suffer the consequences of her own propensity for jealousy and tolerance for deceit.

Lois the Witch, like *Ruth*, replicates Gaskell's interests in advancing the heterosexual economy while enticingly visiting the potentially dangerous intimacy of women's romantic friendships. Faith Hickson, like Bellingham, is never really punished for her deceit although she does lose Nolan. He was transfixed by Lois and so perhaps Faith was spared suffering for her unrequited attraction. The novella also offers us grieving male figures at women's gravesites. Ralph Lucy and Captain Holderness (who represent the trope of the ethical if not naïve male) arrive in Salem far too late. Ralph Lucy renounces heterosexual romantic life and in an inversion of Chaucer's merry *The Canterbury Tales* becomes the "grave miller of Avonside" (223).[37] Captain Holderness, who was raucous and irreverent during the stiff dinner prayers when he dropped Lois off in Salem, becomes reverent in his old age. Here Gaskell's narrators appear to caution the reader about being too flippant about the power of faith or too dismissive of its rituals.

Even the skeptical Ralph Lucy vows to mark the day and pray for Justice Sewall's forgiveness because "She would have willed it so" (226). Lucy is venerating Lois's angel in the house predilections. Ruth and Lois are posthumous emblems of virtue and forgiveness, having been schooled harshly in the lessons of the grave consequences of deceit and failure to participate in a sustained manner in the heterosexual economy.

Notes

1. Margaret Lane, "Introduction," Elizabeth Gaskell, *Ruth* (Northampton: J. M. Dent, 1967), 8.

2. The protracted death scene of Jane's beloved Helen at the infamously cruel Lowood is one of the most distressing scenes in *Jane Eyre*.

3. Quoted by Alan Shelston, "Introduction," Elizabeth Gaskell, *Ruth* (Oxford: Oxford Univ. Press, 1985), xix.

4. Simon Schama, *Rembrandt's Eyes* (New York: Alfred A. Knopf, 1999), 416.

5. Schama, *Rembrandt's Eyes*, 416.

6. Although dehydration, dizziness and faintness are symptomatic of typhus fever and she could have been bitten by an infected louse while sharing crowded quarters with the other oppressed seamstresses, here Ruth seems to be suffering from emotional exhaustion and stress and not typhus fever at this early point in the novel.

7. Clayton Thomas, ed., *Taber's Cyclopedic Medical Dictionary* (Philadelphia: F.A. Davis Company, 1989), 1010.

8. Even Bellingham's mother has stayed at Jenny's Inn before. Bellingham has consorted with women at Jenny's Inn in Wales: "You will not induce me to venture over into those rooms, whose dirt I know of old" (63). The inn is so overcrowded that when Belllingham first arrives with Ruth he has to coax Jenny into moving some of her less illustrious customers into even more disheveled rooms. The narrator also observes that it was continuously raining in Wales that July and all of the hotel customers were confined inside. These unclean conditions would be the ideal feeding ground for typhus fever bearing louses. The servants are hard pressed to keep up with the hunger of the guests: "How many dinners were hastened that day, by way of getting through the morning, let the poor Welsh kitchen-maid say!" (62) They probably did not have enough time left over to keep up with the washing of the linens of the congested, damp inn. Bellingham's "brain fever" may not be typhus fever but he has transported Ruth to an Inn where he is exposing her to moral and possibly physical danger. He is "punished" for this carelessness with illness, just as Ruth will later be punished for sexual and emotional involvement with Bellingham with disease, poverty and death.

9. Here the reader cannot help but remember Ophelia's watery grave. Consider the seductiveness of the erotic injunction in Song of Solomon: "He pastures his flock among the lilies" (*New Oxford Annotated Bible*, Song of Sol. 2: 16). However, even the Old Testament narrator is aware of how sensual love may be fraught with danger: "As a lily among brambles so is my love among maidens" (*New Oxford Annotated Bible*, Song of Sol. 2:2).

10. I. Edward Alcamo, *Fundamentals of Microbiology*, third edition (New York: The Benjamin/ Cummings Publishing Company, Inc., 1991), 301.

11. Alcamo, *Fundamentals*, 300.

12. Quoted in David Raoult, "The Body Louse as a Vector of Remerging Human Diseases," *Clinical Infectious Diseases*, 29 (1999): 902.

13. Raoult, "The Body Louse," 902.

14. George Cowan, "Rickettsial Diseases: The Typhus Group of Fevers – A Review," *Postgraduate Medical Journal*, 76 (2000): 270.

15. Washington Winn, Jr. *Koneman's Color Atlas and Textbook of Diagnostic Microbiology*, sixth edition (Baltimore: Lippincott Williams & Wilkins, 2006), 1407. Typhus fever is "currently rare in the United States, with only thirty-three cases confirmed between 1976 and

1984" (Alcamo, *Fundamentals*, 301). These encouraging statistics may be misleading however, since many undocumented homeless people in the United States may suffer from body lice afflictions including trench fever (Raoult, "The Body Louse," 888). Typhus group rickettsioses "are treated effectively with doxycline, tetracycline, or chloramphenicol (Youmans, 653). These basic antibiotics were not made available to the refugees living in the Burundi camps during the outbreak (Raoult, "Outbreak," 354).

16. David Raoult, "Outbreak of Epidemic Typhus Associated with Trench Fever in Burundi," *Lancet*, 352 (1998): 353.

17. Cowan, "Rickettsial Diseases," 269.

18. Alcamo, *Fundamentals*, 301.

19. Clayton Thomas, ed., *Taber's Cyclopedic Medical Dictionary* (Philadelphia: F.A. Davis Company, 1989), 1929.

20. Thomas, ed., *Taber's Cyclopedic Medical Dictionary*, 1930.

21. Guy Youmans, *The Biologic and Clinical Basis of Infectious Diseases* (Philadelphia: W. B. Saunders Company, 1975), 652. Endothelial cells line the blood cells. They are essential for the integrity of the blood vessel wall, they keep destructive blood clots from forming and if the cell is disrupted, they help blood clots form so that victims do not bleed out. Ruth's sexual and emotional relationship with Bellingham has harmed her so profoundly that it becomes cellular and deadly.

22. Youmans, *The Biologic and Clinical Basis of Infectious Diseases*, 652.

23. Cowan, "Rickettsial Diseases," 271.

24. Siv Janson, "Elizabeth Gaskell: Writing Against the Angel in the House," *The Gaskell Society Journal*, 10 (1996): 67.

25. Thomas, ed., *Taber's Cyclopedic Medical Dictionary*, 1929.

26. Thomas, ed., *Taber's Cyclopedic Medical Dictionary*, 1929.

27. Alcamo, *Fundamentals*, 301.

28. Thomas, ed., *Taber's Cyclopedic Medical Dictionary*, 1929.

29. Thomas, ed., *Taber's Cyclopedic Medical Dictionary*, 1929.

30. Youmans, *The Biologic and Clinical Basis of Infectious Diseases*, 53.

31. Thomas, ed., *Taber's Cyclopedic Medical Dictionary*, 1929.

32. Raymond McPherson, ed., *Henry's Clinical Diagnosis and Management by Laboratory Methods* (Philadelphia: Saunders Elsevier, 2007), 1004.

33. Cowan, "Rickettsial Diseases," 270.

34. Jenny Uglow, "Foreword," *Lois the Witch. By Elizabeth Gaskell* (London: Hesperus Press, 2003), xi.

35. Janson, "Elizabeth Gaskell: Writing Against the Angel in the House," 6.

36. Janson, "Elizabeth Gaskell: Writing Against the Angel in the House," 72.

37. Gaskell's allusion to Chaucer's *Canterbury Tales* is not gratuitous. Ralph Lucy is the perfect antithesis to the ribald Miller. In between episodes of churlish bawdiness, the Miller observes: "How fancy throws us into perturbation! / People can die of mere imagination" (116). The unscrupulous scholar is able to trick the dull-witted and jealous carpenter into believing that a cataclysmic flood is impending. He then seduces the very willing Alison. The miller further advises that "A man's no cuckold if he has no wife" (103). Ralph Lucy has painfully witnessed how the imagination of the citizens of Salem destroyed Lois. He spends the rest of his life alone.

Deviant Femininity as a Metaphor for Female Liberation in Elizabeth Gaskell's *Ruth*

Rezzan Kocaöner Silkü

I am sure I should have been repulsed by hearing that "a tale of seduction" was chosen as a subject for fiction, – that was the opinion I dreaded; – I felt *almost* sure that if people would only read what I had to say they would not be disgusted – but I feared & still think it probable that many may refuse to read any book of that kind.[1]

This quotation from Jenny Uglow's biography of Elizabeth Gaskell well explains what Gaskell had in mind when writing *Ruth*. At this time, writing about "sex" was an improper subject and "a site of anxiety and guilt for a respectable Victorian woman"; yet, as Uglow suggests, by "identifying with her heroine," Gaskell became fully aware of "her own sexuality."[2]

Just like Eve, who was banished from the garden of Eden upon eating the forbidden fruit in the Biblical account of Original Sin, Ruth became an outcast on being seduced by Mr. Bellingham. Uglow asks, "If sex has seemed natural to Ruth, is female desire itself then 'innocent'?"[3] She further adds,

Our reading of *Ruth* is inevitably affected by changed social mores, and a diminution of the sense of sin. The most painful aspect for a modern reader is not Ruth's transgression but the way Gaskell shows how women's natural impulses are transformed under the pressure of internalized values into something monstrous. A personality can split under such pressure.[4]

Gaskell personifies the abstract notions of good and evil in terms of an analogy between body and soul. Ruth, as a fallen woman, represents physical decay and corruption but her soul is pure and innocent, whereas her seducer, Mr. Bellingham, suffers from moral and spiritual degeneration.

There were varying responses to *Ruth* after its publication in 1853: "The respectable condemned her immorality, the liberal praised her courage, the radical regretted her feebleness."[5] After reading *Ruth*, Elizabeth Barrett Browning sent her compliments to Gaskell: "'I am grateful to you as a woman for having treated such a subject – Was it quite impossible but that your Ruth should *die*? I had that thought of regret in closing the book – Oh, I must confess to it – Pardon me for the tears' sake!'"[6]

The nineteenth century was the crossroads at which British women writers developed new strategies in their approach to the subject of women. In the context of various representations of Victorian femininity in the works of Victorian women writers, Gaskell's disguised character, Ruth, turns out to be a metaphor to explore the border-line between the Victorian cult of domesticity and disruptive female sexuality.

As Lyn Pykett emphasizes in her essay "Women Writing Woman," "such disruptive figures [like prostitutes, hysterical or mad women, and bad mothers] were not simply alternatives to normal, respectable femininity; rather normative maternal Woman was constructed in relation to her deviant others"[7] as a threatening image to the future of the race. Yet, such negative attributions or labels were nothing but patriarchal strategies to impose the doctrine of domesticity on Victorian women, by threatening them with the myth of feminine deviance. The idea was to suppress any attempt at working outside the family household that would end women's economic dependency on their husbands. Dani Cavallaro in *Critical and Cultural Theory* also states, "the Other is the person or group that confers meaning upon the subject by either helping it or forcing it to adopt a particular world view and to define its position therein."[8] In this regard, "fallen women," like Gaskell's Ruth, assist the dominant Victorian ideology to sustain its discourse of the cult of domesticity epitomized in the expression "The Angel in the House" by constituting a model to avoid.

This paper aims to study how Gaskell, by emphasizing Ruth's innocence and victimization, employs a strategy to subvert the "fallen woman" discourse of Victorian ideology, which undermines women's potential for social and economic development. I will also discuss how Gaskell gives voice to the female Other through disruptive, deviant femininity, which, in the process of legitimating itself, could only raise the consciousness of younger women and ultimately provoke social change.

Joanne Shattock observes in *Women and Literature in Britain: 1800-1900*: "the polarization of the 'public' (male) and the 'private' (female) sphere [was not only] part of Victorian ideology, but [also] … it was a very real part of nineteenth-century experience."[9] She further notes: "The power structures inherent in the domestic household, and the codes of social conduct, … were aspects of life from which no nineteenth-century woman was immune."[10] Pykett adds that

> Women writers' representations of women, Woman, the feminine, and female sex-
> uality were also shaped by the unstable, contradictory and "uneven" conceptualiza-
> tions of feminine gender and female sexuality which proliferated in the male-con-
> trolled domains of the law, social analysis, medicine, science and the emerging field
> of psychoanalysis, in all of which Woman was constructed as a "relative creature,"
> who was defined through biological, affective and legal relationships to others.[11]

Nineteenth-century British fiction was very much concerned with the issues of
gender and sexuality. But prominent women novelists of the Victorian period like
Charlotte Brontë and Gaskell dealt with questions regarding women from different perspectives. Their examples varied from the rural to the urban and from the
working class to the middle class. Therefore, the representations of women in
their novels had a colourful diversity. As Pykett categorizes the heroines of nineteenth-century British fiction, they range from

> the womanly woman ... [to] the fallen woman; [from] the domestically impris-
> oned wife ... [to] the self-sacrificing maternal angel; [from] the histrionic, non-
> maternal, "fast" "Girl of the Period" ... [to] the scheming assertive, often sexually
> exploitative sensation heroine ... [or to] the "revolting daughters" of the 1880s
> and 1890s who rejected the models of femininity espoused by their mothers,
> sought independence, education and entry to the professions.[12]

Cavallaro claims that "social identities are not centred on fixed properties
acquired at birth and bound to remain stable thereafter ... [since people play]
multiple and shifting roles ... in both private and public contexts on the basis of
their genders and sexualities."[13] Yet, through binary oppositions like "normality
and deviance," societies try to "normalize ... the plural and culturally determined
character of gender and sexuality."[14] Such "normalizing strategies ... [originate
from] the ... legacy of sexual morality ... [which] seeks to define what sexual
activities are permissible, and who is ethically or legally entitled to take part in
them" since illegitimate sexual relationships are believed to "loosen the social fabric."[15] Thus, the novels of Victorian women writers like Eliot, Gaskell, and Brontë
well represent how "sexual morality has benefitted men at the expense of
women."[16] Consciously or unconsciously, these women writers, with novels like
Ruth or *North and South*, contributed to the struggle for

> women's rights to social, political and economic equality; the enhancement of
> their educational and professional opportunities; the assertion of their sexual
> autonomy and reproductive rights; their protection from physical and psycholog-
> ical abuse; the rejection of male-dominated forms of language; and the decon-
> struction of denigrating representations of femininity.[17]

Ruth, in addressing questions of female transgressiveness, aims to sensitise its readership, inspire sympathy and tolerance, and instil a sense of progress that is intrinsically proto-feminist. Ruth is an orphan. After her apprenticeship to a dressmaker, she is blinded by her love for Mr. Bellingham and accepts his proposal to go to London. Her seduction by Bellingham becomes a turning point in Ruth's life. Bellingham's brain fever is a punishment for his guilt, but he is easily convinced by his mother that he has been misguided by Ruth. This unfair treatment brings Ruth to the edge of death as she attempts to commit suicide. But she survives and thereafter owes much to Mr. Thurstan Benson, who provides her with a new life and identity disguised as a widow named Mrs. Denbigh in the northern English parish of Eccleston, so as to protect her illegitimate child, Leonard, from any possible social constraint. She becomes a governess for the Bradshaw daughters in Mr. Benson's parish. When her secret is revealed and she is disgraced, she devotes herself to the victims of typhus and eventually dies of it (ironically) while nursing her seducer.

As Nancy Henry explains Gaskell was first inspired by "a servant named Anne" in her creation of Ruth.[18] As Gaskell's curiosity about the mystery of Anne's affair with her baby's father remained unresolved, she turned her attention to another young seamstress known as Pasley, whose situation was similar to Ruth's. Gaskell put the blame on society for her character's moral corruption, since parents neglected to equip their daughters with an education. Ruth had to face all her misfortune as a motherless, powerless, and uneducated young woman.

In *Ruth*, Gaskell illustrates the changing panorama of British society during the industrialization of the nineteenth century. Many landowning families sold their houses to move to London and the county-town lost its charm. Those houses from then on were occupied by new dwellers like "the professional men and their wives, the shopkeepers and their spouses."[19] Under these circumstances of daily rush, it is easy to understand how a character could be shaped by such external influences as the poverty and disease of the 1840s.

Kathryn Gleadle discusses the employment of working-class women as factory workers, domestic servants, dressmakers, or miners during the first half of the nineteenth century: "The dreadful exploitation of these workers was such that, as the investigative journalist, Henry Mayhew, revealed ... in 1849-50, many needlewomen – whose work was highly irregular due to the vagaries of the London season and the international markets – were forced to supplement their wages through prostitution."[20] As an apprentice to the dressmaker Mrs. Mason, Ruth had to struggle a lot to overcome the difficulties in her life:

> Ruth Hilton passed wearily one January night, now many years ago. I call it night;
> but, strictly speaking, it was morning. Two o'clock in the morning chimed forth

the old bells of St Saviour's. And yet more than a dozen girls still sat in the room … not daring … [to] show any outward manifestation of sleepiness. They only sighed a little when Ruth told Mrs. Mason the hour of the night … for they knew that … the work-hours of the next day must begin at eight, and their young limbs were very weary. (5)

Ruth's journey to Shire Hall was a turning point in her life. It was the first time she encountered Mr. Bellingham, who was attracted to Ruth as she mended the dress of a lady called Miss Duncombe, whom he accompanied. In Bellingham's eyes, "the kneeling figure, that, habited in black up to the throat, with the noble head bent down to the occupation in which she was engaged, formed such a contrast to the flippant, bright, artificial girl, who sat to be served with an air as haughty as a queen on her throne" (15). During the ball, Ruth realized that there were two worlds: inner and outer. "Outside all was cold, and colourless, and uniform. … But inside it was warm, and glowing, and vivid" (14).

Ruth had always suffered from Mrs. Mason's scolding and oppressive attitude. Gaskell uses the "caged bird" metaphor for Ruth's loneliness as an orphan in Mrs. Mason's workhouse, the "press[ing] against [the window] as a bird presses against the bars of its cage" (6). On Sundays, she was accustomed to sitting at the window of her workplace room, reviving her memories, reading the Bible, and creating stories about the lives of the passers-by. In this regard, she had a very romantic nature for a common girl. Ruth's future was not shaped by her own free will but by coincidence at Shire Hall, as she met Mr. Bellingham waiting for his prey. Thomas, the poor labourer of Ruth's father, was an eyewitness to Ruth's approaching tragedy, as he saw Mr. Bellingham "look at [him] … with a strange, grave air of dissatisfaction"; then he warned Ruth through "the language of the Bible: 'My dear, remember the devil goeth about as a roaring lion, seeking whom he may devour; remember that, Ruth'" (44).

Ruth was dismissed upon Mrs. Mason's discovery of her affair with Mr. Bellingham, despite the fact that she was a penniless and homeless girl who had no other alternative but to go with Mr. Bellingham. During their stay in North Wales, Ruth was too innocent to understand that she had been an object of gossip and interest at the inn, "where many watchers stood observing her, and commenting upon her situation or her appearance" (61). Gentlemen found her young, "lovely," and "innocent-looking in her white gown," whereas some others considered it a shame to allow "such wickedness under the same roof!" (61). Ruth for the first time in her life realized that she had done wrong. From then on she would be labelled "a bad, naughty girl" (61), in the words of young Harry at the inn. Thereafter the arrival of Mrs. Bellingham at the inn, on account of her son's illness, became a turning point in Ruth's life. Mrs. Bellingham, as a rich widow, considered Ruth an indecent, wretched girl making plans to marry her beloved son.

By juxtaposing two different women, Gaskell elaborates on the marriage institution. Mrs. Bellingham, an upper-class lady, represents prearranged marriages for the economic benefit of the family: to sustain the family's welfare by arranging a marriage between her son and Miss Duncombe. On the other hand, Ruth symbolizes pure love, which is not allowed to survive in competition with the customary institution of marriage. Ruth's middle-class background and present working-class situation do not meet the expectations of an upper-class mother, who refuses to consider her a prospective bride for her son. Mrs. Bellingham is described as a strong mother figure to compensate for her weak son. Mr. Bellingham's romantic tendencies are balanced by Mrs. Bellingham's realistic and materialistic endeavours. In this regard, both Mr. Bellingham and Ruth are victimized by the established, conventional Victorian morality and the cult of domesticity.

During the time of Ruth's suffering, Mr. Thurstan Benson becomes a determining force to give her "hope," "chance," and "liberty" (85). Mr. Benson, unlike the typical patriarch of the period, identifies Ruth's case in terms of her having to live with the consequences of her choices. Being a mother requires greater responsibility and from Mr. Benson's perspective, the illegitimate child must be protected from any negative consequences in the outside world. In Mr. Benson's view, "the little helpless baby, about to enter a cruel, biting world ... need never know its illegitimacy" (103).

As Gail Marshall states in *Victorian Fiction*, "in the early 1850s paintings of the Pre-Raphaelite Brotherhood ... female sexuality is represented as dangerous primarily to the women themselves."[21] "The Fallen Woman" image of these paintings paved the way for the 1857 Divorce Act, which aimed to punish adventurous women. As Marshall further explains, Victorian women novelists, however, were more concerned to "save their fallen women ... [even through] death [which can be interpreted as a kind of] redemption."[22] For such deviant women, motherhood was also another way of redeeming themselves from their sinful state. For example, Ruth, as Leonard's mother, has "a life of moral purity and service" in her disguise of a governess and a widow.[23] Although the novel was burned by "some of Gaskell's neighbours in Manchester," *Ruth* still gained the "sympathy and understanding" of most because of the novel's moral ending, and because she remained "curiously unsensual, untouched by her fall."[24]

Racheal Bloom, discussing the similarities between the paintings of the Pre-Raphaelite artists and Gaskell's novel-writing, also claims that Ruth "defies traditional categorisation as a fallen woman [because of] her outward appearance [and] her behaviour."[25] Thus, innocence and beauty become a resistance strategy for Gaskell against "class and convention."[26] That is to say, in challenging the conventional Victorian norms and biased attitudes toward fallen women, Gaskell uses beauty as "a narrative device and visual aid" to make Ruth more sympathetic.[27] "With her ... figure, her striking face, with dark eyebrows and dark lashes, combined with auburn hair and a fair complexion" (11), Ruth is likened to "a flower... [an example of] natural beauty,"[28] yet, in contrast to the Pre-Raphaelite artists, "objectifying the woman [as] a mark of male aesthetic creation." Gaskell attempts to attribute meaning to Ruth's existence "in [the] socially determined world" of mid-nineteenth-century England.[29] Thus, Ruth is not a mere object of men's aesthetic and sexual pleasure, but a strong female protagonist who acts in her society to regain the sympathy of both Victorian and contemporary readers. Ruth's innocence is a significant element in distinguishing her from the stereotypical representation of the fallen woman. Ruth is neither a prostitute nor a *femme fatale*, since, as Bloom claims, she does not have "the self knowledge of sexual power."[30] For Ruth, so-called deviancy becomes a catalyst in liberating her from the biased attitudes of Victorian society.

Audrey Jaffe also emphasizes the significance of "infection" as a metaphor for fallenness, which is "everyone's problem" in Gaskell's *Ruth*.[31] Yet, it is only Ruth who must be punished at the end as a fallen woman. Thus, infection is associated with contamination as a threat to the orderly moral structure of Victorian society. However, as Jaffe further states, Ruth is an emblem of the transformation of fallenness into sympathy in the novel. By learning "to discipline resentful feelings and accept her 'station,'" Ruth becomes a role model who "radiates feelings of serenity and cheerfulness ... [and] disseminates familial harmony."[32]

Gleadle claims that "prostitution held an enduring fascination in the Victorian public imagination, capturing as it did the very antithesis of cultural proscriptions of refined and pure womanhood."[33] And Pykett suggests that prostitution was a possible form of feminine deviance, "threatening the future of the race by spreading venereal disease, either by infecting middle-class men who subsequently infected their wives and children, or ... by spreading disease to their [own] husbands and offspring."[34] Therefore, the aim of the Contagious Diseases Acts of 1864 and 1866 was to prevent prostitution; yet they "humiliat[ed] women and restrict[ed] their civil rights."[35] These acts authorized magistrates "to detain for compulsory medical inspection and treatment any woman deemed to be a prostitute."[36] However, such discriminatory acts stimulated the Victorian proto-feminist movement's fight for women's liberation and individual rights.

Because of the humiliating effects of the Contagious Diseases Acts (1864-86), there occurred a strong repeal movement by the proto-feminists, since such acts caused great intolerance towards prostitutes:

> In drawing upon melodramatic … narratives of women's sexual exploitation by upper-class "rakes," feminists were able to forge a brief alliance with working-class radicals – a coalition which helped to preserve women's own identity within the middle-class repeal movement … [with the hope] that … [this coalition] would foster a model of cross-class sisterhood.[37]

The Contagious Diseases Acts were repealed by 1886 through the efforts of some prominent, "religiously inspired" women like Josephine Butler.[38] And, although Gaskell has been criticized for compromising the dominant patriarchal ideology by killing her heroine, the novel had an impact on women's reaction to the Contagious Diseases Acts, and paved the way for the feminist movement's fight for women's liberation.

As Gleadle further states, the "radical unitarians" inspired by a Unitarian preacher, William Johnson Fox of South Place Chapel in Finsbury, played a significant role in the advancement of women's liberation movements in Victorian England.[39] Under the influence of "the Unitarian tradition of Enlightenment," which emphasized "the rights of the individual and the importance of education," the radical Unitarians in the 1840s "campaigned for reform in the laws concerning prostitution, female adult education and reforms to married women's legal position."[40] Proto-feminists of the 1850s, like Bessie Rayner Parkes and Barbara Smith Bodichon, were influenced by the radical Unitarians of the previous decade.[41]

Besides elaborating on gender roles in *Ruth*, Gaskell also treats politics and its impact on the welfare of the nation. The opposition between the Tories and the Whigs is represented in the discourse of Mr. Bradshaw, who prepares his house for "electioneering" purposes as a man of the manufacturing class with a reforming spirit (212). The objective of the Liberal Party and its candidates like Mr. Donne, the Dissenting man of Eccleston, "is to reform the law of England … [and to] get a majority of Liberal members into the House … in order that the next generation might be taught better" (214-19).

Mr. Bellingham and Ruth Hilton's meeting at the Bradshaws' sea-side house, as Mr. Donne and Mrs. Denbigh, is only by coincidence. Ruth never forgives him for "the burden and the shame" (229) she experienced in the past. Yet, she has never lost her confidence in herself to "look up straight at his face [during breakfast, and Mr. Donne] … thought this Mrs. Denbigh was certainly like poor Ruth; but this woman was far handsomer … quite queenly! A governess in Mr. Bradshaw's family! … [H]ow the devil had she played her cards so well as to be governess?" (233-34). Mr. Bellingham, having confessed his weakness to propose to Ruth in the past, now "offer[s] to marry [her]" to guarantee her and her illegitimate son's future (253). Ruth for the first time in her life challenges him by saying

"You have humbled me – you have baited me … the fault is yours" (254). Gaskell thus criticizes the patriarchal discourse of the period, which victimized women and reduced them to objects.

In the nineteenth century, deviant femininity was a common theme, which could be taken as an act of resistance to the cult of domesticity and motherhood in mid-nineteenth-century Victorian society. Those who did not act in accord with the normative behaviour of womanhood were doomed to be isolated from society as the Other, by being kept in such places as the Fordham Penitentiary of Manchester. Thus, exiling the "Fallen Woman" was a way of imposing "The Angel in the House" myth on prospective Victorian mothers and wives, who would raise the sons and daughters of the monarchy by showing the possible misfortunes and sufferings of the sinful and illegitimate Others.

Thus, "the Other is the factor that enables the subject to build up a self image … [and] in Western culture, dominant ideologies have … defined themselves in relation to a subordinated Other."[42] Having emphasized the significance of alterity in gender politics, Cavallaro also contends that "there are various versions and degrees of otherness; the ways in which a particular woman experiences her alterity relate not only to her biological sex and her gender position within a culture but also to her ethnic background, education, profession, social class, and both physical and psychological abilities and disabilities."[43] Considering theories about "the concept of 'difference' as an internal condition, rather than a matter of external attributes," Cavallaro further observes that "we discriminate against, or indeed abuse, other people … [or] find them threatening and react to them violently because we have difficulties negotiating the stranger in us."[44] Then, in accordance with such a psychoanalytic explanation, Victorian society's treatment of Ruth as a "fallen woman" "mirrors … her [own] fears and desires."[45]

Being a spinster is another form of deviance in nineteenth-century British society. For example, Faith Benson stands for a single young Victorian female who has sacrificed her happiness to take care of her brother, Mr. Benson, who, in turn, suffers from a physical deformity. Sally, the servant in the Bensons' house, is another example of a woman who has preferred to maintain a single life as the daughter of a parish clerk rather than marry a man and be dependent on him. Even Sally has a very sarcastic tone in telling how she has had her first proposal from Mr. Dixon, who thinks he has done a great favour to her. Sally declares: "'I've no wish to change my condition just now'" (142), suggesting that there are other ways for young women to survive: through hard work as servants, governesses, or needle-women. Women's contribution to the national economy, through savings, became important during the period of industrialization. They tried to overcome dependency on their husbands, since individual liberation is closely related to women's economic freedom.

Ruth is offered a new position as a governess by the Bradshaws. For her, working in the Bradshaw household as the teacher of their daughters is an opportunity to obtain her economic freedom. Yet, her conflicts mainly derive from the question of whether she is good enough to be a teacher for the Bradshaw girls, since her state as a "fallen woman" contradicts Mr. Bradshaw's understanding of life. Mr. Bradshaw symbolically stands for the dominant patriarchal ideology as a "severe … man … [too] unpitiful a judge" to forgive Ruth (167). In any case, he discovers the mystery about her past.

Jemima, the eldest daughter of the Bradshaw family, seems to be a promising bride for a man like Mr. Farquar, the business partner of Mr. Bradshaw, who considers marriage, like Mr. Bradshaw, as a business matter. Yet, Jemima's attitude of questioning authority disturbs Mr. Farquar, who expects a submissive girl as his prospective bride, one not to be "guided by [her] impulse[s]": "Mr. Farquar had been taught to dread impulses as promptings of the devil" (181-82). Although Jemima is very pleased by the idea of Mr. Farquar's special interest in her, she thinks he has a "cold calculating feeling … a pattern idea in his mind, trying to find a wife to match" (185).

Men like Mr. Bradshaw, who represents the Victorian patriarchal ideology, will never understand Ruth. But his daughter Jemima feels pity for her, though she knows that her own marriage plans with Mr. Farquar will not be fulfilled because of his interest in Ruth. As a female eyewitness, Mrs. Bradshaw is aware that Ruth is wiser and stronger than she was in the past to carry her burden and stand against its consequences. Having heard about Ruth's sin, Jemima herself learns to be tolerant in her relations with others, and not to treat anyone else in a prejudiced manner. Jemima understands Ruth even to the point of challenging her father for his ignorance of her situation. Her visit to Ruth on the eve of her marriage to Mr. Farquar to ask Ruth's forgiveness is an expression of her courage and humility. Mr. Farquar's and Jemima Bradshaw's marriage is the fulfilment of ideal Victorian family unity, since Jemima, as the rich daughter of the Bradshaws, marries her father's business partner, Mr. Farquar, to maintain the family name and status. Although Jemima can be described as a young girl, her distinction lies, as she herself expresses, in her "headstrong and passionate" (305) impulse to question authority. Therefore, Jemima's marriage to Mr. Farquar fulfils the expectations of the dominant ideology, but Jemima would never marry him if she weren't in love with him "since the days when [he] first brought [her] pistachio-candy from London – when [she] was quite a little girl" (314).

Most of the female characters created by nineteenth-century women writers, like Gaskell's Ruth, generally suffer from orphanage, seduction, and betrayal, which victimize them as the sinful mothers of illegitimate children. However, such deviancy has a productive side, for women, in developing such masculine traits as anger and violence, transgress against the stereotypical representations of Victorian femininity. Thus, insanity or other types of deviancy become a kind of liberation from the manacles of patriarchy. Yet, once women deviate in a conservative society, the only way out for them is, ironically, through death, as the resolution of Gaskell's *Ruth* suggests. Such an ironic ending is foreshadowed in Ruth's words when she regretfully says, upon the discovery by the Bradshaws of her sin and the illegitimacy of her son, Leonard: "Oh! would that I had died – I had died, in my innocent girlhood!" (286). Here Gaskell associates "innocence" with love and devotion, an alternative to a pre-arranged marriage in the Victorian age which bans typical married women from expressing such desires publicly, and labels any deviants as adulterous. Being a good wife in Victorian society means to disguise one's real emotions and keep one's silence. However, authenticity requires breaking the silence and expressing one's true feelings and thoughts. Therefore, Mrs. Bradshaw's protesting against her husband's cruel treatment of her son is an expression of her liberation from the bondage of the Victorian cult of domesticity: "I've been a good wife till now … I have done all he bid me, ever since we were married. But now I will speak my mind" (341). Women's speaking out is considered to be a kind of challenge and rebellion against the dominance of Victorian patriarchy. Thus, to suppress such attempts, Victorian ideology represents women who voice their minds as deviant and wild. When Ruth speaks out as a mother, begging God's assistance to have the strength to bring up her son properly, Gaskell describes her as "a wild creature" (285).

As Nancy Henry states, "Gaskell uses the imagery of an opium-induced delusion – of golden mists, stunned conscience and dreams – to emphasise that Ruth is not conscious of her actions."[46] Ruth wants to maintain her life through moral repentance and by hiding her identity as a "fallen woman." In *Ruth*, Gaskell also discusses the consequences of transgression and suggests that the only form of redemption is punishment through an epidemic – a punishment that may raise the moral consciousness of the younger generation. Ruth sacrifices her own life for the welfare of the community during the outbreak of the typhus epidemic in the country. Her death at the end is both her reward and punishment.

Ruth was not born a "fallen woman," but she became one. She was guilty of being an orphan, and loving a man from the upper class whose mother considered marriage as an economic investment to sustain the welfare of the family name and property; she was guilty of giving birth to her seducer's child, and raising him with her own limited earnings by working as a governess; and eventually she was guilty of nursing her seducer while he was suffering from typhus, thereby causing her own death.

Notes

1. Elizabeth Gaskell quoted in Jenny Uglow, *Elizabeth Gaskell: A Habit of Stories* (London: Faber and Faber, 1999), 322.

2. Elizabeth Gaskell quoted in Uglow, 322.

3. Elizabeth Gaskell quoted in Uglow, 325.

4. Elizabeth Gaskell quoted in Uglow, 335.

5. Elizabeth Gaskell quoted in Uglow, 342.

6. Uglow, 1999, 340.

7. Lyn Pykett, "Women Writing Woman: Nineteenth-Century Representations of Gender and Sexuality," *Women and Literature in Britain: 1800-1900*, ed. Joanne Shattock (Cambridge: Cambridge Univ. Press, 2001), 81-82.

8. Dani Cavallaro, *Critical Theory* (London: The Athlone Press, 2001), 121.

9. Joanne Shattock, ed., *Women and Literature in Britain: 1800-1900* (Cambridge: Cambridge Univ. Press, 2001), 3.

10. Shattock, 4-5.

11. Pykett, 79.

12. Pykett, 94.

13. Cavallaro, 109.

14. Cavallaro, 109.

15. Cavallaro, 109-111.

16. Cavallaro, 111.

17. Cavallaro, 111.

18. Nancy Henry, "Introduction," *Ruth*, Elizabeth Gaskell (London: Everyman Paperbacks, 2001), xxiv.

19. Elizabeth Gaskell, *Ruth* (London: Everyman Paperbacks, 2001), 3. Henceforth parenthetically cited in the text.

20. Kathryn Gleadle, *British Women in the Nineteenth Century* (New York: Palgrave, 2001), 20.

21. Gail Marshall, *Victorian Fiction* (London: Arnold, 2002), 44.

22. Marshall, 45.

23. Marshall, 45.

24. Marshall, 45.

25. Racheal Bloom, "Elizabeth Gaskell, the Pre-Raphaelite Author of *Ruth*: Natural Beauty and That Pre-Raphaelite Stunner … Ruth," *Perspectives: Journal for Interdisciplinary Work in the Humanities* (July 23, 2000): 2.

26. Bloom, 2.

27. Bloom, 2.

28. Bloom, 2.

29. Bloom, 4.

30. Bloom, 4.

31. Audrey Jaffe, "Infection and Feeling in Mrs. Gaskell's *Ruth*," *The Victorian Web: Literature, History, and Culture in the Age of Victoria* (September 6, 2006): 1.

32. Jaffe, 1.
33. Gleadle, 99.
34. Pykett, 82.
35. Gleadle, 100.
36. Gleadle, 165.
37. Gleadle, 165.
38. Gleadle, 165.
39. Gleadle, 76.
40. Gleadle, 76.
41. Gleadle, 77.
42. Cavallaro, 121-22.
43. Cavallaro, 123.
44. Cavallaro, 129.
45. Cavallaro, 129.
46. Henry, xxviii.

Class Act: Servants and Mistresses in the Works of Elizabeth Gaskell

Dorice Williams Elliott

In the first chapter of Gaskell's *Cranford*, the narrator describes a party at Mrs. Forrester's "baby-house of a dwelling."[1] While Mrs. Forrester is obviously poor and has only a small charity-school girl to help her, both she and her genteel visitors maintain the fiction that they are "aristocratic" and "that our hostess had a regular servants' hall, second table, with house-keeper and steward … though she knew, and we knew, and she knew that we knew, and we knew that she knew that we knew, she had been busy all the morning making tea-bread and sponge-cakes" alongside her one young servant. Servant, mistress, and visitors all act the necessary roles that maintain their class positions, poverty and reality notwithstanding.[2]

This incident is emblematic of a central tension in Gaskell's work, the contradiction between the actual relationship between servants and mistresses and the necessary fictions that preserve the mistress's class position. In her representations of servants in both her letters and her fictional works, Gaskell frequently portrays them as "friends" whose relationships with their mistresses are based on loyalty, respect, and affection. Women who treat their servants as paid employees, such as the second Mrs. Gibson in *Wives and Daughters*, are seen as morally suspect and vulgar rather than truly genteel. However, Gaskell's depiction of ideal servant-mistress relations characterized by mutual respect and regard is also a fiction that covers over the power differential, market relations, and competition that are built into dealings between servants and mistresses. The tension between her desire to represent and treat servants as equals and friends and the necessity of having servants who were willing to act the role of subservient, loyal dependent in order to maintain her own class position – as well as her ability to write professionally – is ultimately unresolvable. Thus, in her representations of servants,

113

Gaskell comes close to recognizing that social class is constructed and fictional, but she ultimately backs away from that recognition.

Gaskell's description of the Cranford ladies taking tea at Mrs. Forrester's is significantly placed in the first chapter. It foregrounds, from the very beginning of the story, the fictions these poor but genteel older women know they are performing in almost every aspect of their current lives. The repetition of "she knew, and we knew, and she knew that we knew, and we knew that she knew that we knew" destroys any direct correlation between the social ritual they are performing and the reality that ought to lie underneath it. In what is literally an *act* of desperation, the women pretend to each other that their social position is stable and invulnerable, though they all know that this is not the case. The other key player in the scene, of course, is Mrs. Forrester's "little charity-school maiden." Without her, in fact, the play could not be performed. She stands in for the "regular servants' hall, second table, with housekeeper and steward" that are absolutely necessary but significantly absent from Mrs. Forrester's "baby-house." Whether the charity-school maiden is a willing or self-conscious actor in the scene is uncertain. But her "request that she might get the tea-tray out from underneath" the sofa on which the ladies are sitting is the only visible act of labor in the scene. The Cranford ladies "perform" class by pretending not to work; the servant performs in another sense, by actively doing the work that marks her class position as different from theirs.

In her important study of nineteenth-century middle-class women, *Nobody's Angels: Middle-Class Women and Domestic Ideology in Victorian Culture*, Elizabeth Langland makes a crucial point about the duties of middle-class women like the Cranford ladies and Gaskell herself:

> Running the middle-class household, which by definition became 'middle class' in its possession of at least one servant, was an exercise in class management, a process both inscribed and exposed in the Victorian novel. Although the nineteenth-century novel presented the household as a moral haven secure from economic and political storms, alongside this figuration one may discern another process at work: the active management of class power.[3]

Although Mrs. Forrester can only afford a "charity girl," that is, a very young girl – probably nine or ten years old – fresh from a charity school or the workhouse, who would be at the rock bottom of the servant scale both in terms of skills and pay, it is vital to maintaining her position as a "lady" that she retain at least this one servant. This enables her to meet the minimum criterion for the middle-class. A more affluent woman like Gaskell, with "five women-servants, and an out-of-doors-man, or gardener," was constantly preoccupied with hiring, firing, training, and managing her servants, as her letters make manifest.[4] As Langland makes clear, this meant that Gaskell was not only a professional writer, but a professional employer and manager of labor, but also of the signs of class.[5] Decoding the signs of the middle-class home makes it recognizable "as a theater for the staging of a family's social position, a staging that depends on a group of prescribed domestic practices."[6] Langland's reference to the home as a "theater" emphasizes not only the constructedness of the ideal home, but also the performative nature of mistress-servant relations. Langland focuses most of her attention on representations of class difference. Gaskell, on the other hand, tried to minimize difference in her portrayals of mistresses and servants; significantly, though, even that is another way of performing her own privileged position.

In literary study, the theory of performativity is most often discussed in relation to gender or race. Among the most prominent of the theorists of performativity is Judith Butler, who argues that gender, traditionally perhaps the most basic aspect of human identity, is performed rather than naturally occurring in the body or consciousness. As she explains it, gender is not "a stable identity or locus of agency from which various acts proceed; rather it is an identity tenuously constituted in time, instituted in an exterior space through a *stylized repetition of acts*."[7] Similarly, race is now recognized as a "cultural category [that] cannot be sustained by its often purported basis in 'nature,'" but is, like gender, constructed, though in a different way.[8] Social class too is constructed and performed, even more obviously than gender and race. In fact, in *Performance: A Critical Introduction*, Marvin Carlson suggests that "social performance" is "the recognition that our lives are structured according to repeated and socially sanctioned modes of behavior" and thus "*all* human activity could potentially be considered as performance."[9]

While the formulation of gender as performance was a strikingly new idea in the 1980s, when Butler first began writing about it, theorists have recognized for some time that social class was constructed and performed. Combining insights from theatre and sociology, Erving Goffman, for instance, wrote in 1959 that social roles could be defined as "the enactment of rights and duties attached to a given status." Each social role, Goffman continues, "will involve one or more parts and … each of these different parts may be presented by the performer on a series of occasions to the same kinds of audience or to an audience of the same persons."[10] Because it was evident that not only actors and con men, but also the newly rich or socially mobile person could learn the "part" of a new social position (or at least have it taught to their children by masters and governesses), many, including Gaskell, were at least close to recognizing that class is performative as early as the middle of the nineteenth century. When Gaskell has the Cranford ladies and their charity-school maid-of-all-work self-consciously perform a ceremony that affirms their social status, she demonstrates that their identities as gen-

teel ladies and loyal servant are neither natural nor stable, but based on what Butler calls the "stylized repetition" of particular and mutually recognized acts.

Despite the fact that they may have recognized that social class was not actually an identity rooted in nature, Gaskell and her contemporaries, as Langland
and others emphasize, obviously had their reasons for continuing to perform the
rites of class distinction in both their everyday lives and in the political and economic realm. Kevin R. Swafford points out that

> For Victorians of all sorts and conditions, the public discourse concerning class
> was articulated as anything but contingent and performative ... [yet] the sense
> that one must *perform class*, through a host of symbolic actions, practices, beliefs,
> tastes, and desires, was an unspoken source of anxiety that was often avoided and
> repressed within the ruling classes of Victorian society and culture.[11]

Thus, while they might not actually believe in the absolute correspondence
between the social actions they perform and the reality of social status – when, for
instance, ladies like the ones in Cranford know that they are too poor to be secure
in their gentility – they nonetheless believe in the concept of gentility and the
importance of maintaining the fiction that it is a God-ordained and thus natural
system of establishing difference. The tension this paradox created appears both
in Gaskell's fictional works and her letters and diaries. Representing mistress-
servant relations as based on the performance of friendship rather than on economics or coercion was her way of resolving the paradox and was a logical extension of, among other things, her religious views.

For Gaskell, a professing Christian and the wife of a Unitarian minister, religion might ordain the God-given place of the poor and the rich, but it also argued
for the equality of all souls before God.[12] Believing in the responsibility this
entailed to help the poor, Gaskell herself, like several of her fictional characters,
was active in performing charitable works and supported various philanthropies.
In her dealings with the poor, however, Gaskell felt strongly that they should be
treated as friends, not inferiors. In an 1859 letter to Charles Eliot Norton, she
praises her daughter Meta because she "has poor old people whom she goes to see
regularly, as a friend not as a benefactor."[13] This attitude is also represented in
North and South, where Margaret Hale must, like Meta, learn to visit the working-class Higgins family as a friend, not a patroness.[14]

In addition to visiting "poor old people ... as a friend," Gaskell's daughter
Meta also "reads with and teaches Elliott every night," in the same spirit of friendship. Elliott was one of the Gaskells' servants, and Mrs. Gaskell's praise of Meta's
friendship with the family's waiter echoes her representations in her letters of her
own relationships with her servants. In the same letter, for instance, she mentions
that Elliott often asks after Mr. Norton and gives Elliott's opinion on some pho-

tographs Norton has sent – discussing the servant much in the same way she does the rest of her family or other acquaintances.[15] Biographer Jenny Uglow notes that "However much she joked or fretted, during all her married life Elizabeth was closely involved in her servants' lives"; she "cared for her servants" and "depended on them … not merely for practical help."[16] Of all her servants, Gaskell was particularly close to her children's governess, Miss Barbara Fergusson, and Ann Hearn, who was a servant of the Gaskells for over fifty years.

Gaskell wrote in 1857 that her "dearest friends, all throughout [her] life, have been governesses, either past, present or future."[17] While not exactly a servant, a governess like Miss Fergusson was an employee of the family who was not an equal. Although Gaskell eventually decided she had to let Miss Fergusson go because she was not qualified enough to teach Gaskell's daughters in the way she wanted them taught, she continued to write to the former governess frequently, calling her an old nickname – "Daddy" – and urging her to indulge the same level of intimacy and friendship they enjoyed while Miss Fergusson was still in her employ. In an 1845 letter addressed to "My dearest Daddy," Gaskell chastises her for the formality of a previous letter: "Don't be mine 'very sincerely,' again there's a good girl."[18] Gaskell ends the letter with "Goodbye, dear – Ever your very affect friend."[19] In a letter of 1846, Gaskell, who was away from home, sent the governess a whole list of instructions to give to the servants, ending with a concern that the governess will "not think me very troublesome in making you the medium."[20] Her solicitude suggests that Gaskell wanted to preserve the relationship with Fergusson as one of friend asking a favor of a friend, not a mistress dictating to an employee. When she was about to fire Miss Fergusson, Gaskell wrote at length to her friend Fanny Holland about her complicated sense of friendship for her governess:

> so few people can understand how *deeply* I, personally, regret her loss, and yet how desirable I feel it to be on the children's account. … I disapprove and see more and more the bad effects of her mode of treatment; and yet I, my own self, scarcely dare to look forwards to the time when she will no longer be our intimate, and my dear household friend. … However I do try to look stedfastly [sic] to the right for my children; and I am comforted by Miss F's *own* right *understanding* of my different feelings, and own agreement of judgment with mine, as to her not managing the girls well.[21]

Here Gaskell overtly describes the inherent tension between the friend and the employer. Only by assuring herself that her "friend" agrees with her decision as "employer" can she convince herself that she is doing the right thing. Representing her "real" self – "I, personally" and "I, my own self" – as a friend, she attempts to neutralize what seems the more crass performance of her duty as an employer, a duty which she also justifies using the rhetoric of motherhood. Miss Fergusson, at least in Gaskell's account of it, performs her part by approving her mistress's decision and accepting her own incompetence.

While Gaskell's splitting of herself into two personae, a "real" self and an employer-self, emphasizes the performative nature of her role as mistress of servants, it does not mean that she was insincere or hypocritical in her performance of friendship. Goffman's *The Presentation of Self in Everyday Life*, which "turn[s] the question [of performance] around and look[s] at the individual's own belief in the impression of reality that he attempts to engender in those among whom he finds himself," notes that "the performer can be fully taken in by his own act; he can be sincerely convinced that the impression of reality which he stages is the real reality" – and that it is the "typical case" for the audience to be convinced as well.[22] While Gaskell's Cranford ladies, including Mrs. Forrester, the chief actor, are certainly not "taken in" by her performance of affluence, it is difficult to tell whether Gaskell herself recognized that her "I, my own self" was also a performance that involved the counter-performance of her consenting and believing audiences, Miss Fergusson and Fanny Holland. As one of her letters to her friend Eliza Fox reveals, Gaskell was certainly aware that her "self" was split into many roles:

> thats [sic] the haunting thought to me; at least to one of my 'Mes,' for I have a great number, and that's the plague. One of my mes is, I do believe, a true Christian – (only people call her socialist and communist), another of my mes is a wife and mother, and highly delighted at the delight of everyone else in the house. … Now that's my 'social' self I suppose. Then again I've another self with a full taste for beauty and convenience whh [sic] is pleased on its own account. How am I to reconcile all these warring members?[23]

While a recognition that the self is multiple is not quite an awareness of its construction, Gaskell certainly realizes that she performs different roles and that her relationship to those for whom she is performing them determines to a large extent which "me" is in play at a given moment. In the case of Miss Fergusson's dismissal, at least three of these "mes" – the employer, the mother, and the attached friend – are acting as "warring members."

The performing of the mistress-servant relationship as friendship is even more evident in Gaskell's association with Ann Hearn over more than 50 years. Gaskell's letters are peppered with references to "our dear Hearn" as an indispensable part of the "family."[24] In 1859, for instance, Hearn was trusted as sole chaperone and attendant for Gaskell's oldest daughter Marianne when she fell ill and was left in Germany for an extended period.[25] There are several mentions of Hearn going on holiday, leaving Gaskell in "an unusual state of *busy-ness*" and the house in "a continual Panic."[26] Later, in a letter to her sister-in-law Anne Robson in 1865, Gaskell wrote that "Hearn is not well at all just now, as much depression of spirits as anything, I think. – She wants some change of thought and scene, & we have a variety of plans for giving her it, as she has no home to go to, now-a-days [since the death of her mother]. She is a dear good valuable *friend*."[27] Gaskell emphasizes that, although Hearn is a valuable servant, she is even more important as a friend.

It is not only the beloved governess Fergusson and the faithful Hearn who are represented as friends in Gaskell's letters and diaries. In 1837, when her oldest daughters were still very young, Gaskell wrote of losing her "servant Bessy, who was obliged to leave us, being wanted at home, in consequence of the death of a sister. But we still keep her as a friend, and she has been to stay with us several weeks this autumn."[28] When Mary, the cook, became engaged to a "very suitable" widower in 1851, the family dined early "altogether, so as to make less work while the gentleman is here."[29] The thoughtful consideration for Mary and her fiancé, as well as the involvement of the whole family, is apparent: "Mary's 'husband' as the children will call him is arrived, & meets with Flossy & Baby's approbation. Papa is to marry her,\ from here of course/ & there is some talk of Flossy & Baby being bridesmaids!!!" (163). In Gaskell's representation, Mary seems to have no family or friends of her own, the Gaskells supplying all that she needs in the way of true friends. In all of her references to servants, and there are many in the letters and the diary, Gaskell represents herself as a kind, understanding, and thoughtful friend, as well as a fair, if firm, mistress. The exchange of money seems to have little or nothing to do with their relationships. A rare reference to how much the servants are paid displaces any concern about money onto her husband: if a new cook is not allowed to come by a certain date, they "should have to pay her 8s a week till she came; which *Papa* in his present frame of mind does not like."[30]

Like the representations of her own servants in her letters and diary, the servants and mistresses in many of Gaskell's fictional works are depicted as friends rather than employed and employer.[31] The most obvious are Martha and Miss Matty in *Cranford*, Dixon and Mrs. Hale in *North and South*, and Sally and the Bensons in *Ruth*. Martha, though a country girl with rough manners, gradually becomes a devoted friend to Miss Matty, especially after Miss Matty's encounter with her old lover Mr. Holbrook leads her to identify with the girl and lift her lifelong rule about "no followers" (40). Martha is so devastated at the news that her mistress has become bankrupt because of the failure of the Town and Country Bank and can no longer afford to retain her as a servant that she compels her fiancé, Jem Hearn, to marry her and rent Miss Matty's house so that they can provide her a home as lodger. This in effect causes a complete inversion in their relationship; instead of servant and mistress, they are now landlady and lodger, though Martha continues to serve Miss Matty as she did before. When Mary Smith, the narrator, breaks the news of Miss Matty's change of fortune to Martha, she says, "I tell you this, Martha, because I feel you are like *a friend* to dear Miss Matty" (129, my emphasis). Later, when Martha has borne her first child, named "Matilda" after Miss Matty, the former mistress becomes the god-mother of the child, which is "as much at home in her arms as in its mother's" (155). When Miss Matty's brother Peter returns from India to take care of her, she will not hear of a separate household for Martha and Jem. Martha has become the daughter she never had and baby Matilda her granddaughter, but their official relationship is restored to its original basis of mistress and servant.

Like Gaskell's servant Hearn, Mrs. Hale's servant Dixon in *North and South* stays with her throughout her life. When the Hales, like Miss Matty, experience a reversal of fortune, Dixon insists on staying on, even though she must now perform the much more lowly role of maid-of-all-work instead of lady's maid. Margaret, Mrs. Hale's daughter, who desires to nurse her mother through her fatal illness, has to argue against the force of her mother and Dixon's relationship as friends with Mrs. Hale's doctor:

> "My dear young lady, your mother seems to have a most attentive and efficient servant, who is more like her friend – "
> "I am her daughter, sir." (125)

Once Margaret and Dixon share the secret of Mrs. Hale's terminal illness and have joined forces instead of doing a jealous dance around each other, Dixon says to herself about Margaret, "Bless her! … She's as sweet as a nut. There are three people I love; it's missus, Master Frederick, and her. Just them three. That's all. The rest be hanged, for I don't know what they're in the world for" (130). Dixon's proclamation identifies her with those she serves and distances her from any in her own class. Her mistress, and then her mistress's children, have become her only friends. Significantly, though, as Gaskell represents it, Dixon does not want to be an equal. She finally comes to respect Margaret enough to see her as her mistress when Margaret shows "a bit of a spirit. It's the good old Beresford blood" – the blood of the "last Sir John but two" who shot his steward for some just criticism and advice (130). Dixon wants to be a friend, but she also wants her mistress to play the role of superior.

Many Gaskell critics have noticed the delightful characterization of the faithful servant Sally in *Ruth*. According to Winifred Gérin, Sally, with her "forthright manners, northern dialect, and rough independent honesty [is] a creation of real genius."[32] Coral Lansbury deems her "a magnificent creation in the long tradition of comic domestics."[33] Again like Gaskell's own servant Hearn, Sally is a lifelong member of the Benson family, having been in their service for 49 years at the beginning of the time period covered in the novel, waiting on Thurstan and Faith in both their childhood and adult homes.[34] From the first mention of Sally, as a topic of discussion for Mr. Bradshaw, Thurstan Benson's wealthiest and most self-righteous parishioner, we learn that the Bensons "might get a far more efficient and younger servant for the money" (125). Money, though, however scarce it might be with the Bensons, has nothing to do with their relationship to Sally, who is, of course, seen as a friend, not a servant. Indeed, Sally speaks to Miss Faith Benson "quite in the tone of an equal, if not of a superior," and Miss Faith, in turn, confides in Sally her secret worries about beginning to look old (137, 206-207). When Ruth comes into their lives and becomes a part of the family as well, Sally takes it into her own hands to cut Ruth's hair and buy her widows' caps to sustain her new image as a young widow, and she is second only to his mother in influence over Ruth's young son, Leonard. Gaskell devotes many pages to Sally's storytelling, another factor that emphasizes her important role in the family and the novel. She in essence takes over narrative authority when she recounts her experiences with her sweethearts and her youthful spiritual realization of the worth of her work as a servant (165-70; 174-76; 192-96). The Bensons are as respectful of Sally's opinion and solicitous for her needs and feelings as they are for anyone in their circle, making the line between friend and servant very thin. Significantly, however, in company Sally diligently performs her role as servant. When Ruth first arrives, for instance, we are told that after the stranger is put in a chair in the parlor, Sally drops "the more formal 'you,' with which at first she had addressed Miss Benson, and thou'd her quietly and habitually" (137). And, while Sally is definitely a part of the family, she does not join them when they sit in the parlor; she acts as "hostess" when she is in the kitchen and sits as an equal only when Miss Benson and Ruth join her there (192, 381).

While most readers have noticed Gaskell's portrayal of Sally as the loyal servant-cum-friend of the Bensons in *Ruth*, another character who plays that role is Ruth herself. Although she helps with the housework, often under Sally's direction, she is not considered a servant by the Bensons; rather, they treat her as an equal, though they know little of her background and she certainly has no economic claim to middle-class status. When she becomes nursery-governess to the Bradshaws, however, she performs the part of employee and servant. She is hired there in the first place because Mr. Bradshaw wants to free his own daughter from supervising her younger sisters' education and wants "some one above a nurse-maid to sit with them while their masters are there – some one who would see about their learning their lessons, and who would walk out with them" (197). In other words, he wants someone to train them in performing the manners, bearing, and etiquette of the upper middle class. Exactly why Ruth fits this description is somewhat unclear; her own parents were small farmers and she was trained briefly as a seamstress, but has no particular claims to gentility except her natural beauty and grace. She has received a bit of education from Mr. Benson, in order to teach her son, but in outward qualifications, she seems to have little more claim to being a lady than Sally, who was, as she is proud to remind people, the daughter of a parish clerk (148). It is difficult to tell where Ruth has gotten her ability to perform gentility, whether it is indeed innate, along with her beauty, or learned. The novel suggests that she has learned it from the Bensons, although the Bensons treat her as a lady from the beginning, implying that perhaps she acquired some of her outward gentility from being the mistress of a gentleman. The narrator is clear, however, about her being a lady after Leonard is born:

> And although she had lived in a very humble home, yet there was something about either it or her, or the people amongst whom she had been thrown during the last few years, which had so changed her, that whereas, six or seven years ago, you would have perceived that she was not altogether a lady by birth and education, yet now she might have been placed among the highest in the land, and would have been taken by the most critical judge for their equal, although ignorant of their conventional etiquette. (209)

Accordingly, Ruth is hired by the Bradshaws for the gentility she can impart to her young charges, and she becomes first best friend and then bitter rival to the eldest daughter, Jemima – both positions of equality. Eventually, Mr. Bradshaw even invites her to the family's evening parties. Her former lover Mr. Bellingham, now Mr. Donne, is so impressed at her newfound gentility – she is "altogether a more refined-looking person" than he remembers – that he offers to marry her, though she takes the moral high road and refuses him, preferring her status as a good Christian woman and a nursery governess (278, 302). Ironically, when Mr. Bradshaw eventually learns about Ruth's past as a fallen woman and physically casts her out, he claims that she has been acting a part to deceive him: "'I saw her daily – I did *not* know her. If I had known her, I should have known she was fallen and depraved, and consequently not fit to come into my house, nor to associate with my pure children'" (350). The irony here, of course, is that what Mr. Bradshaw saw is not what the novel classes as a performance, but rather Ruth's "true self." Her performance of the role of genteel governess and family friend is seen as natural and God-given. Yet the source of her "natural" gentility is unclear, though even Mr. Bradshaw finally comes to believe in it. In any case, Ruth's gentility, whether learned or natural, strengthens the notion that servants should be treated as friends, not subordinates or inferiors. Ruth is clearly portrayed by the novel as superior to all of the Bradshaws, so any treatment of her as an inferior is clearly a performance and a bad one at that.

The faithful servant who is more a friend than a servant is also found in several of Gaskell's short stories, including Peggy in *Half a Life-Time Ago*, Betty in

Cousin Phillis, and the narrator in *The Old Nurse's Story*.[35] In *Lois the Witch*, even the half-civilized Indian servant Nattee becomes a friend when she and Lois share a prison cell and Lois devotes herself to comforting the frightened woman all through the night before her execution as a witch (189). Besides these and other portrayals of the servant and her mistress as friends, rather than employee and employer, Gaskell also uses her fiction to criticize women who do not treat loyal servants as friends. Most notably, the second Mrs. Gibson in *Wives and Daughters* fires Betty, the long-time servant who has been a friend to Mr. Gibson's daughter Molly – competing with the governess, in fact, for Molly's affection (33-34). Mrs. Gibson refuses to accept an apology from Betty for her "impertinence" and bargains for the services of a maid she considers "such a genteel girl! – always brings in a letter on a salver!" (183). Both Molly and the narrator clearly disapprove of such behavior, which implicitly marks the new Mrs. Gibson as vulgar in her slavish imitation of Lord Cumnor's family, where she herself formerly served as governess. Betty, who relies on her position as friend, loses her post to another servant who is willing to play a different servant part, the role of the stylish servant to the aristocracy – a sign of her mistress's pretensions to gentility that is too obvious to be genuine.

While sincere friendship between mistress and servant might seem, in Gaskell's representations of her own experience as well as those in her fiction, to meliorate mistress-servant relations, it also conceals key aspects of that relationship. Despite the appearance of genuine friendship between mistress and servant, the relation between the two still involved an exchange of money for service, a real difference in power, and a struggle over conditions of work and the control of representations, since the "character" the mistress gave of the servant determined her future as well as her present employment. Moreover, even if Gaskell herself had unusually cordial ties with her servants and believed in the model of friendship that she represented in her fiction as the best solution for class divisions, that model itself was a convention that she inherited from a long line of prior literary representations of servants. As Bruce Robbins has pointed out, "Rather than take up the life of the domestic as a subject in its own right, the [nineteenth-century] novel turned back to literary tradition: … to the much-repeated master-servant tropes and devices that earlier novelists had already borrowed from Shakespeare and Molière."[36] One thinks especially of servants like the nurse in *Romeo and Juliet*, who, though certainly a comic character like Sally in *Ruth*, performs the role of friend and surrogate mother to the young Juliet. "Even Dickens and Gaskell," argues Robbins, "reinscribe and rejuvenate the conventions of the literary servant." If Gaskell's representations of servants, both literary, and, as I contend, her non-literary or autobiographical depictions, are "stylized repetitions" or reiterations of long-standing conventions, then the friendship between mistresses and servants is as much a performance as is the handing of letters on salvers or the pretence that a charity-school maid-of-all-work stands in for a houseful of well-paid retainers. While Gaskell may perform the part of friend under the assumption that she is treating her servants as equals, her performance nonetheless maintains the hierarchy of class relations just as surely as Lord Beresford shooting his steward.

Continuing to perform the rituals of class involved in the employment and management of servants, however softened or mystified, was, of course, crucial to maintaining Gaskell and other middle-class women's own social status. As a number of historians have remarked, the middle classes were defined by their employment of servants.[37] However, as Langland argues, for middle-class women it was not only the actual employment and management of servants that mattered, but the way they were deployed as cultural signs of status: "Through precise signifying practices, servants were installed within a rigid class hierarchy where a moral vocabulary performed the function of naturalizing an elaborate system of beliefs about men and women, middle and lower classes."[38] While the "moral vocabulary" Langland refers to reinforces the differences, both moral and bodily, between working-class and middle-class women, for Gaskell the moral differences seem, at least in the case of her friend-servants, less pointed; in some cases, as we have seen, she even represents servants and mistresses as moral equals. This, too, however, is implicated in reinforcing class differences. As Langland states elsewhere, what women like Gaskell, who belonged to the "genteel bourgeoisie," were doing was not so much to prove their difference from the working classes as "to police the borders of polite society from the incursions of the vulgar middle class or the petite bourgeoisie."[39] Kind treatment that disguised the economic and power relations behind cordial servant-mistress relations, ie treating and representing servants as friends, was a way to stage or perform the family's status as not only middle-class, but *genteel* middle-class. This performance distinguishes truly genteel women like Margaret Hale from vulgar upstarts like Fanny Thornton, even though the real gentlewoman might not have as much money, or, as in the case of Mrs. Forrester, might even be very poor. Really genteel women avoided treating their servants as inferiors and in the process performed the role of natural and inbred gentility, rather than manners learned from etiquette books.

It was not only genteel middle-class women, however, who performed their class position through servant-mistress relations. The working-class women employed in domestic service were also willing to self-consciously perform their status because they needed the jobs or the security of the position, or because it gave them a measure of power and authority. Servants, too, had a stake in the way the drama of the middle-class home was staged. Dixon in *North and South* and Martha in *Cranford*, for instance, are willing to perform the role of loyal and devoted servant even when it may be to their economic disadvantage. Sally in *Ruth*, unbeknownst to her employers, saves up most of her earnings to leave to Mr. and Miss Benson in her will. Their knowing, self-conscious performance of the role of servant, especially the servant-as-friend, allows them to define their position as voluntary. If the servant's performance is voluntary and not forced, even by economic circumstances, then she can avoid defining herself as inferior to her mistress. While Dixon, Martha, and Sally seem, in Gaskell's representations, to be perfectly willing to acknowledge and perform their inferiority, in fact that very performance could be seen as saving them from the "reality" with which the performance supposedly corresponds.

One of Sally's stories in *Ruth* demonstrates the way that a servant could perform her position in a way that avoided "real" inferiority even in the process of acting it out. When Sally perceives Ruth moping about her household duties and lamenting her fate as an unwed mother, she tells her a story from her very young days as a servant when she, too, moped about her duties and performed them badly because she was concerned about her soul after having dropped her charge, Master Thurstan, and causing his lifelong deformity. Her kind mistress takes her aside and reminds her about the line in the Church of England catechism in which the catechumen responds, "'to do my duty in that station of life unto which it shall please God to call me'" (176). Proud of her standing in the Church of England, while her employers are all dissenters, Sally responds favorably to this principle. Her mistress continues, "'well, your station is servant, and it is as honorable as a king's, if you look at it right; you are to help and serve others in one way, just as a king is to help others in another.'" While of course this line of reasoning is ideal for keeping people in their place by convincing them that inequality is God-ordained, as Mrs. Benson says, "if you look at it right" it can be used in another way. For Sally, a meal cooked well or a floor well-scrubbed gives her a certain kind of power – not only the internal advantage of feeling proud of herself for a job well done, but the right to talk back to her employers, as she does when Faith Benson tries to persuade her that having Ruth in the house will mean no extra trouble:

> "Well, I never! As if I minded trouble! You might ha' known me better nor that. I've scoured master's room twice over, just to make the boards look white, though the carpet is to cover them, and now you go and cast up about me minding my trouble. If them's the fashions you've learnt in Wales, I'm thankful I've never been there." (139)

Sally goes on to tell her mistress to her face that she has half the sense of her brother and accuses Faith of treating her "like a babby," unusually blunt back-talk from a servant. Sally earns her right to say what she will and do essentially what she wants by the quality of the work she does. Independent enough to turn down two marriage proposals (though admittedly one was from a madman who went about "on all fours") and to lord it over her employers much of the time, Sally manages, at least in Gaskell's representation of her, to make her own choices and live as she wishes, only occasionally choosing to perform the role of inferior before strangers. Her performance of her class status seems to be under her own conscious control and her position as free a choice as any woman of her day had.

That there could be a real struggle over the meaning of the performance of class in the servant-mistress relation, however, is revealed in Gaskell's report in a letter to Miss Fergusson of her cook Anne's pregnancy. Gaskell had discovered that the unmarried Anne was with child and she and her husband had asked a Mr. Curtis to

> go & rummage up the man & tell him her state, and *ask* not *urge* him to marry her; for she had told us she had not seen him for months & that her [sic] knew nothing of her condition, – told it again & again and once most solemnly – Well! Mr. C went. The man of course refused to marry her, but worst of all it came out he knew all about her state – when she expected to be confined, – and she had been at his lodging only the Sunday previous, although she told me she had no idea where he was, & thought he had left Manchester.[40]

Gaskell responded to Anne's lie with anger and hurt: "and all this when I was so full of sorrowful pity for her, – it makes one feel so angry to be deceived, & so uncertain as to where the deceit begins or ends that I was nearly throwing up the case in despair, but I did not – " (37).

Anne's lie is so significant because it exposes the relation of friendship that Gaskell portrayed in her novels and her correspondence as usually one-sided and unequal. While Gaskell supposedly performed the role of friend in good faith, the cook consciously manipulated that role for her own protection and mercenary gain. The cook chose to perform another role for her mistress, that of the wronged and abandoned fallen woman that Gaskell herself represents in *Ruth*. Gaskell's discovery that Anne's performance of this other role was not sincere undermines the performance of friendship that Gaskell uses to conceal the real power relations between the servant and her mistress. Presumably, Anne lied about her relations with her lover in order to retain Gaskell's protection and sympathy, and, more practically, to secure her mistress's financial help. Her consciously deceitful performance of the fallen woman narrative reveals that the mistress and servant are not "friends" but competitors. They are struggling over who will get the best bargain in monetary terms; in essence, they are competing for the right to earn money for their stories. In her own mind, Gaskell manages to win this battle by insisting on being Anne's friend even after the "truth" is revealed. As she says, despite feeling angry and hurt, she was "*nearly* throwing up the case in despair – but I *didn't.*" So important is the performance of friendship to Gaskell's class position and her image of herself that she continues as Anne's benefactor despite her lies. She gives the servant money and removes her from Manchester to Knutsford, where her story will have no currency. Though it costs her money, Gaskell uses the friend's story as a performance of power over her servant. The servant, however, apparently managed to get what she wanted out of Gaskell, so in essence, her manipulative and deceitful performance achieved its desired effect. Like Mrs. Forrester's party in *Cranford*, however, the incident clearly reveals the difference between the performance of mistress and servant roles and the realities that underlie the performances.

Gaskell's writings, both her fiction and her letters and diaries, indicate that she recognized that there was no real inequality between mistresses and servants. Both were God's children and it was the forces of economics, education, and position that differentiated them. Their roles as mistress and servant were performative and made it *seem* as if there were inherent differences between them, but those differences could be bridged through friendship. However, friendship itself was also a performance, played according to time-honored conventions that themselves signified distinctions within the middle class, as well as between the middle- and working-class woman. And for Gaskell, keeping up this class act enabled her not only to preserve her position as a genteel upper-middle class lady, but also to have the leisure to write stories about servants and mistresses.

Notes

1. Elizabeth Gaskell, *Cranford* (Oxford: Oxford Univ. Press, 1972), 3.

2. Julie Nash, in *Servants and Paternalism in the Works of Maria Edgeworth and Elizabeth Gaskell* (Aldershot, Hampshire: Ashgate, 2007), 6, also comments on this passage. Nash's book contains many valuable insights into Gaskell's relationship with her servants, but unfortunately was not available before this article went to press.

3. Elizabeth Langland, *Nobody's Angels: Middle-Class Women and Domestic Ideology in Victorian Culture* (Ithaca: Cornell Univ. Press, 1995), 8.

4. *The Letters of Mrs. Gaskell*, ed., J.A.V. Chapple and Arthur Pollard (Cambridge, MA: Harvard Univ. Press, 1967), 618. Hereafter *Letters*.

5. Monica Cohen also writes about women's "professional domesticity."

6. Langland, *Nobody's Angels*, 9.

7. Judith Butler, *Gender Trouble: Feminism and the Subversion of Identity* (New York: Routledge, 1999), 179, emphasis in original.

8. Richard Schechner, *Performance Studies: An Introduction* (London: Routledge, 2002), 133.

9. Marvin Carlson, *Performance: A Critical Introduction* (London: Routledge, 1996), 4, emphasis mine.

10. Erving Goffman, *The Presentation of Self in Everyday Life* (Garden City, NY: Doubleday, 1959), 16.

11. Kevin R. Swafford, "Performance Anxiety, or the Production of Class in Anthony Trollope's *The Claverings*," *Journal of the Midwest Modern Language Association*, 38.2 (2005), 45-58; 46.

12. Patsy Stoneman, *Elizabeth Gaskell* (Bloomington: Indiana Univ. Press, 1987), 60, discusses how Gaskell's Unitarianism was "potentially subversive … of class and gender."

13. *Letters*, 537.

14. See Dorice Williams Elliott, *The Angel out of the House: Philanthropy and Gender in Nineteenth-Century England* (Charlottesville: Univ. Press of Virginia, 2002), 135-58.

15. *Letters*, 536.

16. Jenny Uglow, *Elizabeth Gaskell: A Habit of Stories* (New York: Farrar, Strauss, and Giroux, 1993), 263. Pauline Nestor, *Female Friendships and Communities: Charlotte Brontë, George Eliot, Elizabeth Gaskell* (Oxford: Clarendon 1985), 40, also comments on Gaskell's bonds with her servants.

17. Quoted in *Further Letters of Mrs. Gaskell*, ed. John Chapple and Alan Shelston (Manchester: Manchester Univ. Press, 2000), 28, note 1. Hereafter *Further Letters*. See also, John Chapple, *Elizabeth Gaskell: The Early Years* (Manchester: Manchester Univ. Press, 1997), 171.

18. *Further Letters*, 27.

19. *Further Letters*, 28.

20. *Further Letters*, 32.

21. *Further Letters*, 34, emphasis in original.

22. Goffman, *The Presentation of Self in Everyday Life*, 17.

23. *Letters*, 108.

24. *Letters*, 631, 107, 180. Gaskell's biographers likewise mention Hearn frequently. See Winifred Gérin, *Elizabeth Gaskell: A Biography* (Oxford: Clarendon, 1976) and Uglow, *Elizabeth Gaskell*.

25. *Letters*, 632.

26. *Letters*, 344.

27. *Letters*, 760, emphasis in original.

28. Elizabeth Gaskell and Sophia Holland, *Private Voices: The Diaries of Elizabeth Gaskell and Sophia Holland*, ed. J. A. V. Chapple and Anita Wilson (New York: St. Martin's, 1996), 63. Hereafter *Diary*.

29. *Letters*, 162.

30. *Letters*, 620, my emphasis.

31. On Gaskell's servant characters, see Stoneman, *Elizabeth Gaskell*, 47-48; Uglow, *Elizabeth Gaskell*, 263-64; Felicia Bonaparte, *The Gypsy-Bachelor of Manchester: The Life of Mrs. Gaskell's Demon* (Charlottesville: Univ. Press of Virginia, 1992), 40-41; and Coral Lansbury, *Elizabeth Gaskell: The Novel of Social Crisis* (London: Paul Elek, 1975), 65.

32. Gérin, *Elizabeth Gaskell*, 128.

33. Lansbury, *Elizabeth Gaskell*, 63.

34. Elizabeth Gaskell, *Ruth*, ed. Alan Shelston (Oxford: Oxford Univ. Press, 1985), 145.

35. All these stories are from Elizabeth Gaskell, *Cousin Phillis and Other Tales* (Oxford: Oxford Univ. Press, 1981).

36. Bruce Robbins, *The Servant's Hand: English Fiction from Below* (New York: Columbia Univ. Press, 1986), xi.

37. See Pamela Horn, *The Rise and Fall of the Victorian Servant* (New York: St. Martin's Press, 1975), 17, and Theresa M. McBride, *The Domestic Revolution: The Modernisation of Household Service in England and France 1820-1920* (New York: Holmes & Meier, 1976), 18.

38. Langland, *Nobody's Angels*, 15.

39. Langland, *Nobody's Angels*, 17.

40. *Further Letters,* 37, emphasis in original.

North and South: an Industrial Version of the Victorian Gentleman

Raffaella Antinucci

On the mutable backdrop of the Victorian social landscape, the heated debate revolving around the idea of the gentleman can be regarded primarily as a nostalgic attempt to revive and re-imagine British traditional values. Running through the lines of novels, conduct books, and newspapers between 1840 and 1870 such an "anxiety of definition" becomes the point of intersection between cultural and political discourses aimed at facing and containing the epistemological repercussions of the Industrial Revolution. Within the framework of a wider European phenomenon that marked the decline and fall of the aristocracy, the English gentleman embodies, in a Greenblattian sense,[1] the Victorian negotiation of aristocratic and bourgeois demands, emerging as a further cultural reformulation of the 'Victorian compromise.' The unique permeability of Victorian society, based on "a system of removable inequalities,"[2] intensified the survival of respect and deference towards the aristocracy – in Gladstone's words "a sneaking kindness for a Lord" – along with an alluring fascination for its way of life, within reach of every upstart.[3] As a consequence, contrary to Marx's predictions, in England the aristocratic *Weltanschauung* was not as much rejected as absorbed by the middle classes. In a social context wherein "no man [could] safely boast of his ancestors,"[4] the figure of the gentleman was evoked to provide new parameters of distinction, as is apparent in the semantic shift from a designation of rank to a set of moral qualities.

Fiction played an important part in the process of dynamic circulation of interests and concerns that not only mirrored but also shaped the social trends, disclosing the vital importance of being a gentleman. Reducing the friction between the aristocrats and the capitalists, the fictional gentleman proved an effective and powerful instrument that was employed to exorcize the ghost of an internal revolution. In spite of its diverse characterization, it is possible to identify some recurring features which I would like to call "coefficients of characterization": confronted with the Victorian antinomies of city–country, industrialism–rural economy, north–south, and present–past, all encompassed in the main antithesis of chaos versus order, the gentleman is usually connected with the second term of each dyad, offering the reassuring image of the British keeper of tradition.

Moving from these considerations, I will highlight Elizabeth Gaskell's contribution to the debate on gentlemanliness, as well as investigate to what extent her fiction, especially *North and South*, subverts some recurring elements in the literary fashioning of the Victorian gentleman, while at the same time sanctioning his conventional role as social tuner. I will limit my discussion to the different representations of gentlemanliness displayed and demolished in the novel, setting Gaskell's discourses against the reflections of the so-called Victorian prophets: Mill, Ruskin, Newman, and Smiles. It is my objective to establish that in the characters of Thornton and Higgins, Gaskell produces the first attempt to mould an industrial gentleman, associated with the elements of North, city, industry, present, and workshop.

The first meta-narrative indicators of Gaskell's approach to the gentleman idea can be detected in her use of techniques that apply this "principle of misunderstanding" and narrative inversion to the compositional process. As a result, the novel offers an ideal model "in progress" in a double sense: on the one hand, Thornton's "gentlemanliness" is shown in its development, whilst on the other, his inner features transpire through the looking-glass of other masculinities; that is, by means of the progressive demolition of pre-arranged polarities. From its very title, *North and South* shows a dyadic structure built around complex networks of diegetic oppositions and shifting symmetries. As a long critical tradition has underscored, the major *topoi* of Milton and Helstone are simultaneously paralleled and contrasted with the two minor *topoi* of Oxford and London, unfolding conflicting pairs that are often re-arranged in conformity with different criteria. Hence, the main contrast between the north and the south, personified in the characters of Thornton and Margaret, generates the satellite oppositions of industry and agriculture and urban and rural space, which, in economic and topological terms, place London and Milton against the country setting surrounding Helstone and Oxford. Concomitantly, characters, especially male ones, are inflected by the overlapping categories of masters and hands, "shoppy people," and gentlemen. Eventually, these two planes intersect and converge into the political metaphor that posits Milton as "the hands" for manufacturing ruling Britain.

Not only are these binomial paradigms reversed and crossed, but they are also dismantled as oppositions. The theory of interpenetration between public and private spaces that Susan Johnston opposes to Gallagher and Schor's "separatist" readings of the novel's ending, can be applied to the whole set of analogies.[5] In other words, Gaskell erects a system of dichotomies and multi-fashionings that are deconstructed throughout the narration as false oppositions. Particularly revealing is the symbolic reversal of Helstone, the Hampshire birthplace of the Hales, turned from the paradise lost of Margaret's childhood into an *inferno* dominated by "practical paganism"[6] and endowed with the hellish connotations hidden in its very name. Thornton's "northern" characterization is permeated with "southern" components, such as his love for the classics, pertaining to Mr. Bell or Mr. Hale. In this regard, I would like to stress Gaskell's awareness of the cultural nature of these topological associations and conflicting dualities. Like Margaret and Thornton, the reader is misled by the title: the discrepancy between appearance and reality staged in the plot contains, in embryo, the very method of composition. It follows that "North" and "South" should not be decoded as conflicting cultural artefacts; rather, the reader is invited to interpret them in more literal terms, replacing the disjunctive conjunction *versus* with the more welcoming conjunctive, Milton *and* Helston, city *and* country, masters *and* hands, men *and* gentlemen, Thornton *and* Margaret.

The second meta-narrative aspect of the novel I would like to examine is closely linked to the gentleman's characterization. Fluctuating between social status and moral conduct, its meaning in the nineteenth century was gradually shifting from birth to character, or, according to Castronovo, "from condition to process."[7] Differently from most Victorian novels, *North and South* presents a hero whose gentlemanly status is not assumed from the beginning. On the contrary, Thornton's genteel-ization is literally enacted through the female gaze and detailed in every step.

An underrated element of the novel, the feminine perspective adds to the "singularity" of Gaskell's representation of the gentleman: not only is his figure viewed through the female gaze, but it is also the result of a process of mutual acquaintance. Thornton's fashioning as a gentleman tags along Margaret's growth as a gentlewoman. In many ways, *North and South* can be justly defined a "double *Bildungsroman*" wherein romance and public plot overlap and intermingle through domestic metaphors and political tropes.[8] Moreover, the "gentleman-liness" of the male is tested by his relationship with the woman, usually his wife. The gentleman model is thus deeply entangled with the issue of the woman's role within marriage as a counterpart of the process of epistemological readjustment brought about by the Industrial Revolution, involving re-fashionings of both masculinity and femininity.

After her first encounter with Thornton, Margaret hastily imparts his "ungen-tlemanlike" condition to her mother: "'About thirty – with a face that is neither exactly plain, nor yet handsome, *nothing remarkable* – not quite a gentleman, but that was hardly to be expected.'"[9] Almost sinking into Thornton's character, Margaret's description proceeds from outward appearance, with information concerning his age and looks, to focus on inner qualities, inferred from their brief talk. Significantly, in her judgment are inscribed some crucial notions informing Margaret's pre-Victorian idea of the gentleman, grounded in rank, class, and education, which throughout the narration will give place to a more democratic and character-based conception of gentlemanliness. First of all, Margaret's comment that Thornton is "nothing remarkable" points to his depreciation as an ordinary man. In fact, since the Middle Ages individualism has underpinned any fashioning of male excellence as its ontological precondition: the medieval knight, the Renaissance courtier, and the nineteenth-century gentleman share the implication of models who stand out from the mob. During the Victorian period, writers and thinkers such as Carlyle, Ruskin, and Arnold variously reassert the primacy of individuality and originality as values to oppose a standardized and standardizing society. However, John Stuart Mill's "On Liberty" (1859) can be considered the most seminal essay for promoting the emergence of a new image of masculinity hinging on virtue and inner worth. Without overtly mentioning the gentleman, Mill envisages a new spiritual loftiness attainable by anybody, replacing Carlyle's "hero worship" with the elevation of the "average man":

> The initiation of all wise or noble things, comes and must come from individuals, generally at first from some one individual. The honour and glory of *the average man* is that he is capable of following that initiative; that *he can respond internally to wise and noble things*, and be led to them with his eyes open.[10]

The pre-eminence given to inward merits, detectable in the reiteration of the adjective "noble" in its single character connotation, is indicative of an altered view of "gentility" that, hovering between utilitarianism and idealism, runs parallel to older concepts championed by Margaret in the first half of the novel. Significantly, the last part of Margaret's sentence – "but that was hardly to be expected" – makes apparent the fact that she is referring to a traditional meaning of the lexeme, voicing her prejudice against the northern world of industry and trade. Earlier in the novel, at her mother's complaint about the impracticability of seeing the wealthy Gormans, she had declared her aversion against the new rich: "'I'm glad we don't visit them. I don't like shoppy people. I think we are far better off, knowing only cottagers and labourers, and people without pretence.'"[11] Margaret's repulsion for riches and "shoppy" people, "testing everything by the standard of wealth,"[12] bespeaks the wider phenomenon of the "English disease,"[13] a renowned expression used by Correlli Barnett to define the axiological displacement through which England dismissed the factors – in the first place economic

– that had made possible its rise to "the workshop of the world," to embrace a bucolic view of its essence, supported by the everlasting myth of "merry England." The resulting conflicts of social values gave rise to the cultural symbols of "workshop" and "garden" matched by what Donald Horne renamed the "northern" and the "southern" metaphors, in a passage that demands complete quotation:

> In the *Northern Metaphor* Britain is pragmatic, empirical, calculating, Puritan, bourgeois, enterprising, adventurous, scientific, serious, and believes in *struggle*. Its sinful excess is a ruthless *avarice*, rationalized in the belief that the prime impulse in all human beings is a rational, calculating, economic *self-interest*.
>
> In the *Southern Metaphor* Britain is romantic, illogical, muddled, divinely lucky, Anglican, aristocratic, traditional, frivolous, and believes in *order and tradition*. Its sinful excess is a ruthless *pride*, rationalized in the belief that men are born to serve.[14]

According to this epistemic subdivision, Gaskell's novel, often labelled as the Victorian re-writing of *Pride and Prejudice*, could be more aptly retitled "Pride and Avarice," reviving the poles of Horne's topological excesses. On a superficial level, *North and South* is organized around the conflicting subcultures mirrored in the two intertwined perspectives of Thornton and Margaret. Whereas the former conceives life in Darwinian terms, the latter is proud of her role of pre-eminence in the small community of Helstone: as the daughter of the first gentleman in the village, her duties include visiting the poor, dispensing charity, and giving good advice. In social terms, although such dichotomies are part of the overall Victorian web of contradictions, in the long run it is the southern metaphor that proves successful, begetting the surfacing of the gentleman as the restorer of "order and tradition." An antidote to the several "Victorian disharmonies,"[15] his model of exemplary moral conduct bolsters the idyllic icon of rural Britain.

From this angle, Gaskell's literary efforts are not so much directed to the creation of a "northern" gentleman, as to his colonization with northern elements that materialize a de-located and porous idea of inner "gentility": in the end north and south are dispelled and integrated in the foundation of a common ground where Margaret's and Thornton's modified attitudes can converge. Thus, Gaskell uses the topographical dualistic staging as a starting point to challenge and rupture automatic associations deeply ingrained in the distorted "countryside of the mind" of Arcadian Englishness.

As pointed out by Martin Wiener, the "decline of the industrial spirit"[16] led to an increasing disdain for personal ostentation and riches, which accounts for the purely instrumental value attached to the pursuit of material gain, replaced by a kind of "economic chivalry" which incited upstarts and plutocrats to emulate and even exceed aristocratic luxury, through the acquisition of a country estate or a coat of arms. If Margaret's southern vision, including her dislike for the Gormans, will reveal itself to be myopic and one-sided, nevertheless Gaskell seems to subscribe to her exposure of economic repression, forging in Thornton a modern paragon of gentlemanliness who is not ashamed to display the origins of his wealth, but, on the contrary, rejoices in placing his home inside the scene of labour – the precincts of his mill – merging house and factory within a social space that is simultaneously private and public.[17]

Margaret's southern perspective functions as a mirror on which Gaskell's version of gentlemanliness can be projected and refracted, bolstering new modes of characterization. Implied in her loathing for the Gormans's assumed "pretensions" is a deterministic outlook on social inequalities underlying a rigid hierarchy by which class is inherited and divinely sanctioned. On the horizon of a pyramid system that implements paternalism and enforces deference to the leisured classes, any rise in rank signifies a Promethean act of rebellion, as such, a sin against the established order. From this social slant, Margaret's southern views are clearly out of sync with the emergent "gospel of work" and its philosophical corollary, the doctrine of *self-help*, preached by Samuel Smiles to the working men of Leeds during the same years. In Victorian England's social magma the climbing to gentility is not only perceived as a proper ambition, but also, according to John Ruskin, a duty nobody could or would avoid. As he writes in his essay "Pre-Raphaelitism" (1851):

> Now that a man may make money, and rise in the world, and associates himself, unreproached, with people once far above him ... it becomes a veritable shame to him to remain in the state he was born in, and everybody thinks it is his duty to try to be a 'gentleman.'[18]

The theory of social predestination belies a despotic relationship between the upper classes and their enslaved subordinates that collides with the liberal state of industrial economy founded on consent and contract. It is worth noting the fact that Margaret's conservative code of gentleness does not so much depend on rank as on education, a controversial issue whose manifold facets are woven into the fabric of the novel.

As is evident, the preordained framing of the hereditary system entails the exclusion of some professions from the realm of gentility. In Margaret's opinion, manufacturers cannot be gentlemen, since education seems pointless for them. When her father informs her about his new job as a private tutor for Milton's working men, she retorts, "'What in the world do manufacturers want with the classics, or literature, or the accomplishments of a gentleman?'"[19] Gaskell's *North and South* presents itself as a bid to answer this question, instilling new sap into the controversy on the British educational system and on the need of its reorganization through the university reform promoted by the "Royal Commission for Enquiry" in 1850. At several points, Gaskell's narrative unveils the faults of the hidebound education given in the public schools, focused on the study of the classics – Greek and Latin – and on an in-depth knowledge of the Bible. After the creed of Thomas Arnold, master at Rugby from 1828 to 1841, the purpose of formal education was to follow a definite hierarchical order: "first, religious and moral principle; secondly, *gentlemanly conduct*; thirdly, intellectual ability."[20] Indeed, Arnold's words echo in Ruskin's unequivocal apothegm: "A youth is sent to Universities not to be apprenticed to a trade, nor even always to be advanced in a profession, but always *to be made a gentleman and a scholar*."[21] The priority assigned to the Christian and moral formation, to the detriment of scientific and professional training, was perpetuated in the numerous associations for the promotion of the working classes, styled on Maurice and Kingsley's "Working Men's College," as well as in the parish schools, where the acquisition of expertise and professional abilities was regarded incidental.

Gaskell's novel addresses both Christian Socialism and the Ox-bridge ethos to question the real significance of education. In this respect, Mr. Hale and Mr. Bell serve as the prime vehicle for Gaskell's criticism. The former, in Margaret's eyes "a complete gentleman,"[22] is turned into the ironic personification of Cardinal Newman's idea of the gentleman as "one who never inflicts pain."[23] Himself a converted clergyman, Mr. Hale emblematizes a bygone model: his erudition confines him to a "dreamy,"[24] literary world far removed from reality. Despite his religious "dissent," his feminized masculinity prevents him from establishing a true dialogue with his wife or with the working men. Tellingly, he chooses to lecture at a local Lyceum on Ecclesiastical Architecture, an unsuitable subject for the working men, and completely unrelated to their daily experience. Similarly, on her last visit to Helstone, added by Gaskell in her revision for the book edition (1855), Margaret is confronted with an educational method that, instructing the country children on grammar and nomenclature, equally fails to meet their more practical requirements.[25]

Both episodes obliquely confirm Margaret's perplexities about the opportunity of educating the working classes, insofar as they advocate the demand for a more balanced educational system comprising useful subjects like farming and political economy. Although questioned, traditional education is not easily rejected.[26] Instead, Gaskell suggests a new, and I would add topical, concept of education, that, beyond "reading and writing," will combine schooling with social learning, literacy with experience, expanded, in Kuhlman's analysis, through the triple action of event, dialogue and movement.[27] As the twin *Bildungen* of Margaret and Thornton demonstrate, besides a new vocabulary, southern and northern people need a new semantics, a grammar of customs to cross the bridge between classes and separate social spheres.

The new stress laid on the educational experience reverts the subject to the reviewed pattern of past and present and gender role expectations. At every turn, old-fashioned convictions are cast against a new mindset, to the point of re-titling the novel after one of its chapters, as "Once and Now."[28] Nowhere is the dissatisfaction for traditional education and southern world-view more embedded in the vexed question of gentility as in Thornton's defence of northern values. To Mr. Bell, the Oxford man who, despised by Mrs. Thornton for "living a lazy life in a drowsy college," considers education as an end in itself, Thornton's replies:

> 'Remember, we are of a different race from the Greeks, to whom beauty was everything. … I don't mean to despise them. … But *I belong to Teutonic blood* … we don't look upon life as a time for enjoyment, but as a time for *action* and *exertion*. Our glory and our beauty arise out of our *inward strength*. … If we do not reverence the past as you do in Oxford, it is because we want something which can apply to *the present* more directly.'[29]

The centrality of such lexical items – "action," "exertion," "present," and "inward strength" – depict a new form of northern "gentility," distinguished from the spurious models of the *snob* and the *self-made man*, respectively scrutinized by Thackeray and Smiles. The reference to the Teutonic blood reinforces Samuel Smiles's *Self-Help* in its role of Gaskell's major hypotext within the novel's intertextual conflation. In the chapter "Industry and the Peerage" the British aristocracy is similarly likened to "the fabled Antaeus," who derived and renewed his strength mingling with "that most ancient order of nobility – *the working order*," fostering the current notion that valued the "aristocracy of character" as the true heraldry of man.[30] To some extent, the Victorian *pater familias*, the super-hero, the "muscular Christian," the knight, and the *gentleman* stem from the northern mythology that, as Smiles reminds us, not accidentally numbers among its deities, "a god with a hammer," immediately evoked by Mr. Bell some lines after.[31] These ideal models share an undisputed superiority that is character-centred, rooted in behaviour and in the qualities of the mind which, in Smiles's words, form the very "manly character" Thornton set against Margaret's old variant of the gentleman.[32] Contradicting her first impressions, Margaret's later definition of Thornton as "a very remarkable man"[33] shifts to his being "very kind and attentive,"[34] up to the complete acknowledgment of his qualities in the dialogue with her "absent" brother, Frederick:

> "I fancied you meant some one of a different class, not a gentleman; somebody come on an errand. He looked like some one of that kind," said Frederick, carelessly. "I took him for a shopman, and he turns out a manufacturer." Margaret was

138

silent. She remembered how at first, *before she knew his character*, she had spoken and thought of him just as Frederick was doing.[35]

Once again, Gaskell accentuates the progressive nature of Margaret's and Thornton's, but also Thornton's and Higgins's mutual knowledge and understanding, positing an unstable social space inside and outside the family based on what Smiles termed "a system of mutual dependencies"[36] and celebrated in Madox Brown's painting, *Work*. Overcoming their first mis-perceptions, masters and hands, like husband and wife, become the repository of a new partnership – economical as well as emotional – wherein not only cooperation, but also discussion and dissent are encouraged to stave off violent antagonism. Gaskell uses unstableness to fight social unrest.

Even if subverting many of the traits of its Victorian predecessors, the industrial gentleman foreshadowed in the figures of Thornton and Higgins retains his role of social harmonizer. The crucial aspect of Gaskell's representation lies in the shift, within the synecdochal relationship of individual with community, from the vertical paternalism of the father-son relation to the horizontal line of the "marriage metaphor" that places workmen and gentlemen, masters and servants, men and women, on equal terms. The hymeneal trope used by Gaskell in *North and South* sheds new light on the gentleman as the by-product of Victorian re-negotiations of masculinity and femininity. Not only is his growth traced through the female gaze, but his features are made visible through a sequence of mis-oppositions with false or "anti-types": both Captain Lennox and Henry Lennox are rejected as true exemplars of gentlemanliness on account of their respective notions of woman as a charming object to flaunt and as a dependent creature dwelling in the domestic space.

Against the hedonistic, animal life of unlimited pleasure and acquisition pursued by Lennox and the Shaws, and encapsulated in their very name, Gaskell's industrial gentleman fulfills "a dream of order," in which masters and hands can speak to each other "beyond the mere 'cash-nexus,'"[37] as "from man to man."

Notes

1. Stephen Greenblatt, *Shakespearean Negotiations* (Oxford: Clarendon Press, 2001).

2. Edward George Bulwer-Lytton, *England and the English* (London: Bentley, 1933), 24.

3. Quoted in Asa Briggs, *Victorian People. A Reassessment of Persons and Themes 1851-67* (Harmondsworth: Penguin, 1990), 19.

4. Shirley Robin Letwin, *The Gentleman in Trollope* (London: Macmillan, 1982), 8.

5. See Susan Johnston, "'We too are men': Enacting Revolution in *North and South*," *Women and Domestic Experience in Victorian Political Fiction* (Westport: Greenwood Press, 2001), 103-34.

6. Elizabeth Gaskell, *North and South*, ed. Patricia Ingham (London: Penguin, 1995), 381. All further references will be to this edition.

7. David Castronovo, *The English Gentleman. Images and Ideals in Literature and Society* (New York: Ungar, 1987), 15.

8. Susan Zlotnick, "*North and South*, Nostalgia and Dissent: Gaskell's Double Bildungsroman," *Women, Writing and the Industrial Revolution* (Baltimore: The Johns Hopkins Univ. Press, 1998), 99-122.

9. *NS*, 65, emphases added.

10. J. S. Mill, "On Liberty," in *On Liberty and other essays* (Oxford: Oxford Univ. Press, 1991), 74, emphases mine.

11. *NS*, 20.

12. *NS*, 88.

13. Correlli Barnett, "Obsolescence – and Dr Arnold," *Sunday Telegraph*, 26 January 1975, reprinted in Patrick Hubter, ed., *What's Wrong with Britain?* (London: Sphere, 1979), 29-34.

14. Donald Horne, *God is an Englishman* (Sydney: Angus & Robertson, 1969), 22-23. Emphases in the text.

15. See Francesco Marroni, *Disarmonie Vittoriane* (Rome: Carocci, 2002).

16. Martin J. Wiener, *English Culture and the Decline of the Industrial Spirit 1850-1980* (Harmondsworth: Penguin, 1985).

17. See Johnston, "We too are Men," 103, and Doris Williams Elliot, "The Female Visitor and the Marriage of Classes in Elizabeth Gaskell's *North and South*," *The Angel out of the House: Philanthropy and Gender in Nineteenth-century England* (Charlottesville, VA: Univ. Press of Virginia, 2002), 135-58.

18. John Ruskin, *Works*, ed. E. T. Cook and Alexander Wedderburn (London: George Allen, 1903-1912), 12: 342.

19. *NS*, 40.

20. Arthur Stanley, *The Life and Corrispondence of Thomas Arnold, D.D.* (London: Murray, 1887), 1: 107, my italics.

21. *The Works of John Ruskin*, 20: 18, my italics.

22. *NS*, 27.

23. J.H. Newman, *The Idea of a University*, ed. I.T. Ker (Oxford: Clarendon Press, 1976), 179.

24. *NS*, 242.

25. On Gaskell's revision, see Larry K. Uffelman, "Elizabeth Gaskell's *North and South*: the Novel in Progress," *Gaskell Society Journal*, 14 (2000): 73-84.

26. On the theme of education, see Wendy Craik, "Lore, Learning and Wisdom: Workers and Education in *Mary Barton* and *North and South*," *Gaskell Society Journal*, 2 (1988): 13-33.

27. See Mary H. Kuhlman, "Education through Experience in *North and South*," *Gaskell Society Journal*, 10 (1996): 14-26.

28. *NS*, 46, 375.

29. *NS*, 327, emphases mine.

30. "One reason why the Peerage of England has succeeded so well in holding its own, arises from the fact that, unlike the peerages of other countries, it has been fed, from time to time, by *the best industrial blood of the country* – the very 'liver, heart, and brain of Britain.' Like the fabled Antaeus, it has been invigorated and refreshed by touching its mother earth, and mingling with that most ancient order of nobility – *the working order*" (Samuel Smiles, *Self-Help*, 103-104, emphases mine).

31. "Well, at any rate, I revoke what I said this morning – that you Milton people did not reverence the past. You are regular worshippers of Thor" (*NS*, 327).

32. "'I take it that "gentleman" is a term that only describes a person in his relation to others; but when we speak of him as "a man." We consider him not merely with regard to his fellow-men, but in relation to himself – to life, to time, to eternity. A cast-away lonely as Robinson Crusoe – a prisoner immured in a dungeon for life – nay, even a saint in Patmos, has his endurance, his strength, his faith, best described by being spoken of as "a man." I am rather weary of this word "gentlemanly," which seems to me to be often inappropriately used, and often, too, with such exaggerated distortion of meaning, while the full simplicity of the noun "man," and the adjective "manly" are unacknowledged – that I am induced to class it with the cant of the day'" (*NS*, 163).

33. *NS*, 88.

34. *NS*, 232.

35. *NS*, 252.

36. Smiles, *Self-Help*, 186. See Margaret's assertion: "God has made us so that we must be mutually dependent" (*NS*, 122).

37. *NS*, 420.

38. *NS*, 175.

The Conflicted Duties of the Caretaker in Elizabeth Gaskell's *Life of Charlotte Brontë* and Letters

Amanda J. Collins

The friendship of Elizabeth Gaskell and Charlotte Brontë, though short-lived, appears to have been a warm and relatively harmonious one. The two writers began to correspond in November 1849, after the publication of Brontë's novel *Shirley*, and met on five separate occasions before Brontë's death in March 1855. They exchanged news about their families and health. They lent each other books, sent their own published works as gifts, shared anecdotes about their lives and their experiences as authors, and exchanged opinions about contemporary works of literature. Each time they met, the two women came away from the experience with sincere feelings of warm respect. To her publisher, George Smith, Brontë remarked that "Mrs. Gaskell herself is a woman of whose conversation and company I should never soon tire – She seems to me kind, clever, animated and unaffected."[1] Similarly, Gaskell recognised the potential for friendship after their first meeting: "She and I quarrelled & differed about almost every thing, – she calls me a democrat, & can not bear Tennyson – but we like each other heartily I think & I hope we shall ripen into friends."[2]

Their bond is constructed as a site of harmony and congruity in *The Life of Charlotte Brontë*:

> Copying this letter has brought the days of that pleasant visit very clear before me, – very sad in their clearness. We were so happy together; we were so full of interest in each other's subjects. The day seemed only too short for what we had to say and to hear.[3]

Gaskell's reminiscence undoubtedly testifies to the intensity of her private intellectual and emotional affinity with her friend. Yet her trope of sentimental friendship is arguably also part of a public strategy to promote the intimate and unique quality of her friendship with Brontë. For in claiming a "special" relationship with her biographical subject, Gaskell publicly authorizes her memorializing role. She thus cloaks her public role and ambition in private terms and presents a one-dimensional, domestic portrait of a friendship free of conflict and dissonance.

Yet as various critics have pointed out, the relationship of Gaskell and Brontë was a complex and conflicted arena in which issues of caretaking, rivalry, ambivalence, and literary authority were played out. This paper builds on the scholarship of Deirdre D'Albertis, Pamela Corpron Parker, Linda K. Hughes, and Michael Lund, who tease out the contradictions in Gaskell's response to Brontë within the public sphere of literary production.[4] It explores some of the conflicted spaces in Gaskell's public and private relationships with Brontë, particularly as they are evidenced in her early letters on Brontë. These letters encapsulate many of the thematic, rhetorical, and emotional strategies and concerns of the first edition of the *Life*, and reveal how Gaskell's "caretaking" of Charlotte Brontë is complicated by her ambivalence towards the author and her novels, by her awareness of her status as Brontë's professional peer, and by her desire to promote and legitimize her own literary vocation and reputation.

> I am half amused to find you think I could do her good. (I don't know if you exactly word it so, but I think it is what you mean,) I never feel as if I could do any one good – I never yet was conscious of strengthening any one, and I do so feel to want strength, and to want faith. I suppose we all do strengthen each other by clashing together, and earnestly talking our own thoughts, and ideas. The very disturbance we thus are to each other rouses us up, and makes us more healthy.[5]

Gaskell had been so fascinated by an earlier letter from Lady Kay-Shuttleworth, that on this occasion she could not resist "the impulse to write 'on the rebound,' just as if I were talking to you" (115-16). Among the various snippets of information in Lady Kay-Shuttleworth's letter was the compelling news of Charlotte Brontë's visit to her estate in Lancashire in March. An ardently curious Gaskell desired "to hear a great deal more about her, as I have been so much interested in what she has written" (116). Unfortunately for Brontë, her hosts were instrumental in authorizing and disseminating various lurid and tragic tales about her life and family, and Gaskell was to prove their enthusiastic and credulous proselyte. Amidst rumours of Brontë's emotionally deprived and physically oppressed existence, a small network of (mostly) women sprang up, determined to "strengthen" and to do the "poor poor creature" some good.[6] These women, many of whom belonged to the socially progressive Unitarian community,[7] positioned them-

144

selves as supportive caretakers of a benighted literary prodigy. Harriet Martineau was one of the more active participants in this network, repeatedly defining Charlotte as unfortunate or deserving of compassion and aspiring to be of "great use to her."[8]

Brontë was herself only too painfully aware of this network of care, which, seeking to rescue "Charlotte Brontë" and redeem "Currer Bell," simultaneously supported and constrained her by continually casting her in the role of invalid. In a letter to George Smith, Brontë complained of the intrusive "care" of Martineau and Gaskell: "two ladies – neither of them unknown to fame" who "seem determined between them that I shall be a sort of invalid." This had led to Brontë being

> occasionally kept in hot water by people asking me how I am. If I do not answer the letters of these ladies by return of post … flying rumours presently reach me derogatory to my physical condition. Twice – kind but misled strangers living in Southern Counties have with the greatest goodness written to ask me to their houses for the benefit of a milder climate – offering every "accommodation suitable to an invalid-lady." This, in one sense touches me with almost painful gratitude – but in another – it makes me a little nervous. Why may not I be well like other people?[9]

Brontë's mock quotation of typical newspaper advertisements for accommodation "suitable to an invalid-lady" reveals her bitter awareness of such a simplistic and patronizing formulation of her by her contemporaries.[10]

The *Life* stands as the public apotheosis of this network and discourse of care. In it, Gaskell sought to take care of Brontë by sanitizing, reinterpreting, and memorializing her friend and fellow writer. Through a contextualizing methodology in which the Brontë novels are repeatedly "cradled" within detailed vignettes of the "wild," "rough," and "primitive" Yorkshire environment,[11] Gaskell endeavours to displace and to exonerate the Brontës and their fiction from contemporary accusations of coarseness and morbidity. An impassioned Gaskell argues that it was

> not from the imagination – not from internal conception – but from the hard cruel facts, pressed down, by external life, upon [the Brontës'] very senses, for long months and years together, did they write out what they saw, obeying the stern dictates of their consciences. (*Life*, 272)

Yet this focus on the bleak external life of the Brontës, coupled with Gaskell's publicly inscribed sororal empathy for and care of Charlotte Brontë, inevitably resulted in the recuperation and inscription of a quintessentially pathologized and victimized Brontë.

The doomed portrait of Charlotte Brontë that appears in the *Life* is already strikingly evident in the series of letters that Gaskell dispatched to her female friends immediately after her meeting with Brontë in August 1850.[12] To Catherine Winkworth, Gaskell remarked on the resemblance she detected "in character & ways" between Charlotte and her close friend Eliza Fox, "if you can fancy Miss Fox to having gone through suffering enough to have taken out every spark of merriment."[13] She noted this resemblance again in her letter to Eliza Fox: "Like you, Tottie, without your merriment: poor thing she can hardly smile she has led such a hard cruel (if one may dare to say so,) life."[14] Of course, Gaskell first met Brontë at a time when Brontë was still grieving intensely for the loss of her siblings, but the analogy between Brontë and an Eliza Fox "with every spark of merriment" taken out, heightens the sublime tragedy of Brontë's history by reminding her readers of the auspicious potential of Brontë's life and character. As Gaskell tells Charlotte Froude in a letter which is, in many ways, a recapitulation of her much lengthier one to Catherine Winkworth, Brontë is "truth itself – and of a very noble sterling nature, – which has never been called out by anything kind or genial."[15]

To both Winkworth and Froude, Gaskell shamelessly relayed the prurient gossip about Brontë and her family which Lady Kay-Shuttleworth had in part reported back to her "with all the malicious glee of a sitting-room gossip."[16] Much of Lady Kay-Shuttleworth's information about Brontë's childhood and family came from "an old woman at Burnley" who had nursed Brontë's mother in her last illness but was later dismissed. Her stories have frequently been discredited as the malicious rantings of a disgruntled former employee.[17] The gossip constructs a nightmarish domestic tableau at Haworth that contains the seeds of the Gothic melodrama that would emerge in the *Life*. Here in Gaskell's early correspondence is the grim external world in all its magnificent barrenness and austerity. Details of the parsonage sitting-room looking into the churchyard "filled with graves" elide all boundaries between inner and outer worlds.[18] A pathologised Charlotte emerges from this world: "stunted" and "undeveloped," her blighted stature is ascribed to the physical deprivations endured at Cowan Bridge School[19] and reflects the struggle of nature to exist in such an adverse environment; "their parsonage facing the North – no flowers or shrub or tree can grow in the plot of ground, on acct of the biting winds."[20] Her own visit to Haworth later compelled Gaskell to revise this statement and in the *Life* we read of a narrow flower-border "carefully tended in days of yore, although only the most hardy plants could be made to grow there."[21] The image of the "hardy" plant takes on a metaphoric intensity in Gaskell's biography, signaling the unfledged and stoic nature of her heroine and the fundamental environmental influences shaping the character and writings of the Brontës.

These early letters also document Gaskell's genuine feelings of admiration and awe for Charlotte, living as she did in such an unpropitious situation. In her letter to Tottie Fox, she praises Brontë for being

> sterling and true; and if she is a little bitter she checks herself, and speaks kindly and hopefully of things and people directly; the wonder to me is how she can have kept heart and power alive in her life of desolation.[22]

Viewed from the perspective of her own conventional domesticity as mother of four children and wife of a gentle, active, and upright Unitarian minister, we can almost feel Gaskell shudder at what she perceived to be such a bleak prospect, especially when she had once admitted to being "glad and thankful to Him that I am a wife and a mother and that I am so happy in the performance of those clear and defined duties."[23] Gaskell later confessed to Lady Kay-Shuttleworth that she was convinced she could not have borne "even with my inferior vehemence of power & nature," Brontë's life "of monotony and privation of any one to love."[24] Interestingly, Gaskell privately recognises her friend's inherent and superior resilience, as Jenny Uglow has similarly noted: "in many ways Charlotte was the tougher of the two. Elizabeth's migraines and neuralgia and feelings of total lassitude were often the results of stress."[25]

While privately Gaskell acknowledged Brontë's greater resilience, publicly in the *Life* she is more ambivalent. Gaskell's role as literary caretaker and her consequent debilitation of Brontë in the *Life* stand as potent and public disavowals of the superior capacity for endurance in her friend. Superior is the word to note here, because Gaskell does not deny – in fact she highlights – Charlotte's womanly patience and fortitude in the *Life* as part of her overall design to protect and vindicate her subject. Hughes and Lund remark on the biography's "catalog of unremitting sickness, solitude, and depression" and suggest that Brontë's endurance and triumph over these handicaps "exists only because she first enacted feminine sacrifice to duty."[26] The noble portrait of female self-renunciation and submission that emerged from the *Life* led Sir James Kay-Shuttleworth to express the hope that A. B. Nicholls would "learn to rejoice that his wife will be known as a Christian heroine, who could bear her cross with the firmness of a martyr saint."[27] In a no less reverential tone, Martineau described the biography of Charlotte Brontë as the "story of a life bravely spent" and pronounced it to be a sort of secular hagiography: "little as Charlotte Brontë knew it, she was earning for herself a better title than many a St. Catherine, or St. Bridget, for a place among those noble ones whose virtues are carved out of rock, and will endure to the end."[28]

Yet in Gaskell's August 1850 letter to Tottie Fox, the tale of heroic endurance and duty that would emerge in the *Life* is subtly undercut by the possibility of

Brontë's residual bitterness: "if she is a little bitter she checks herself." Here we have an inkling of the ambivalence towards Brontë that would emerge in Gaskell's later letters and in the *Life*, where she would applaud her friend's inestimable courage and determination, but criticize if not condemn what she saw as Brontë's morbid disposition and frequently introspective and self-indulgent way of coping. In the biography, Gaskell stresses the "peculiarly unfortunate circumstances" of her subject's life: "her feeble constitution of body, her sufferings by the death of her whole family, and the secluded and monotonous life she led" that had induced and fuelled what she identifies as Brontë's morbid sensitivity and had shaped the emotional and narrative force of her art.[29] However, while she frequently attributes her subject's chronic depression and ill health to the lack of external contact and stimulation – noting, for example, that "the usual effects" of Charlotte's "solitary life, and of the unhealthy situation of Haworth Parsonage, began to appear in the form of sick headaches, and miserable, starting wakeful nights" in the Autumn of 1851 (*Life*, 391) – Gaskell is also at pains to identify this oppressive and debilitating isolation as the trigger rather than the underlying cause of Brontë's (morbid) depression. Thus, we read of Ellen Nussey urging her friend to leave home "when these constitutional accesses of low spirits preyed too much upon her in her solitude" (400).

Gaskell herself sought to channel any restless or rebellious feelings through an active engagement with the outside world – whether that be the company of her friends, family, writing or involvement in one of the many pressing philanthropic projects of the day. Gaskell's "social" behaviour and convictions were undoubtedly shaped by her extroverted personality and her Unitarian background which preached that every human being possessed "the qualities – reason and love – for self-government and social responsibility."[30] In her evident capacity "for self-government and social responsibility," Gaskell implicitly saw herself as superior to a morbid and bitter Charlotte. Hence, in her 7 April 1853 letter to Lady Kay-Shuttleworth, where she extols Brontë's superior "vehemence of power & nature," Gaskell nonetheless implicitly faults Charlotte for her wilful dissatisfaction:

> her life sounds like a fulfilment of duties to her father, to the poor round her, to the old servants … that I can not help hoping that in time she may work round to peace, – if she can but give up her craving for keen enjoyment of life – which after all comes only in drams to anyone, leaving the spaces between more dreary & depressing.[31]

Although she immediately and self-consciously retreats from her own criticisms: "Still it is easy to talk & arrange another person's life for them," Gaskell's private remarks are a compelling utterance of her ambivalence towards her subject as well as a cogent statement of biographical intent.

The concept of morbidity, of repression, introspection, and physical dis-ease, not only ran counter to Gaskell's philosophy of personal duty but also to that of writing and publication. As D'Albertis has convincingly argued, Gaskell regarded literary production and duty as "other-regarding," as a service to others and thus as a "passport to the world outside a vulnerable sentient self, a license (indeed an injunction) to help, by representing others who suffer."[32] Gaskell sets out two competing models of female literary authority in the *Life*. The first is a male-inflected, solipsistic, Romantic model, to which Brontë, with her "melancholic absorption in literary self-objectification" subscribed (*Life*, 34); the other, which Gaskell advocates, is "based on a commitment to social realism and service through one's literary talents" (32).[33] However, this literary model of public duty was not solely confined to configurations of feminine duty and authority, but "invariably paralleled or even intersected with paradigms of masculine duty and literary culture" (22) promulgated by professional men of letters such as Thomas Carlyle.

Gaskell's ambivalence towards Brontë's writing, which resulted in her tendency to emphasize what she perceived as the morbidity of Brontë's artistry and to contrast it with her own, is manifest in her 7 April 1853 letter to Lady Kay-Shuttleworth. Gaskell comments on the difference between herself and Brontë as women writers. This forms a preamble to her critique of *Villette*:

> The difference between Miss Brontë and me is that she puts all her naughtiness into her books, and I put all my goodness. I am sure she works off a great deal that is morbid into her writing, and out of her life; and my books are so far better than I am that I often feel ashamed of having written them and as if I were a hypocrite.[34]

Her remarks partly constitute an implicit rebuttal of the connection that reviewers made between the coarseness and morbidity of Currer Bell's writings and character – all Brontë's "naughtiness" goes into her books, leaving her life and character unblemished. Yet her comments are also evidence that Gaskell regarded Brontë's life and writings in much the same troubled way as her contemporaries – "she works off a great deal that is morbid into her writing, and out of her life." Writing provides an outlet for Brontë's constricted psychological and physical systems. Yet Gaskell's trope of catharsis evokes images of excess, eruption, and of diseased alterity, especially when juxtaposed with her own moderate and altruistic literary production. Gaskell complains of feeling like a "hypocrite" because she puts all her "goodness" into her works. What Gaskell implies here is that in contrast to the solipsistic, introspective nature of Brontë's literary approach (which Gaskell is implicitly criticizing), writing for Gaskell is ostensibly a social act. Her belief that her "books are better than I am" is a recognition of the altruistic and reformative impulses of her works. As she wrote to her friend, the artist Tottie Fox: "first we must find out what we are sent into the world to do, and define it and make it clear to ourselves, (that's the hard part) and then forget ourselves in our work, and our work in the End we ought to strive to bring about." [35]

Interestingly, Gaskell deployed the same equivocal defence of Brontë in a letter to the Christian Socialist lawyer and critic John M. F. Ludlow. Gaskell's letter is a response to Ludlow's *North British Review* article on *Ruth* in which he had encouraged unmarried women to turn from the "morbid" preoccupations of authorship to "living and practical affections and duties."[36] While Ludlow praised *Jane Eyre* and *Mary Barton* as the "two novels which are perhaps most likely of all to survive in England from the present day" (167), he had expressed his preference for the married Gaskell over the single Brontë, claiming that Brontë's works "have in them a something harsh, rough, unsatisfying, some say all but unwomanly, as compared with the full, and wholesome, and most womanly perfection of the other" (169). In defence of Brontë, Gaskell deploys many of the same rhetorical strategies that she would use to vindicate Charlotte (and to manage her own ambivalence towards her subject) in the *Life*:

> Then again, though perfectly agreeing in the sense of what you say about writing being a bad occupation for unmarried women, I feel a little as if there was a slight tone of contempt in that part of the article … and besides all this, I should like to tell you a good deal about Miss Brontë, – & her wild sad life – and her utter want of any companionship … I mean literally companionship, – for she lives alone, (although in the house with an old blind father); the last of six children, – in ill-health; & after all she is so much better, & more faithful than her books; you should know how the poor & they that have none to help in the great desolate parish speak of her![37]

Gaskell commences her defence by stressing the "wild" sadness of Brontë's life – her utter solitude and ill-health. She then asserts that Brontë "is so much better, & more faithful than her books" and invokes the testimonies of the parish poor to adduce Brontë's active womanly goodness.[38] However, we witness once again Gaskell's equivocal response to Brontë's writing in the distinction she makes between the author and her work. Indeed, Gaskell adopts the same phrase that she used in her letter to Lady Kay-Shuttleworth to describe this disjunction:

> She puts all her naughtiness into her books; when the suffering that falls so keenly on one of her passionate nature, pierces her too deeply "sits by her bed & stabs her when she awakes" (to use her own words,) & when others could go to some friend, & claim sympathy and receive strength her only way of relieving herself is by writing out what she feels, & so getting quit of it. I know what you will say, – but she does cling to God, as to a father, in her life & in herself – but somehow she only

writes at her morbid times. I am going to stay with her on Thursday. I wish I could make her known to you.[39]

Although Gaskell is quick to counter any accusation of religious or filial impiety in her friend, her observation that "somehow she only writes at her morbid times" together with the images of passion that Charlotte's "own words" evoke, effectively pathologizes Brontë's character and writing practice once again.

Another way in which Gaskell dramatizes her opposition to Brontë's "morbid" literary practice, as D'Albertis contends, is through the process of memorialization: she "willfully repress[es] her subjectivity as a biographer in order to represent and, in some sense, 'heal' the fissures in Brontë's divided consciousness."[40] While I agree that Gaskell uses the biographical form to express and validate her socially-inflected sense of feminine duty and literary authority and to distinguish herself from her introspective subject, my own reading of the *Life* more closely corresponds with Angus Easson's assessment that Gaskell "never meant it, overtly or covertly, to be an unfeelingly objective account of her friend. The work is openly subjective and fully romantic."[41] Indeed, the phrase "willfully repress[es] her subjectivity" that D'Albertis uses, suggests an inward – as much as an outward-directed act: the conscious and deliberate repression of one's subjectivity foregrounds that which is being suppressed. Thus, when Gaskell tells the reader of her decision to privilege Brontë's texts over her own: "[a]cting on the conviction, which I have all along entertained, that where Charlotte Brontë's own words could be used, no others ought to take their place" (*Life*, 231), her declaration dramatizes the deliberate suppression of her own voice. Though it appears to be an act of self-effacement, Gaskell's statement actually serves to inscribe her subjective presence in the biography and, crucially, to underline her biographical integrity and care. Gabrielle Helms argues that "in observing and constructing her subject's life, the narrator assesses her own position in the act of telling and becomes a personalized character that stands out against Charlotte's life."[42] Gaskell constructs herself as an engaged, committed, other-directed literary caretaker of her friend and peer, but her self-reflexive utterances of biographical intent and engagement in fact reinscribe her strategic, textual presence.

Further valuable insights into Gaskell's self-authorizing tactics as well as her consequent textual disempowerment of her subject emerge from the treatment of Brontë's letters in the *Life*. Positioning herself as the narrator-interpreter of Brontë's texts enables Gaskell to mask her own contradictory responses to Brontë. Frequently in the *Life* Gaskell tells readers why she has included a particular letter as well as outlining its significance (as she sees it): "Commonplace as this extract may seem, it is noteworthy on two or three accounts" (98); "I will insert two or three of Miss Brontë's letters to her publishers, in order to show" (259); "I give these letters with particular pleasure, as they show her peculiarly womanly character" (346). These palimpsestic and dialogic episodes assert the biographer's narrative and textual presence and thereby displace, if not obscure, the centrality and authority of her subject's voice. Gaskell projects herself into the biography – her personality, thoughts and commentary mediate between the reader and Brontë's texts.

Some of the rhetorical and textual strategies of public self-authorization that Gaskell deploys in the *Life* are brilliantly captured in her August 1850 letter to Catherine Winkworth. This letter is the most impassioned and stylized of the four letters that Gaskell wrote after first meeting Brontë. In its self-conscious literary artistry, we find the biographer's craft and self-legitimization prefigured in private discourse. Gaskell begins her letter by adopting a similar journey motif to approach her subject as she uses in the *Life*. It is worth quoting the beginning in full.

> I went on Tuesday afternoon. Dark when I got to Windermere station; a drive along the level road to Low-wood, then a regular clamber up a steep lane; then a stoppage at a pretty house, and then a pretty drawing room much like the South end one, in which were Sir James and Lady K S, and a little lady in a black silk gown, whom I could not see at first for the dazzle in the room.[43]

As Uglow argues, this gradual advance towards her subject is common to almost all of Gaskell's novels and short stories: "author and reader slowly approach the subject and learn the lie of the land until, at a moment of crisis, a door suddenly seems to open, like Sesame, and we step into new terrain – melodrama, mystery, intense emotion or fantasy" (256). In the *Life*, the reader retreats from an urbanised space, moving inexorably forward into a more primitive social space, before finally arriving at the threshold of death – the Brontë family crypt. Gaskell's epistolary account of her journey to the Kay-Shuttleworths is handled in a similarly skilful and dramatic manner. "Dark when I got to Windermere station" – the emphasis on darkness, together with the reiteration of the adverb "then," adumbrate the mystery surrounding Brontë as well as Gaskell's excitement and anticipation – at long last, Gaskell stands at the threshold of the secret that is the author of *Jane Eyre*. Yet upon arrival at the Kay-Shuttleworths' residence, Gaskell is temporarily blinded by the brightness of the room which, by implication, eclipses rather than foregrounds the "obscurity" of her subject, dressed as the "little lady" is in a black silk gown. Desire is deferred a little longer, leading Brontë to approach Gaskell instead: "she came up & shook hands with me at once."[44] For one brief moment, Gaskell is the observed rather than the observer, the sought rather than the seeker, situated at the textual centre rather than at the margins of the narrative. Although the narrative focus shifts back to Brontë, at that critical moment of first encounter and ontological negotiation, Gaskell asserts her primacy.

Gaskell then proceeds to provide Catherine Winkworth with a detailed description of Charlotte's appearance:

> She is, (as she calls herself) undeveloped; thin and more than ½ a head shorter than I, soft brown hair not so dark as mine; eyes (very good and expressive looking straight & open at you) of the same colour, a reddish face; large mouth & many teeth gone; altogether plain; the forehead square, broad, and rather overhanging.[45]

Gaskell reproduced much of this passage in the biography (*Life*, 352). In both letter and biography, Gaskell subtly juxtaposes her subject's unappealing and asymmetrical physical attributes with the harmony of her voice and mode of expression:

> She has a very sweet voice, rather hesitates in choosing her expressions, but when chosen they seem without an effort, admirable and just befitting the occasion. There is nothing overstrained but perfectly simple.[46]

In the *Life* Gaskell similarly observed: "Any one who has studied her writings, – whether in print or in her letters; any one who has enjoyed the rare privilege of listening to her talk, must have noticed her singular felicity in the choice of words" (246). Gaskell brings her own acute consciousness of Brontë as a writer to these texts and emphasizes the congruence between the external world and Brontë's linguistic representation of it. It is a neat inversion of Gaskell's customary practice of privileging the supernal domestic achievements of Brontë over the literary prowess of Currer Bell and serves to foreground the literariness of subject and text. Hence, Gaskell positions and authorizes herself as the reader and writer / interpreter of Brontë the author as well as the woman.

Within the parsonage walls, so Gaskell's letter discloses, the "strange half mad" father rages, sawing off backs of chairs, and setting fire to hearth-rugs, thereby aiding and abetting the untimely death of his wife, "a 'pretty young creature' brought from Penzance by the Irish Curate."[47] True to her storytelling instincts, Gaskell eagerly recounts the affecting death-bed scene of Mrs. Brontë, and the mother's stricken cries of "Oh God my poor children – oh God my poor children!" (447) haunt the text. In the midst of the adult, patriarchal environment of violence, female oppression and neglect: "Mr. B has never taken a meal with his children since his wife's death, unless he invites them to tea, – never to dinner" (448), the children get by as best they can. The girls are given scant education: "only the servant taught them to read & write" (448). Charlotte at twelve years of age proves the most intrepid and resourceful of the group, petitioning the patriarch to send them to school and much later, the "shy & silent" heroine travels alone to Brussels via London: "She had never been out of Yorkshire before; & was so frightened when she got to London" (448). Returning to Haworth, Brontë resumes the shackles of domestic care, tending to the needs of her near blind father and consumptive sisters at the same time as she endeavours to forge a career first as an artist and then as an author. Gaskell's letter to Catherine Winkworth continues with the sisters' collaborative attempts to write and publish novels: "They used to read to each other when they had written so much" (448). After *Jane Eyre* is published and proves a literary and commercial success, Charlotte seeks and gains her ultimate reward – the paternal blessing. As Shirley Foster remarks, the news of Charlotte's success is "dramatized in a fictionalized way" and presented as a dialogue between father and daughter "which though avowedly authentic is also an instance of careful imaginative construction."[48] Alas and woe! At the very moment of success, Charlotte's much-loved sisters rapidly succumb to the ravages of consumption, "unattended by any doctor." Gaskell concludes her melodramatic rendition with the ominous words: "There seems little doubt she herself is already tainted with consumption"[49] – a piece of gossip that proved most damaging to Brontë's marriage prospects: "it convinced Mrs. Smith that Charlotte was unmarriageable and her son in need of protection."[50] Gaskell's 'public' sympathy in this instance proved to be unfortunate, to say the least.

The graphic depictions of the Yorkshire environment, the melodramatic declamation of Maria Brontë, and the stylized disclosure of Brontë's authorship in the letter foreground the narrative and rhetorical skill of Gaskell and implicitly assert her literary authority. The ensuing gossip about Brontë's home and family which "Lady K S described … to me" further confirms Gaskell's self-appointed cultural role as the repository and disseminator of stories about Brontë, and in depicting Brontë's friendly overtures – "she came up & shook hands with me at once" – Gaskell similarly gestures to her subject's ready acquiescence in this literary caretaking dynamic.[51]

In sum, it is arguable that alongside her desire to support and defend Brontë, one of the purposes of Gaskell's letter to Catherine Winkworth was to articulate and affirm Gaskell's caretaking and storytelling capacities, as well as to locate and confine "poor Charlotte" and "eloquent Miss Brontë" within these processes. Gaskell exploited all her narrative, and rhetorical abilities to achieve these goals, so that the letter may be considered the rhetorical, narrative and thematic prototype of the *Life*. It is a testimony to Gaskell's considerable skill that both public and private texts elicited the desired response from readers. Charles Kingsley spoke for many of his contemporaries when he warmly complimented Gaskell on her biography. As a Christian Socialist, one who was actively involved in social reform, Kingsley read the biography in terms of its moral and social caretaking potential:

> Be sure that the book will do good. It will shame literary people into some stronger belief that a simple, virtuous practical home life is consistent with high imaginative genius; & it will shame, too, the prudery of a not over cleanly, though carefully whitewashed age, into believing that purity is now (as in all ages until now) quite compatible with the knowledge of evil.[52]

For Kingsley, as for Margaret Oliphant who declared that *The Life of Charlotte Brontë* was a plea for "every woman dropped out of sight," Gaskell had achieved her proto-feminist agenda.[53] She had seemingly proved to an apprehensive and ambivalent public that a woman's literary genius and aspirations could be reconciled with her domestic responsibilities. Thus, the anonymous critic for the *Economist* proclaimed the *Life* to be "a great practical protest against the assumption that there is any real incompatibility between the common duties that fall to the lot of all women and those peculiar ones which belong in addition to women of genius."[54] Moreover, the construct of Charlotte in the *Life* as tragically dutiful daughter, sister, and wife – "iconic in its power of endurance and personal resolution"[55] – enabled those like Kingsley who had "[given] up the writer & her books with the notion that she was a person who liked coarseness," to read the less "good and pleasant" aspects of Brontë's novels as the product of a unique environment and strict sense of duty, not as the manifestation of a coarse mind.[56]

We do not know how Catherine Winkworth responded at this time to Gaskell's letter. She did, however, forward the note to her sister Emily, who replied:

> Thanks for Mrs. Gaskell's. Poor Miss Brontë, I cannot get the look of the grey, square, cold, dead-coloured house out of my head. One feels as if one ought to go to her at once, and do something for her. She has friends though now, surely? I wonder whether she has any unmarried ones; people who could go and look after her a little if she were ill. Oh dear, if the single sisters in this world were but banded together a little, so that they could help each other out as well as other people, and know how important they were, and what a quantity of work lies ready for them! One feels that her life at least almost makes one like her books, though one does not want there to be any more Miss Brontës.[57]

There are several important points to note about this passage. Firstly, the austere landscape and domestic environment, which Gaskell had so vividly outlined in her letter, resonates powerfully with the visual and sympathetic imagination of the reader. The external world portrayed in *The Life of Charlotte Brontë* would prove equally effective. Secondly, Emily's ambivalent, closing comment that "one feels that her life at least almost makes one like her books, though one does not want there to be any more Miss Brontës" underlines an interpretative, contextualizing approach to Brontë and her novels that was implemented and authorized by Gaskell's biography. For Emily Winkworth and her contemporaries, Brontë's history and Gaskell's interpretation of it offered the reader a more sympathetic understanding of the novels but this contextualizing process inevitably mediated between the reader and Brontë's works. In an anonymous review of the biography for the *North American Review*, Margaret Sweat recognised this mediation: "We find in it, not only the satisfaction of an urgent curiosity upon many points of personal history, but a key to Currer Bell's fictions, which sends us to their reperusal with a new and more tender interest."[58] Finally, Gaskell's letter achieved its affective goal. It elicited the compassionate and "caring" sensibilities of the reader, prompting Emily Winkworth likewise to place and constrain Brontë within a caretaking circle: "One feels as if one ought to go to her at once, and do something for her."

The 25 August 1850 letter to Catherine Winkworth is a text that purports to outline Gaskell's literary as well as emotional support of Brontë and it consequently authorizes a discourse and dynamic of care in relation to Brontë. It is doubly ironic, therefore, that much of the material in this letter should end up being reproduced in a gossipy and scandalous article entitled "A Few Words About 'Jane Eyre'" in *Sharpe's London Magazine* for June 1855.[59] A close comparison of the obituary with Gaskell's letter to Winkworth and another that appears in the *Life* (353), reveals compelling similarities. The content of the two passages is virtually identical: Charlotte organizes for herself and her sisters to be sent to school, her elder sisters die, and her remaining siblings contract consumption while at school, and both passages conclude with a near identical quotation on Charlotte's need of income:

"At nineteen," continued Charlotte, I should have been thankful for a penny a-week. I asked my father; but he said, "What do women want with money?" ("A Few Words," 341)

"At 19 I should have been thankful for an allowance of 1d a week. I asked my father, but he said 'What did women want with money.'" (Smith, 448)

Although in revisiting the controversy surrounding the authorship of this obituary and its close connection with Gaskell's 1850 letter, Dennis Robinson first discounts Gaskell and suggests instead that Catherine Winkworth wrote this obituary, his alternative conjectures seem more plausible given the factual inaccuracies in the Sharpe's article:

Catherine freely allowed the letter to circulate and did not herself object to someone else making use of it, or that it fell into someone else's hands in an accidental
fashion and they had even fewer scruples about consulting its author or recipient
before publishing its contents.[60]

Indeed, we know for a fact that Catherine Winkworth forwarded Gaskell's 25
August 1850 letter to her sister Emily. Whoever its author, reading the *Sharpe's
London Magazine* article with its "tissue of malignant falsehoods" caused Ellen
Nussey, Brontë's intimate friend, much pain and hurt. It was this very article that
motivated Nussey to write to Charlotte's husband, demanding that "an attempt
be made to do justice to one who so highly deserved justice." "You will be certain
to see the article," she wrote to A. B. Nicholls soon after its publication, "and I
am sure both you and Mr. Brontë will feel acutely the misrepresentations and the
malignant spirit which characterises it."[61]

The great irony, as critics such as Sharps and Barker have noted, was that Ellen
suggested Gaskell be commissioned to publish a defence, to give "a sound castigation to the writer."[62] Nussey recommended Gaskell on the basis of her "personal acquaintance with Haworth, the Parsonage, and its inmates."[63] Yet it was
this selfsame "personal acquaintance" that implicitly nurtured and authorized
much of the gossip surrounding the Brontës and it was Gaskell's letters that were
the probable sources for the magazine article. As Hughes and Lund suggest, the
fact that Gaskell did not acknowledge the obituary's source when she accepted the
biographical commission (though it would have been unlikely for Gaskell to have
remained ignorant of the *Sharpe's* article given her interest in other obituaries of
Charlotte Brontë) and then proceeded to adhere to the "outlines of the account
that upset Nussey in the first place is to suggest a writer who harbored depths on
depths rather than a cheerful housewife bustling about to assuage hurt feelings"
(130).

The genesis of the *Sharpe's* magazine article and *The Life of Charlotte Brontë*
resides in the early letters of Gaskell. They testify to the intensity of Gaskell's
imaginative and emotional engagement with Brontë as well as to her ambivalence
towards Currer Bell. Many of the rhetorical and textual strategies that emerge in
the *Life* first appear in these letters – deployed to defend and to criticize one artist,
to authorize, and inscribe another. Gaskell's insistence on a tragic and morbid
vision of Brontë in the correspondence arose from and fostered the network of
care that simultaneously supported and constrained Brontë. When Gaskell wrote
that famous passage in the *Life* about the separate duties of writer and woman –
"not opposing each other; not impossible, but difficult to be reconciled" (271) –
she was arguably not only reflecting upon her own difficulty in integrating her
familial and parish duties with her desire to write, but was also perhaps meditating

on her struggle to reconcile her personal and professional motives and feelings towards her subject. As the early letters reveal, this was a struggle that haunted Gaskell from her very first encounter with Brontë.

Notes

1. Letter dated 1 July 1851 in Margaret Smith, ed., *The Letters of Charlotte Brontë: With a Selection of Letters by Family and Friends. 1848-1851* (Oxford: Clarendon Press, 2000),2: 655.

2. Elizabeth Gaskell to Charlotte Froude, undated, in J. A. V. Chapple and Arthur Pollard, eds., *The Letters of Mrs. Gaskell* (Manchester: Mandolin, 1966, 1997), 129. Henceforth *Letters*.

3. Elizabeth Gaskell, *The Life of Charlotte Brontë*, ed. Angus Easson (Oxford: Oxford Univ. Press, 1996), 404.

4. D'Albertis views the biography as a "disguised form of literary competition with Brontë" in which Gaskell "subordinate[s] the other woman as the subject of her text" (20) and examines how Gaskell's pathological portrait of Charlotte Brontë is both a critique and authorization of romantic morbidity and creativity in the woman writer (Deirdre D'Albertis, "'Bookmaking out of the Remains of the Dead': The Life of Charlotte Brontë," *Dissembling Fictions: Elizabeth Gaskell and the Victorian Social Text* [New York: St. Martin's Press, 1997], 19-43). Linda K. Hughes and Michael Lund explore Gaskell's negotiations of the Victorian literary marketplace, arguing that Gaskell responded to the obituaries and criticisms of the Brontës in *The Life of Charlotte Brontë* and thereby "intervened in public discourse on Brontë's as well as her own behalf" (Linda K. Hughes and Michael Lund, "Engendered Lives: Gaskell's *Life of Charlotte Brontë*," *Victorian Publishing and Mrs. Gaskell's Work* [Charlottesville: Univ. Press of Virginia, 1999], 144). Similarly, Pamela Corpron Parker recognises the *Life's* mixture of "privacy and publicity, tragedy and triumph, personal identification and professional dissociation" which reflect the conflicted nature of Gaskell's response to Brontë (Pamela Corpron Parker, "Constructing Female Public Identity: Gaskell on Brontë," *Literature and the Renewal of the Public Sphere*, ed. Susan Van-Zanten Gallagher and M. D. Walhout [Basingstoke: Macmillan, 2000], 80).

5. Elizabeth Gaskell, letter to Lady Kay-Shuttleworth, 14 May 1850 (*Letters*, 116).

6. Elizabeth Gaskell, letter to Lady Kay Shuttleworth, 12 December 1850 (*Letters*, 139).

7. See Stoneman for a discussion of the Unitarian circle to which Gaskell belonged. Apart from Gaskell and Martineau, Stoneman lists the Winkworth sisters, Eliza (Tottie) Fox, Barbara Bodichon, Emily Shaen and Parthenope Nightingale as members of this "network" (Patsy Stoneman, *Elizabeth Gaskell* [Brighton, Sussex: The Harvester Press Ltd., 1987], 26).

8. Elizabeth Gaskell, letter to Anne Shaen, ?20 December 1849 (*Letters*, 96).

9. Smith, 606.

10. Smith, 607, n. 3.

11. Henry F. Chorley, "Rev. of The Life of Charlotte Brontë, by E. C. Gaskell," *The Athenæum*, 1536 (4 April 1857): 427.

12. There are four extant letters: to Catherine ("Katie") Winkworth, 25 August 1850 (Smith, 2: 446-50), to Charlotte Froude, wife of J. A. Froude (*Letters*, 128-129), to an unknown recipient (*Letters*, 126-127; *Life*, 353) and lastly to Eliza ("Tottie") Fox, [27] August 1850 (*Letters*, 129-31).

13. Smith, 447.

14. *Letters*, 130.

15. *Letters*, 128.

16. Juliet Barker, *The Brontës* (London: Weidenfeld and Nicolson, 1994), 107.

17. see Barker, 106-8.

18. Elizabeth Gaskell, letter to Winkworth, 25 August 1850 (Smith, 448).

19. Elizabeth Gaskell, letter to Charlotte Froude, undated (*Letters*, 128); Elizabeth Gaskell, letter to Catherine Winkworth, 25 August 1850 (Smith, 447).

20. *Letters*, 128.

21. *Letters*, 12.

22. *Letters*, 130.

23. Elizabeth Gaskell, letter to Lady Kay-Shuttleworth, 14 May 1850 (*Letters*, 118). But as Uglow has pointed out, Gaskell herself struggled with reconciling her professional and domestic responsibilities, sometimes expressing considerable irritation and resentment at the disruptive effect of domestic and parish duties on her writing (Jenny Uglow, *Elizabeth Gaskell: A Habit of Stories* [London: Faber & Faber, 1993], 45-46; 249).

24. 7 April 1853 (*Letters*, 229).

25. Uglow, 266.

26. Hughes and Lund, 135.

27. William Gaskell, letter to Ellen Nussey, 15 April 1857 in Thomas James Wise and John Alexander Symington, eds., *The Brontës: Their Lives, Friendships and Correspondence* (Oxford: Basil Blackwell, 1933, 1980), 222.

28. Harriet Martineau, "Rev. of The Life of Charlotte Bronté, by E. C. Gaskell," *Westminster Review*, n.s., 12 (1 July 1857): 295.

29. Miriam Allott, ed., *The Brontës: The Critical Heritage* (London: Routledge & Kegan Paul, 1974), 302. Lucasta Miller notes that both Martineau and Gaskell sought to dispose of their uneasiness with the "disturbing passion and intensity" of Bronté's work by regarding it as morbid: "the sad consequence of a mind made sick by a life of continual suffering and deprivation ... in this way, they could dissociate themselves from the unpalatable aspects of her work without feeling that they were betraying the cause of women's writing" (Lucasta Miller, *The Brontë Myth* [London: Jonathan Cape, 2001], 28).

30. Stoneman, 60.

31. *Letters*, 229.

32. D'Albertis, 21.

33. Interestingly, Gaskell evokes this model of solipsistic, subjective Romanticism in her description of Haworth and its surrounds. The moors are "grand, from the ideas of solitude and loneliness which they suggest, or oppressive from the feeling which they give of being pent-up by some monotonous and illimitable barrier, according to the mood of mind in which the spectator might be" (*Life*, 11).

34. *Letters*, 228. Felicia Bonaparte argues that "naughty" was the word Gaskell had put in the mouth of the child who first accuses Ruth of sinning and that implicitly Gaskell was suggesting that just as "Ruth had committed a sexual sin, ... so in a sense had Charlotte Bronté, since her fiction, being 'coarse,' was vulgar, gross, indecent, obscene" (Felicia Bonaparte, *The Gypsy-Bachelor of Manchester: The Life of Mrs. Gaskell's Demon* [London: Univ. Press of Virginia, 1992], 242).

35. ?April 1850 (*Letters*, 107).

36. John M. F. Ludlow, "Rev. of Ruth, by Elizabeth Gaskell," *The North British Review*, 19 (May-August 1853): 171.

37. Elizabeth Gaskell, letter to John M. F. Ludlow, ?7 June 1853 (John Chapple and Alan Shelston, eds. *Further Letters of Mrs. Gaskell* [Manchester: Manchester Univ. Press, 2000], 90). Henceforth *Further Letters*.

38. *Further Letters*, 90.

39. *Further Letters*, 90-91.

40. D'Albertis, 39.

41. Angus Easson, *Elizabeth Gaskell* (London: Routledge & Kegan Paul, 1979), 170.

42. Gabrielle Helms, "The Coincidence of Biography and Autobiography: Elizabeth Gaskell's *The Life of Charlotte Brontë*," *Biography*, 18.4 (1995): 354.

43. Smith, 446-447.

44. Smith, 447.

45. Smith, 447.

46. Smith, 447.

47. Smith, 447.

48. Shirley Foster, *Elizabeth Gaskell: A Literary Life* (Basingstoke: Palgrave Macmillan, 2002), 120.

49. Smith, 449.

50. Lyndall Gordon, *Charlotte Brontë: A Passionate Life* (London: Vintage, 1994), 223.

51. Smith, 447.

52. Angus Easson, ed., *Elizabeth Gaskell: The Critical Heritage* (London: Routledge, 1991), 398.

53. Margaret Oliphant, *"The Sisters Brontë," Women Novelists of Queen Victoria's Reign: A Book of Appreciations* (London: Hurst & Blackett, Ltd., 1897), 24.

54. Unsigned "Review of 'The Life of Charlotte Brontë,'" *The Economist* (18 April 1857): 425-6; Easson, ed., *Critical Heritage*, 387.

55. Foster, 120.

56. Easson, ed., *Critical Heritage*, 398.

57. Emily to Catherine and Selina Winkworth, 30 August 1850 in Margaret J. Shaen, *Memorials of Two Sisters: Susanna and Catherine Winkworth* (London: Longmans, Green, and Co., 1908), 60.

58. Margaret J. Sweat, "Rev. of 'The Life of Charlotte Brontë', by E. C. Gaskell and The Brontë Novels, by Charlotte, Emily and Anne Brontë," *North American Review*, 85 (October 1857): 295.

59. "A Few Words About 'Jane Eyre,'" *Sharpe's London Magazine*, n.s., 6 (June 1855): 339-42.

60. Dennis Robinson, "Elizabeth Gaskell and 'A Few Words About 'Jane Eyre,'"" *Notes and Queries*, 23 (September 1976): 397. The similarities between the Sharpe's obituary and Gaskell's letter were first observed in the *Times Literary Supplement* for 1963 by Richard Gilbertson, who argued for Gaskell's authorship of the obituary (Richard Gilbertson, *Times Literary Supplement* [28 June 1963]: 477). J. G. Sharps similarly contended that while the "studied journalistic prose of the first and final paragraphs seems unGaskellian; the middle section … may well be from her pen" (John Geoffrey Sharps, *Mrs. Gaskell's Observation and Invention: A Study of Her Non-Biographical Works* [Fontwell, Sussex: Linden Press, 1970], 576).

61. Thomas James Wise and John Alexander Symington, eds., *The Brontës: Their Lives, Friendships and Correspondence* (Oxford: Basil Blackwell, 1933, 1980), 4: 189.

62. Juliet Barker assigns full responsibility for the article to Gaskell, claiming that she was "the very person who had made [the misrepresentations] public knowledge" (Barker, 780-81).
63. Wise and Symington 4: 189.

Elizabeth Gaskell's Tragic Vision:
Historical Time and Timelessness
in *Sylvia's Lovers*

Francesco Marroni

Sylvia's Lovers (1863) owes its powerful ideological impact to a combination of solid semantic organisation and imaginative range of tragic vision. Such a vision reflects Elizabeth Gaskell's preoccupations with providing a historical reconstruction which highlights the contradictions of the female condition. Whereas the social context of the novel seems governed by repression and negation of individual identity, women's imaginary goes beyond such strictures and barriers in order to evoke the positive values of love, fidelity and moral coherence. Hence the emergence of a conflict which entails an existential code (transgression *vs.* obedience; words *vs.* silence) as well as a topological one (movement *vs.* immobility), directly connected with the peculiarity of the novel's setting. It stands to reason that, both in terms of the private and public spheres, the tragic events of *Sylvia's Lovers* can be regarded as a dramatisation of the negativity of history. Despite the fact that the majority of Victorian intellectuals believed in the notion of historical progress as a metaphysical design, in Gaskell's view, the influence of history on individual destinies can only lead to fatal miscalculation, often culminating in catastrophic choices and self-destruction.

In implicit opposition to the Victorian belief that women should be preserved and protected from the turmoil of history, Gaskell explores the theme of change – and the subsequent crisis brought about by change – mainly from the point of view of her heroine, Sylvia Robson, whose plight is characterised by increasing existential dispossession. Behind the final image of a woman doomed to live in desperate solitude lies an oblique condemnation of egoistical masculinity that was all too ready to reject a female character who did not speak and live in line with the traditional canons of domestic life. This ostracism is the typical fate that all rebellious women are forced to endure. In this sense, Sylvia Robson can be considered the social and ethical fulcrum of the narration, since she directly experiences a shift from the rural world to an urban environment as a progression which, on a temporal level, moves from the carefree existence of childhood to a maturity rife with conflicts and dilemmas. As the title of the novel itself suggests, what makes Sylvia's transition so difficult is an irresolvable emotional problem stemming from her involvement with two men – her cousin Philip Hepburn and the sailor Charley Kinraid – whose personalities and cultures are antithetic, but who both declare their love for her with the same force and conviction.[1] At the same time, however, it is imperative to point out that Gaskell's novel is not a love story as such, but a representation of a gender crisis – womanhood and history are clashing entities whose incompatibility prevents the narrative from reaching a proper gratifying closure.

It is well known that, during her stay in Whitby, Gaskell made detailed research on the coastal town – which is given the fictional name of Monkshaven – and that the novel's composition was to prove to be a long and laborious process.[2] Indeed, such factors testify to the ambitious aim of Gaskell's project to represent the complex network of the visible and invisible relationships connecting great historical events and individual destinies. This is no less the case for the inhabitants of Monkshaven, who seem to witness the Napoleonic wars in Europe at the end of the eighteenth century without being emotionally involved in the historical narration; yet even such a small town on the north-east coast of England, far from the main national currents, will be dramatically caught up in the turmoil of war and change. Thus, the spatial structure of *Sylvia's Lovers* deliberately evinces the extent to which historical processes invisibly connect distant and different places, thereby changing the personal stories of such characters as Sylvia and her two lovers. In particular, Gaskell establishes a coherent metalanguage of place, based on her own experiences of the customs and landscape of Whitby, by laying an emphasis on the dynamic of inclusion and exclusion which, as the novel's ending shows, culminates in the neutralization and demise of what appears to be non-cultural (transgression and revolt against law). In the case of *Sylvia's Lovers*, the farm on the moor where Sylvia and her parents live, better known as Haytersbank, is depicted as the initial centripetal core of the diegesis, and the focus towards which the ambitious desires of the two young men who seek her hand in marriage are drawn. With respect to Haytersbank, Philip Hepburn and Charley Kinraid incarnate two topologically antithetic oppositions, the former embodying the spatial dimension of the city (Philip is a shop-assistant in a drapery in Monkshaven), the latter of the sea (Charley being the chief harpooner of a whale-ship). Consequently, the metalinguistic level is organized

164

according to a strategy that tends to transcend the simple binary opposition town/country. In fact, what is suggested is a more articulated portrayal of the conflicts that arise as a result of the intersections and confrontations in terms of a triadic structure, namely, town–country–Haytersbank.

Apart from the sense of order and tranquillity that characterises the domestic life of the Robson family – and the unity of the household group here is certainly an exception in Gaskell's macrotext – it must be made clear that from a cultural point of view, Haytersbank Farm spatially belongs both to the sea and the mainland. It is therefore a remarkably suggestive universe filled with tales from two quite different ways of conceiving reality. Not only do we immediately learn in chapter 1 that "for twenty miles inland there was no forgetting the sea, nor the sea-trade,"[3] but also that Daniel Robson, the heroine's father himself, epitomises in many ways the double value that now, in his old age, pertains exclusively to his farm:

> One of the farms on the cliff had lately been taken by Sylvia's father. He was a man who had roamed about a good deal – been sailor, smuggler, horse-dealer, and farmer in turns; a sort of fellow possessed by a spirit of adventure and love of change, which did him and his own family more harm than anybody else. (*SL*, 34-35)

As in Sylvia's daily life, there seems to be a permanent interchange of experience between Haytersbank and the expanse of the sea, a richly creative osmosis which produces the effect of a perfect dialogic integration of natural elements. A relationship which, even on a connotative level, comprises the same lexical occurrence: "the wild wide ocean" (*SL*, 6) is paralleled with "the wild bleak moors" (*SL*, 1) which surround both the farm and Monkshaven. It cannot go unnoticed that the ocean and the moors both acquire a connotation (*wild*) aimed at conveying a pervasive sense of primitiveness; it is an untameable world whose mutinous dimension proleptically delineates the sorrowful events that are to befall the heroine. The disorder and restlessness that reign over the intimate space of her family home are symptomatic of her inner confusion, which will eventually lead to her suffering the tragedy of her own self-oblivion and self-dispossession. To further underline the link earth–sea–farm, the lexeme *wild* also occurs in the description of Haytersbank Farm: "The buildings were long and low, in order to avoid the rough violence of the winds that swept over that wild, bleak spot, both in winter and summer" (*SL*, 35). Nevertheless, the inhabitants of this primordial place do not form a homogenous group. If Daniel represents primitiveness – a trait connected with a desire for mobility is transformed into a desire for disorder and discontinuity – his wife Bell has quite a different role, being from Cumberland and thus the guardian of orthodox values which belong neither to the sea nor to the rural world. Her silence – "She was not a great talker" (*SL*, 30) – which is the expression of her inability to adapt to the cross-section of various cultures, prompts her desire for evasion and forces her to look beyond the moorland of her birthplace towards the sea-side town, which promises a more refined and less rough and primitive existence: "Bell was a touch better educated than her husband, but he did not acknowledge this, and made a particular point of differing from her whenever she used a word beyond his comprehension" (*SL*, 43). This explains the positive attitude the woman adopts towards her nephew Philip Hepburn, "a serious-looking young man" (*SL*, 25), who has a good education on his side, together with the desire to perform his work with the utmost zeal, the same scrupulous zeal that he devotes in his coherent application of the rules and behavioural codes of his Quaker religion. By contrast, Kinraid, with his violent rebelliousness, is undoubtedly much nearer the ethos of the "wild north-eastern people" of whom Daniel Robson seems to be the champion. The harpooner reveals the characteristics that make him the hero of the "stirring narrations" that have been circulating from time immemorial among the inhabitants of the coast. In the imaginations of the people who wait for the periodic return of the whale-ship, he is the protagonist of a fabulation that speaks of miracles and astonishing exploits whose setting is the dangerous Greenland seas, where whales are monsters and sailors brave defenders of justice and freedom.

Obviously, Sylvia's initial situation is that of a person who, seemingly placed in a neutral field, is in reality forced to endure the aggression of negative entities. Bell and Philip both seem to embody the gendered values of silence and cold, rational calculation. In this sense, the episode centred on Sylvia who goes to her cousin's shop to buy "duffle for a cloak" (*SL*, 22) is significant: for in advising the young girl to choose a more sober colour than scarlet (her favourite colour), Philip shows that he is strictly respectful of social convention, perfectly on the same wavelength as his aunt Bell. Conversely, Daniel Robson and Charley Kinraid represent primitiveness and intolerance towards any attempt to limit individual freedom. Both of them are, first of all, characterised by their ability as story-tellers. As skilful narrators of fantastic and marvellous stories of the remote northern seas, they evoke an oral tradition in which miraculous visions blend with hyperbolic and seductive phrases. Everything tends towards a romantic portrayal of life which, both for the old sailor and the young adventurous harpooner, is the origin of an infinite fable whose enchanting power and resonances reach the extreme limits of the imagination:

> From smuggling adventures, it was easy to pass on to stories of what had happened to Robson, in his youth a sailor in the Greenland seas and to Kinraid, now one of the best harpooners in any whaler that sailed off the coast.

'There's three things to be afeard on,' said Robson, authoritatively: there's t'ice, that's bad; there's dirty weather, that's worse; and there's whales theirselves, as is t' worst of all: leastways, they was in my day: t' darned brutes may ha' larnt better manners sin'. When I where young they could never be got to let theirsels be harpooned wi'out flounderin' and makin' play wi' their tales and fins, till t' sea were all in a foam, and t' boats' crews was all o'er wi' spray, which t' them latitudes is a kind o' shower-bath not needed.' (*SL*, 99)

The voices of the two men almost merge with the mythical sound of the ocean, creating a linguistic universe laden with metaphors and images that speak of another world. The sailor is the sole person chosen to explore these unknown regions where it is possible to capture whales as well as to understand the mysterious signs of nature. A central element in the narrative is the cultural and rhetorical link established between Daniel Robson and Charley Kinraid who, drawing on popular imagination rather than their own personal experiences, weave oral tales whose dramatic impact is heightened by their use of multiple codes (existential, non-verbal, heroic and phonosymbolic, etc). Hence, a powerful incantatory effect which no one seems able to resist, least of all Sylvia who, in contrast with the silent presence of her mother, sees the harpooner as the heroic protagonist of a romantic love story. Indeed, soon after his arrival she begins to 'interpret' the sound of the surf as an invitation towards an imaginary escape from the narrow limitations which frustrate her desire for richer and more exciting experiences:

The mother and daughter hardly spoke at all when they sat down at last. The cheerful click of the knitting-needles made a pleasant home-sound; and in the occasional snatches of slumber that overcame her mother, Sylvia could hear the long-rushing boom of the waves, down below the rocks, for the Haytersbank gulley allowed the sullen roar to come up so far inland. (*SL*, 97)

The 'specksioneer' breaks the silence of the evening, bringing into Sylvia's household a vitality and energy which, until only a few moments previously, seemed to belong to the increasing roar of the ocean. Consequently, the opposition day *vs.* night generates a series of further homologous binary opposites (light *vs.* dark, life *vs.* death, heat *vs.* ice) which, however indirectly, convey a positive portrait of the young sailor:

To Sylvia the sudden change into brightness and bustle occasioned by the entrance of her father and the specksioneer was like that which you may effect any winter's night, when you come into a room where a great lump of coal lies hot and slumbering on the fire; just break it up with a judicious blow from the poker, and the room, late so dark, and dusk, and lone, is full of life, and warmth. (*SL*, 97)

If, as Bachelard writes, "le feu suggère le désir de changer,"[4] it may be pertinent to conclude that the image which signals the entrance of the harpooner also evokes the heroic qualities assigned to him by Sylvia. Kinraid, in other words, is the fire that lights her soul but is also, proleptically, the fire that tragically destroys everything. Before the skills of his narrative inventiveness she is able to do nothing but listen to his enchanting and magic words: "Sylvia had dropped her work, and sat gazing at Kinraid with fascinated wonder" (SL, 103). Like Coleridge's Ancient Mariner his story-telling is imbued with a visionary tension and, while tempered by realistic descriptions of whale hunting, nonetheless each word immediately evokes the mythical imagination and the timeless struggle between good and evil for the possession of the individual's soul:

> the waters were rocking beneath us, and the sky were steady above us; and th' ice rose out o' the waters, and seemed to reach up into the sky. We sailed on, and we sailed on, for more day nor I could count. Our captain were a strange, wild man, but once he looked a little pale when he came upo' deck after his turn-in, and saw the green-grey ice going straight up on our beam. Many on us thought as the ship were bewitched for th' captain's words; and we got to speak low, and to say our prayers o' nights, and a kind o' dull silence came into th' very air; our voices did na' rightly seem our own. And we sailed on, and we sailed on. All at one, th' man as were on watch gave a cry: he saw a break in the ice, as we'd begun to think were everlasting; and we all gathered towards the bows, and the captain called to th' man at the helm to keep her course, and cocked his head, and began walk the quarter-deck jaunty again. And we came to a great cleft in th' long but weary rock of ice: and the sides o' th' cleft were not jagged, but went straight sharp down into th' foaming waters. But we took but one look at what lay inside, for our captain, with a loud cry to God, bade the helmsman steer nor'ards away fra' th' mouth o' Hell. (SL, 102)

Kinraid's narrative concludes with the death of the captain who had dared "to peep at terrors forbidden to any of us afore our time" (SL, 102), and with his death there is a return to the accepted order of things and the normal rhythms that punctuate the pursuit of the precious cetaceans. Apart from its sensational, and at the same time reassuring, epilogue, what must also be noted is the thematic coherence of his tale of a journey to a land at the other end of the world, a land in which sailors confront rebellious and mysterious forces that no man will ever be able to fully explain. The various allusions and insistent iterations – particularly in the segment that begins "And we sailed on" – the choice of a specialised terminology and the invocations for divine intervention, are all features that evince the expertise and experience of a voice whose aim is to captivate the naïve, primitive sensitivity of its audience.[5] Furthermore, in this skilfully constructed oral narration there emerges a tragic vision that reflects man's eternal struggle with the natural elements which, in this case, seem to be in league with the Evil One.

On a diegetic level, Philip Hepburn conveys values that are totally antithetic to those of Kinraid. The confined and routinary space of Philip's everyday existence is set in contrast with the limitless and adventurous spatial dimensions of the harpooner's life at sea. Philip, who is used to serving the clients at his drapery shop, has a cold calculating personality, partly explained by his profession, which has taught him to control his emotional responses, and partly owing to his effortless acts of dissimulation. In fact, he is able to dominate and 'administrate' his feelings in exactly the same precise way that he displays, measures and cuts his fabrics and decides their price. Ever ready to denounce any form of irregularity or excess – which seem to be above all characteristics of the world of the sailors – Philip believes in cultural growth and moral elevation. For this reason Bell chooses him to teach her daughter to read and write. However, the attempt proves to be so disastrous that it only puts the girl into "a very rebellious frame of mind" (*SL*, 107). It is quite symptomatic of her insubordinate mind when she declares to her cousin mentor that "Greenland is all t' geography I want to know" (*SL*, 108), thereby confessing her exploitation of Philip's lessons for the sole purpose of learning more about the remote world that has enflamed her imaginative spirit. Physically close to Philip as she may be, her dominating desire is to escape from her present circumstances into a reverie in which Kinraid the harpooner increasingly takes on heroic proportions.

Nevertheless, the sea is more than merely the origin of individual mythologies. As Andrew Sanders justly notes, "the sea reflects the restlessness in the novel's characters, and it makes and unmakes their destinies. Like Fate it is uncertain, generous, cruel, impersonal and boundless."[6] Also from the sea come the troublesome press-gangs, whose task it is to force men into recruitment and, in doing so, spread panic among the populations of the seaside towns. Sylvia has a premonition of these events when, after buying the cloth for her cloak, she encounters the funeral of a sailor who was killed by the press-gang for attempting to flee forced recruitment. Her reaction towards the public ceremony, which culminates in her crying out in grief, is a testimony of her participation in the trials of those whose family income depends on the sea. Consequently, the experience of the funeral signals a profound inner revolution in the girl that culminates in a vision of the tragic condition of the whole of humanity:

she had gone to church with the thought of the cloak-that-was-to-be uppermost in her mind, and she had come down the long church stair with life and death suddenly become real to her mind, the enduring sea and hills forming a contrasting background to the vanishing away of man. (*SL*, 75)

In a few words, Gaskell renders, with extraordinary imaginative insight, the transition from euphoria to tragedy. Whereas innocence teaches one to dream, experience teaches one to suffer. Sylvia's mind undergoes a first significant metamorphosis – the structure of the phrases with the iteration of the syntagm "in her mind," particularly emphasises the young girl's spiritual transformation. From this moment onwards the sense of tragedy is indelibly inscribed in her with the sudden vanishing of a human life counteracted by the permanency of the natural world whose indifference before the death scene terrifies her. Yet, apart from her awareness of human finitude, the episode also anticipates the destinies of those who engage in primitive forms of rebellion and refuse to succumb to the laws and decisions of authority. Sylvia, who is by no means intimidated by the risks deriving from the sea and even challenges the forces of destruction – i.e. the press-gang – accepts Kinraid's proposal of marriage since, in her eyes, he is the one man capable of dominating the elements and leaving on them the mark of his strength and courage: "she sate down to meditate and dream about her great happiness in being loved by her hero, Charley Kinraid. ... Her eyes looked, trance-like into a dim, glorious future of life" (*SL*, 208).

The engagement establishes a temporary connection between the marine world and Haytersbank. In terms of the thematic development of the novel it signifies Sylvia's choice to become fully involved in a romance whose formulaic language requires that the woman awaits the return of her dauntless and faithful knight. In the same way, she continually fantasises about the moment the sailors return to Monkshaven with their load of whales and new fantastic stories. However, the fact that "historical necessity is no otherworldly fate divorced from men"[7] does not mean that it takes individual desires into account. This is the lesson the young girl has to learn. Indeed, she is denied the exhilarating experience of Kinraid's return, for at the very moment in which he is about to leave for a new whale hunting season in the waters of Greenland, he is captured by the press-gang. Such a negative impact of history on Sylvia's life is further enhanced by the tragic fate reserved for her father, who is condemned to death after leading a revolt against the press-gang.

Seen from an axiological perspective, the sudden collapse of the homogeneous group Kinraid–Robson corresponds with the automatic emergence of Philip Hepburn. On the surface, Philip appears cold and detached, enclosed within a suffocating puritan severity whose internal landscape is one of icy impenetrability.

Yet, behind the lukewarm and rational modality of his behaviour, he is devoured by a burning passion for his cousin, which induces him to express himself in a language that becomes more and more intense in its religious fanaticism and sexual obsession.[8] In the light of his tormented and sexually frustrated desire to possess Sylvia, Philip interprets Kinraid's capture by the press-gang as a sign of divine will. Sylvia, on the other hand, allows herself to be convinced by the insistent voices of those who would like to imagine that Kinraid has been killed in the violent brawl. Indeed, the discovery of the young man's hat with the ribbon that Sylvia has given him seems to confirm his tragic destiny before the whole community. Philip, however, who has witnessed the crucial moment of Kinraid's kidnapping, knows very well that the latter has not been killed. Not only does he know the truth, but as a result of an ironic coincidence, is entrusted by the harpooner to send a message of his fidelity to the girl. It is no wonder, therefore, that Philip views the exit of his rival as God's acceptance of his own burning desires. As in *Ruth*, Gaskell constructs her novel around a lie – a guilty silence – since Kinraid's voice is submerged by the internal voice of Philip who chooses to pursue the path of simulation and deception – which prepares the way for the final tragedy. Yet, rather than making him "the great sinner of the novel,"[9] Philip's concealing of the truth reveals him to be a character within whom all the dilemmas and conflicts of an axiologically unstable society are made to reverberate. His is therefore the guilty conscience of change.[10]

In Philip's view, his marriage to Sylvia – partly accelerated by the death of her father – marks the accomplishment of a design that he believes has been conditioned by the intervention of divine providence. Furthermore, the collapse of the group of characters epitomising transgression and rebellious wildness, upsets the relationships in the novel, and awakens in Philip a new awareness of his psychological strength. His victory, which is also favoured by Sylvia's mother, configures the victory of a conception of human life intended as a territory marked by silence and the total absence of communication.[11] This is the atmosphere in which, soon after the celebration of their marriage, Sylvia is forced to live:

> She did not tell him; but idea of the house behind the shop was associated in her mind with two times of discomfort and misery. The first time she had gone into the parlour about which Philip spoke so much was at the time of the press-gang riot, when she had fainted from terror and excitement; the second was on that night of misery when she and her mother had gone into Monkshaven, to bid her father farewell before he was taken to York: in that room, on that night, she had first learnt something of the fatal peril in which he stood. She could not show the

bright shy curiosity about her future dwelling that is common enough with girls who are going to be married. (*SL*, 336)

Sylvia's married life is set against a past that has no happy memories for her. In fact, the domestic sphere is characterised by negative valences which anticipate the tragic ending. Philip, by contrast, is convinced that in marrying his idol and placing her in "a befitting shrine" (*SL*, 341) his great dream has finally come true. But he does not realise that, for Sylvia, marriage represents a spatial and psychological contraction which reduces her to an attitude of passivity towards both him and the external world: "She was quiet even to passiveness in all her dealings with Philip" (*SL*, 342). Under the guise of her silence, however, her internal world is pervaded by recurrent premonitions in which the two heroic figures of her life, her father and Kinraid, are continually evoked: "Sylvia, with all her apparent frankness, kept her deep sorrows to herself. She never mentioned her father's name, though he was continually present to her mind. Nor did she speak of Kinraid to human being" (*SL*, 349-50). Her instinctive alternative to such an enclosing and stifling domestic routine is the moor where she abandons herself to haunting thoughts of the past in which Kinraid is the hero of a mythical and remote universe. In this bare primal landscape, even her pain seems to melt away and become transient and insignificant compared with the eternal murmur of the sea; and in her state of self-abandonment Sylvia experiences a freedom otherwise denied her: "she was glad occasionally to escape from the comfortable imprisonment of her 'parlour', and the close streets around the market-place, and to mount the cliffs and sit on the turf, gazing abroad over the wide still expanse of the open sea" (*SL*, 350). It is also true that "the sight and sound of the mother-like sea" (*SL*, 350) remains the sole companion through which she can find relief for the sorrow of her solitude and silence. Her dialogue with the sea is a strategy of survival as well as an escape from her painful condition of estrangement: "she was a prisoner in the house, a prisoner in her room" (*SL*, 350). Not even the birth of her child is able to alleviate the sorrow of her internal struggles as she continues to live in a state of social death which is the result of a marriage dictated not by personal choice, but by a combination of historical and family circumstances. Because of her inability to resist external pressure, Sylvia is a passive witness of the gradual break down of her own self. Only contact with the primitive forces of the elements – which above all means retracing the past – manages to mount some kind of resistance to the oppressive enclosure of her family environment: "She paid for these happy rambles with her baby by the depression which awaited her in the dark confined house that was her home; its very fullness of comfort was an oppression" (*SL*, 360). From a linguistic angle, the proximity of such quasi-synonymous lexical items as *depression* and *oppression* delineates a state of immobility behind which Sylvia's gradual psychic withering is taking place – "she seemed to have no will of her own" (*SL*, 362).

Gaskell is all too ready to underline the pathological nature of Sylvia's experiences, associating her imprisonment with a melancholic condition that signifies her inner death against a tragic background. If, for the heroine, this means witnessing the gradual decline of her spirit – manifested by her silence and the ghostly presence of the harpooner – Philip's psychic drama reveals all its instability in the haunting 'return' of the very obstacle which, with his guilty silence, he thought he had been able to remove. Indeed, such is the hold of the rival on Philip's imagination that he establishes a sort of indirect dialogue with the Other, the real Charley Kinraid and with his return to the Monkshaven scene:

> Over and over again in this first year of married life he dreamt this dream; perhaps as many as eight or nine times, and it never varied. It was always of Kinraid's return: Kinraid was full of life in Philip's dream, though, in his waking hours he could and did convince himself by all the laws of probability that his rival was dead. (*SL*, 343)

The obsession of Philip's nightmares ends with the return of Kinraid in the flesh. Once his lie has been exposed, he is left in an existential desert from which he flees in horror. Sylvia's raging words determine an instantaneous crumbling of Philip's fictional construction and, inevitably, his ontological dissolution:

> 'I'll make my vow now, lest I lose misel' again. I'll niver forgive yon man, nor live with him as his wife again. All that's done and ended. He's spoilt my life, – he's spoilt it for as long as iver I live on this earth; but neither yo' nor him shall spoil my soul. It goes hard wi' me, Charley, it does indeed.' (*SL*, 383)

At this point, realising that his life is a failure under every aspect, Philip disappears and attempts, as a last resort, to construct a new identity, so as to find self-redemption in the eyes of his wife and the community at large, by enlisting "as one of his Majesty's marines" (*SL*, 391) under the name of Stephen Freeman.[12] With no God to protect him any longer, and no ties of affection to support him, there is only the wide horizon of a world in which he can satisfy his desire for a life of wandering – for him the redeeming light is very distant and out of reach; now he is left with the hope of expiating somehow and somewhere his immense and devastating sense of guilt. It is obvious that in his self-inflicted punishment, Philip is masochistically searching for a new life founded not on the pleasures of sex, but on that of humiliation. As for Kinraid, his return does not bring liberation to Sylvia, but the annihilation of those memories in which, in her moral 'imprisonment,' she had hoped for a possible salvation. In many ways, Kinraid kills the very last romance of her happy childhood when, for the second time, he abandons her to a destiny in which she no longer has the possibility of recomposing the fragments of her life. That is why she seems ready to commit suicide: "There was a sure hiding-place from all human reproach and heavy mortal woe beneath the rushing waters borne landwards by the morning tide" (*SL*, 378). But Sylvia's self-destructive compulsion is checked by "perhaps the thought of her sucking child; perhaps her mother; perhaps an angel of God" (*SL*, 378). Here, significantly, the narrating voice abandons omniscience in the attempt to illustrate the obscure and mysterious agents which shape human beings' choices.

Ultimately, Sylvia is tragically alone, dispossessed, lost in a world which is not her own. Even the impenetrable regions of Greenland cannot form a part of her microcosm, since after the 'death' of her hero (a respectable and unromantic Kinraid, now lieutenant of the Royal Navy, decides to marry an heiress in spite of the fact that Sylvia still loves him), and the marvellous stories of the sea reveal all their ethical and axiological inconsistency. At the end of the novel, the heroine is helplessly sucked into an ontological whirlpool from which the only lesson she learns is the ultimate futility of everything. She cannot help but realise now that individual paths are dominated by the great machine of history and that man can choose, consciously or unconsciously, whether or not to adapt to its complex and contradictory movements. To a certain extent, Sylvia's tragedy derives from the fact that she is unable to come to terms with change – she remains anchored to the unreal and fascinating story of a paternal/patriarchal voice, without succeeding in distinguishing a clear line between reality and romance. Given up for dead, Kinraid survives change because he is able to adapt to the most diverse climates and situations and has no difficulty in understanding the directions of historical necessity. The fact that he rises to the rank of lieutenant of the Royal Navy during the Napoleonic wars, is a confirmation of his desire to be wholly integrated into the social system. The same does not apply to Philip, however, who moves in the very opposite direction. In the illusory idea of making his own monological vision dovetail with a model of reality, he forgets that life is much more ambiguous and shifting than his puritan upbringing has taught him. Only when he is on the point of death does he glimpse something of the freedom he vainly sought in his long tormented quest, in his wife's words of forgiveness. By changing his name to Freeman he lays bare his desire to be freed above all from the sin of conceit, that of believing he could shape other men's destinies.

Tellingly, Philip's death does not provide any existential solution for Sylvia. For, instead of reacting positively to the tragic events by rebuilding a life of her own, she becomes increasingly isolated from those around her. Her sole means of defence in attempting to overcome the limits imposed by history is her silence and her relationship with the natural world. It is significant that on the final page of the novel, the narrative voice recalls how "you may hear the waves lapping up the shelving shore with the same ceaseless, ever-recurring sound as that which Philip listened to in the pauses between life and death" (*SL*, 429). After the intricate web of historical circumstances and private events, after so many family adversities which lead to destruction and self-destruction, after the final scene showing a 'stranger' named Stephen Freeman who miraculously saves Sylvia's daughter from drowning, there remains nothing but the rhythmic sound of the sea which is the only dialogic element for "a pale sad woman, always dressed in black" (*SL*, 502).[13] The colour of the novel's beginning – "the red cloth" of Sylvia's euphoric imagination – now becomes the black dress of a speechless melancholy widow. Beneath the surface of her silence lies a final awareness that eternity can be found in the natural world, whereas, essentially, tragedy is the very culminating truth of human predicament.

Notes

1. On the thematics of the lovers' conflict, see Terry Eagleton: "The structure of *Sylvia's Lovers* … is primarily organised around a contrast between Hepburn and Kinraid" ("*Sylvia's Lovers* and Legality," *Essays in Criticism*, 13.1 [1976]: 18). However, it must be added that the rivalry between Hepburn and Kinraid is totally functional to the representation of a world characterised by the instability of ethical and social referents. In fact, from the point of view of their textual functionality, the narrative elements that make up the diegesis go well beyond the simple contrast between the two lovers referred to in the title of the novel.

2. According to A. W. Ward, the editor of the Knutsford Edition of Elizabeth Gaskell's works, the writer spent a great deal of time researching the historical period of her novel (that is the period from 1796 to 1800) to the point of even reading the two volumes of the *History of Whitby* (1817) by George Young. As confirmation of her hard work on the novel there are also the various titles she thought of adopting at different stages of composition: *Philip's Idol, The Specksioneer, Too Late* and *Monkshaven.*

3. Elizabeth Gaskell, *Sylvia's Lovers*, ed. Andrew Sanders (Oxford: Oxford Univ. Press, 1986), 4-5. All subsequent quotations refer to this edition, and page numbers are given parenthetically. Hereafter *SL.*

4. Gaston Bachelard, *La Psychanalise du feu* (Paris: Gallimard, 1949, 1983), 35.

5. See Andrew Sanders, *The Victorian Historical Novel 1840-1880* (London: Macmillan, 1978). In particular, Sanders notes that "Charley delicately relishes the effect he creates; he exchanges accounts of extravagant adventures with Daniel Robson, but he manages to outdare him in imagination, range and variety, producing tales of a whaler's experience as extraordinary as any in *Moby Dick*" (214).

6. Sanders, *The Victorian Historical Novel*, 211.

7. Georg Lukács, *The Historical Novel*, translated by Hannah and Stanley Mitchell (London: Merlin Press, 1989), 58. For many aspects, what Lukács writes on Scott's historical novels, mutatis mutandis, may be applied to the combination of historical necessity and tragic vision in *Sylvia's Lovers*: "Historical necessity in his novels is of the most severe, implacable kind. Yet this necessity is no otherworldly fate divorced from men; it is the complex interaction of concrete historical circumstances in their process of transformation, in their interaction with the concrete human beings, who have grown up in these circumstances, have been *very variously influenced by them, and who act in an individual way according to their personal passions. Thus, in Scott's portrayal, historical necessity is always a resultant, never a presupposition; it is the tragic atmosphere of a period and not the object of the writer's reflections*" (58, italics mine).

8. Margaret Ganz detects a parallelism between Philip Hepburn and John Barton, observing that "both are really destroyed because an obsessive commitment to a particular objective leads them to deny the claims of a higher morality" (*Elizabeth Gaskell: The Artist in Conflict* [New York: Twayne Publishers, 1969], 232).

9. Graham Handley, *Sylvia's Lovers (Mrs. Gaskell)* (Oxford: Blackwell, 1968), 33. Hepburn's contradictory attitude has been rightly noted by Angus Easson, *Elizabeth Gaskell* (London: Routledge & Kegan Paul, 1979), 175: "Philip's decision to lie (more properly remain silent and so suppress the truth: another instance of his restraint) does not make him unfeeling – his heart goes out to Sylvia when he sees her grief over Charley's supposed death." See also J. G. Sharps, *Mrs. Gaskell's Observation and Invention: a Study of her Non-Biographical Works* (Fontwell, Sussex: Linden Press, 1970), 440: "Unsure whether or not he had explicitly pledged to give Sylvia her lover's last message, Philip deferred making a decision for the

moment, only to overhear, at the end of the day, a bar-room jest about Kinraid's light ways with women. Thereafter he made himself believe that, for his failure to communicate to the Robsons the news of the impressment, impersonal forces were responsible."

10. Various critics have proposed gender readings of the novel by stressing the opposition between the sexes. However, such reductive approaches, to my mind, do not do justice to the complexity of its thematic developments. From an interpretative viewpoint, if we want to do justice to *Sylvia's Lovers*, we need to recognise the tragic vision it is built upon. As Patsy Stoneman, *Elizabeth Gaskell* (Manchester: Manchester Univ. Press, 2006), comments: "Extreme gender-polarisation creates an atmosphere in which each sex admires in the other the qualities from which it is excluded" (97). In my opinion, basing an analysis of *Sylvia's Lovers* on gender interpretations is like looking at the events in the novel through a keyhole. Useful and stimulating though such readings may be, they should be made without over-looking a more dynamic and articulate *Weltanschauung*.

11. Shirley Foster justly observes: "The portrayal of their marriage, the result of Sylvia's final volitionless accession to Philip's overmastering will, highlights the narrative's concern with failure of communication and ideological entrapment" ("Introduction," *Sylvia's Lovers*, ed. Shirley Foster [Harmondsworth: Penguin, 1996], xxv).

12. As far as Philip Hepburn's psychological and behavioural transformation is concerned, Gaskell accurately describes his oscillations with respect to his decision of disappearing for good, forgetting his past and, ultimately, redeeming himself: "Anything was welcome that severed him from his former life, that could make him forget it, if it were possible … and before Justice Cholmley, of Holm-Fell Hall, he had sworn into his Majesty's service, under the name of Stephen Freeman. With a new name, he began a new life. Alas! the old life lives for ever" (*SL*, 392).

13. It should be noted here that Philip Hepburn's redeeming progress is marked by a coincidence whose ethical and psychological meaning influences Sylvia's moral attitude in the final scene of reconciliation with her rejected husband. In fact, in the melodramatic words of Charley Kinraid's wife, Philip is depicted to Sylvia as a hero who saved Kinraid's life during the Siege of Acre (1799): "'Yes, at Acre, I tell you,' said Mrs. Kinraid, with pretty petulance. 'The Turks held the town, and the French wanted to take it; and we, that is the British Fleet, wouldn't let them. So Sir Sidney Smith, a commodore and a great friend of the captain's, landed in order to fight the French … and the poor captain was wounded, and lay a-dying of pain and thirst within the enemy's – that is the French – fire; so that they were ready to shoot any one of his own side who came near him. They thought he was dead himself, you see, as he was very near; and would have been too, if your husband had not come out of shelter, and taken him up in his arms or on his back (I couldn't make out which), and carried him safe within the walls'" (*SL*, 448-49). Significantly, Sylvia's immediate response reveals the extent to which this final portrait clashes with her own: "'It couldn't have been Philip,' said Sylvia, dubiously" (*SL*, 449). Apart from Gaskell's overworking of the pattern of coincidence, what is important to underline here is that, ironically, the man with blackened face and burnt lips dying on the Monkshaven shore is no longer the effeminate shop-assistant we meet at the beginning of the novel, but a man corresponding to the model of romantic and dauntless hero who inhabited Sylvia's juvenile dreams. Melodramatic though it may be, the episode focused on Philip's rescue of Kinraid evinces the way Gaskell problematises the main protagonists' role and axiology before history.

The Literature of Literacy:
Sylvia's Lovers and *Our Mutual Friend*

Deborah Frenkel

"*Literature*," writes Raymond Williams, in his etymological excavation of the dusty corners of the cultural and social lexicon, "is a difficult word."[1] Those apparent definitional certainties which adhere to the noun in its contemporary usage, he argues, prove less stable as one goes back in time; its edges become fuzzy; and by the time a lexicographical explorer has hit the nineteenth century, what appear to be denotative centralities today are revealed as mere semantic fluff. "*Literature* came into English," notes Williams, "in the sense of polite learning through reading." Prior to the universalisation of textual proficiency throughout English society – a slow process which gathered steam in the Industrial Revolution, and only found its culmination, according to some arguments, in the *Elementary Education Act* of 1870[2] – "*literature* ... corresponded mainly to the modern meanings of *literacy*."[3] Thus 'letters' – spelling out either fiction or fact – could be aligned, and were to some extent interchangeable, with the condition of their own existence. Precisely because it is so hard to quarantine its meaning, the term *literature* has proven, of the entire lexicon, one of the most troubled – and troubling – words.

At a time in which the ability to read and write remained topical, as a moral as well as political debate, this shimmering relationship between literacy and literature necessarily rendered the position of the author somewhat precarious. Writing as part of a textual explosion which saw the novel, in the words of Kathleen Tillotson, develop with "surging variety" into the "dominant form,"[4] Elizabeth Gaskell and Charles Dickens discovered fruitful material for fiction in the anxieties and ambiguities attendant upon this social – and semantic – change. *Sylvia's Lovers* and *Our Mutual Friend*, as mature works, both stage scenes of what one critic broadly terms "reading lessons" – pedagogical dramas which enact processes of textual interpretation and misinterpretation, of the "use and abuse" of ABCs.[5] By the 1863 publication of *Sylvia's Lovers*, overall literacy rates were approaching 70 percent[6]; *Our Mutual Friend*, serialised in 19 installments over 1864 and 1865, could command a reading audience which probably numbered in six figures.[7] Literacy, therefore, was of foremost topicality as the novel developed during the 1860s, and it is not surprising that Gaskell and Dickens, in particular, should both produce texts which reflexively explore its nuances. *Sylvia's Lovers* and *Our Mutual Friend* do not merely reflect attitudes towards *literacy* in the 1860s; they simultaneously refract those ambivalences which clustered around it through the lens of their own materiality as *literature*. In doing so, they raise fascinating questions about the nature of textuality, and textual competence, asking exactly what it means, as Noddy Boffin puts it, for "all print to be opening ahead" of one.[8]

For Dickens, of course, whose fame was consolidated by the 1860s, the immediacy of the "large and attentive audience" which attended his public Readings,[9] as well as a method of serial publication which enabled readerly interpellation of the creative process, engendered a sense of the "openness" of print – an illusion of proximity between the producer and the consumers of literature.[10] "No one thinks first of Mr. Dickens as a writer," commented one contemporary critic. "He is at once, through his books, a friend."[11] But it is this kind of renovation of authority as affiliation, of distance into a Veneering of intimacy, which epitomises the notion of "Society" that the novel is at such pains to discredit. The written word, throughout the work, is hassled by those *literates* who presume to control it; who believe that the relationship between literature and literacy can be a mutually friendly one. When the terms enter *Our Mutual Friend*, therefore – one explicitly, one through contextual implication – Dickens' shuffling together of the two is a nod to a particularly central thematic concern, and Boffin and Wegg enact an exchange which goes beyond, in its import, a joke:

> 'I thought to myself, "Here's a man with a wooden leg – a literary man with – "
>
> "N- not exactly so, sir," said Mr. Wegg.
>
> "Why, you know every one of these songs by name and by tune, and if you want to read or to sing any one on 'em off straight, you've only to whip on your spectacles and do it!" cried Mr. Boffin. "I see you at it!"
>
> "Well, sir," returned Mr. Wegg, with a conscious inclination of the head; "we'll say literary then."
>
> "'A literary man – *with* a wooden leg – and all Print is open to him!' That's what I thought to myself, that morning," pursued Mr. Boffin, leaning forward to describe, uncramped by the clothes-horse, as large an arc as his right arm could make; "'all Print is open to him!' And it is, ain't it?"[12]

180

Open, perhaps, as both Wegg and the reader will discover – but seldom mastered. In endorsing the conflation of 'literacy' with 'literature,' Wegg entertains a fantasy of authority – and, perhaps, authorship – which must remain, for any reader of the novel, forever illusory. "I believe you couldn't show me the piece of English print," he subsequently boasts, "that I wouldn't be equal to collaring and throwing." As if through a process of domestication, that which is animated, alive and wild, Wegg would suggest, can easily be pacified upon the page – even *with* a wooden leg. What Dickens will go on to show, however, is that such professed proficiency, for any of the readers of *Our Mutual Friend*, consists of nothing more than puffery. It will prove impossible to domesticate this text – and strikingly so, given that it belongs to that most *domestic* of genres: the Victorian novel; the "household word."[13] Despite the emphatic homeliness of the stall, described as a kind of literary manger which finds Boffin "nursing his stick like a baby" against the clothes-horse, Dickens' print remains uncollared. Whilst writing may, indeed, prove "open" to its literate friends, it will exact a price of ambiguity, uncertainty and slipperiness in exchange for ease of entry.

Sylvia's Lovers addresses a similar problem relating to the link between the literary, the literate, and the circuitry of power at play between the two. But where Dickens teases apart his own discourse in defiance of those readers who aspire to an authority over language – Wegg, Bradley Headstone, the representatives of "Podsnappery" – for Mrs. Gaskell the ideal of textual proficiency is necessarily associated with a process of gendered socialisation. In late eighteenth-century Yorkshire – a rural past, that is, on the cusp of a commercial future – the learning of letters proceeds "just as a wild animal is tamed,"[14] as an induction of its student into the conventions of the middle-class hearth and home. "Now Sylvia," coaxes her "lover" Philip in one early attempt at instruction, "here's a copy-book wi' t' Tower o' London on it, and we'll fill it wi' as pretty writing as any in t'North Riding."[15] But the meaning of a copy book imprinted with an emblem of imprisonment is not lost upon Sylvia: she refuses to learn how to read or write. In allowing her "dunce" to opt out of the compulsory literacy shared by all her readers, Gaskell opens an uncomfortable gap between the worlds of her protagonist and that of her audience, raising the prospect that the domestic plots which threaten Sylvia's happiness, and from which she so destructively struggles loose, are nevertheless ineluctably *impressed* upon the minds of her audience. Not only are such plots fundamental to the existence of the novel itself, she suggests, they are the very condition of Sylvia's own legibility. This double play of letters – of the literate and the literary – leads the reader of *Sylvia's Lovers* to the unsettling suspicion that even as they read, they are simultaneously being pressed into literature themselves.

Thus Gaskell's pen, like Dickens', is dual-ended. When it produces literature, it does so both reflectively and reflexively. But whereas Dickens allows his coterie of misguided literates to mistake reading for a species of writing, building upon the illusion of the novel as a kind of mutuality, *Sylvia's Lovers* gathers impact from an acute sense of its subject's remoteness. From its opening words, the gulf between past and present emerges with a sharp, statistical clarity:

> On the north-eastern shores of England there is a town called Monkshaven, containing at the present day about fifteen thousand inhabitants. There were, however, but half the number at the end of the last century, and it was at that period that the events narrated in the following pages occurred.[16]

Narrated by whom? is one obvious question which arises for a reader, but it will remain mysterious throughout the novel. Indeed, the book itself seems to have materialised in the passive voice: Mrs. Gaskell's narrator remains palpable yet shadowy, and his or her confident pronouncements upon the past only serve to emphasise the doubled distancing of Sylvia – both within time, and within the language which inscribes that time into history. "In looking back to the last century," the novel continues, "it appears curious to see how little our ancestors had the power of putting two things together ... discrepancies ran through good men's lives in those days."[17] For the narrator, this synthetic ability, or rather its lack, defines a fissured world set in opposition – albeit with gentle irony – to the literate, analytical world of the novel's readers: "It is well for us that we live at the present time, when everybody is logical and consistent."[18] Sylvia's landscape, by contrast, is emphatically one without writing; its topography consists of "traditions" rather than documentation; and its significance as a bastion of literate learning – a 'monk's haven' – is long fallen into "ancient remains."[19] What Mikhail Bakhtin calls a *chronotope* – the space-time continuum within a text which "makes narrative events concrete, makes them take on flesh"[20] – thus functions, in *Sylvia's Lovers*, as a marker of aesthetic distance. The opening chapter's tour of the Monkshaven landscape – the "odd ... expression" in the faces of livestock, the "great ghastly whale-jaws" over gate-posts, the "marvelous" tyranny of the press-gang[21] – lucidly charts the gulf between then and now, between the subjects and the objects of history.

Dickens' opening is equally loaded. Like Gaskell, his concern is with establishing a thematic entrée to the work as a whole; he constructs a bridge between the world inside the novel and its textual exterior. Against the straightforward strangeness of Sylvia's Yorkshire, however, *Our Mutual Friend* proves chronotopically dual: both familiar and alien – *here* and *there* – at the same time. Dickens is explicit: "In these times of ours, though concerning the exact year there is no need to be precise, a boat of dirty and disreputable appearance, with two figures in it, floated on the Thames, between Southwark Bridge which is of iron, and

London bridge which is of stone, as an autumn evening was closing in."[22] In one breath, the world of the novel draws close and cosy beneath the umbral pronoun 'our'; in another, it lurches into an epochal expansiveness, positioning its hazy subjects somewhere between iron and stone, upon a river thick, primevally, with "slime and ooze."[23] In this way, Dickens inaugurates the play of realism and magic, the actual and the fantastic, which will reach, perhaps, its most lurid peak in Bella's discovery in her new house of "a charming aviary" replete with "tropical birds" and "gold and silver fish, and mosses, and water-lilies, and a fountain."[24] This conflation of the metaphorical and the literal – that is, the *lettered* – is already marked in the stone bridges and stone ages, dead bodies and death itself, which blur across the novel's opening pages. Whereas Gaskell's narrator invokes the capacity of the present for "putting things together," *Our Mutual Friend*, in contradistinction, works to prise its chronotope apart – and in doing so it challenges the very legibility of 'literature' itself.

As has been well recognised, the readers of *Our Mutual Friend* come in a variety of flavours.[25] There are the fluent genteel literates such as John Harmon, Eugene Wrayburn and Mortimer Lightwood, who employ a proficiency in language unthinkingly and playfully. There are the aspirants to and hawkers of literacy – Charley Hexam, Bradley Headstone and, above all, Silas Wegg – who consider the mastering of language a means of mastering the world, by converting it into various forms of currency – social capital, sexual fulfilment, money. And then there are those 'readers,' in a broader sense of the word – those for whom literacy involves less an act of mechanical decodage than a leap of faith and imagination, and who discover within it a kind of self-transcendence. Lizzie Hexam, for example, perceives "fancies" in the flames of fires[26]; the orphan Sloppy "beautifully" animates the newspaper ("he do the Police in difference voices")[27]; and Jenny Wren, bent over a book on Riah's roof-garden, is lifted by language into strains of lyrical ecstasy. "You see the clouds rushing on above the narrow streets, not minding them," she describes, "and you see the golden arrows pointing at the mountains in the sky from which the wind comes, and you feel as if you were dead."[28] A number of critics have noted the manner in which the novel's plot carefully sorts these kinds of readers into a hierarchy of literacy, returning John Harmon to his rightful inheritance and Mortimer Lightwood to his rightful profession, joining Sloppy and Jenny in a final "gold image,"[29] and allowing Wegg to decline-and-fall-off into the waste matter from whence he has come.[30] Yet at the same time, however, *Our Mutual Friend* draws within its discourse an additional group of readers, far more pervasive and plural than its characters – those readers, that is, of the novel itself.

It is difficult to determine the precise scope and the nature of the readership of the 1860s. *Our Mutual Friend* was published serially in *All the Year Round* with sales of between nineteen- and thirty-thousand copies[31]; but after the rapid enlargements of literacy over the previous decades, the novel's potential audience exceeded these figures – exceeded them enormously, and, perhaps, threateningly. As Wilkie Collins put it in one 1858 essay, beyond the reach of serials, beyond the circulating library, the book-club and the newspaper, lay "the mysterious, the unfathomable, the universal public of the penny-novel-journals. … A reading public of three millions which lies right out of the pale of literary civilisation."[32] In political terms, this growing population of literates – troped by Collins as a kind of exotic species, from which "specimens" might, zoologically, be taken – arguably resembled, in its abstract expansiveness, the kind of mob which surges through a number of contemporaneous works: the "raging ravening beast" of *Sylvia's Lovers*,[33] or the crowd in Eliot's *Felix Holt* whose behaviour can "hardly be calculated on more than those of oxen and pigs."[34] It is hardly surprising, therefore, that such an anonymous, unknowable mass, bestowed with literacy in all its powers and yet quite alien to "literary civilisation," should present a very real textual hazard.[35] In its propensity to co-opt authorial power by sheer market heft – plagiarists, for example, favoured Dickens' titles[36] – this final species of reader could not, manifestly, be restrained via manoeuverings of plot. *This* kind of aggregate reader – this 'literate' mass – presented a stupendous narrative force, purporting, like Wegg, to "collar and throw" the written word in exchange for its two-shilling cover-price.[37] Even as Dickens steered his characters through "a perfect archipelago of hard words,"[38] therefore, it was necessary to resist, through a kind of literary shadow-boxing, the challenges which mob literacy posed to authorship.

Gaskell's position, by contrast, was less precarious, but more constricted. On one hand, the publication of *Sylvia's Lovers* in three simultaneous volumes avoided the temporal, spatial and narrative lacunae which split apart, in seventeen places, the textual integrity of *Our Mutual Friend*. On the other hand, however, female authorship presented acute contradictions for Gaskell, as her biography of a fellow writer and friend makes clear: "existence became divided into two parallel currents – her life as Currer Bell, the author; her life as Charlotte Brontë, the woman."[39] Publication did not sit comfortably, in 1863, with the private domesticities which society designated as female,[40] and within the world of *Sylvia's Lovers* any association of women with language tends towards a "delightfully" nonsensical whimsy:

> I sent my love a letter,
> But alas! she canna read,
> And I lo'e her a' the better.[41]

Gaskell's inscription of an oral, balladic text about *literacy* into her own work of *literature* opens a fascinatingly reflexive commentary upon the relationship between communication, authority, language and gender, and the necessary partiality of the written word within such a conversation. Like the silenced Jess MacFarlane, the readers and writers of *Sylvia's Lovers* repeatedly encounter external forces which curtail their linguistic powers. Whilst Philip Hepburn prefaces his initial tuition of Sylvia, for example, with an impassioned defence of government "by … a British Constitution,"[42] a little later – having grappled first-hand with the letter of the law – he concedes "never mind about capitals … a man does just as well without them."[43] Alice Rose, similarly, presenting an alternative version of female literacy, nevertheless views language as instrumentally subject to a higher kind of Authorship, to the effect that Sylvia's final acquiescence in her lessons marks her as "one who, from being a pupil, might become a convert."[44] And Bell Robson, "a touch better educated than her husband," quietly submits to Daniel's wilful misappropriation of her language. Sylvia, her father insists, "niver spoke a pretext at all" – and perhaps inevitably so, given that the "domestic business" of daily life limits *textuality* to its purely etymological sense, as something which is woven rather than verbalized – "Bell's knitting" or "Sylvia's spinning."[45] In a novel which situates itself at a moment of social "tyranny,"[46] literacy in this sense offers little more than an additional kind of impressment – as a subjugation, rather than a liberation, of those who purport to possess it. Beneath its veneer of "pretty writing," language arouses a power-play from which no reader – or author – is exempt: "I *can* not (it is not *will* not) write at all," Gaskell admitted, "if I ever think of my readers, and what impression I am making on them."[47] In the business of producing 'impressions' upon an audience, 'Mrs. Gaskell' was nevertheless deeply mindful of her own authorial malleability. As Sylvia says to Philip, "If iver I write thee a letter it shall just be full of nothing but 'Abednego! Abednego! Abednego!'"[48] Authorship, it seems, tends constantly towards the empty citation of someone else's authorities – towards texts, that is, which are inevitably, always, *pre.*

Like *Sylvia's Lovers*, *Our Mutual Friend* recognises language as a form of power, whilst simultaneously conscious of its own dependence, as 'literature,' upon the commercial and social machinery which has carried it into the public sphere. But whilst Gaskell allows that authorship in the mass-market always depends on a concession of authority from elsewhere, and that the novel, accordingly, can never be really *new*, Dickens is less pragmatic. *Our Mutual Friend* addresses itself towards a readership which is threateningly aberrant, thematising situations of "meaning mischief"[49] – of various ways of reading *wrongs*. Headstone, for example – whose very name unifies inscription and death – cannot talk of Lizzie Hexam without "speaking as if he were repeating … from a book"[50]; Mr. Podsnap, more comically, whose facility with "literature; large print"[51] stretches, at a pinch, to translation, misses his interlocutor's equation of the "Constitution Britannique" with horse droppings. ("'We call it Horse,' he responds. 'In England, Angleterre, England, We Aspirate the "H," and We Say "Horse." Only our Lower Classes Say 'Orse!'"[52]). Most stunning of all linguistic depositions, however, and one which transcends Class boundaries in its democratic ordure, is that which Dickens inflicts upon his own public – allowing his Golden Dustman, in duping Bella and Wegg, to pull his miserly wool over the reader's eyes as well.

> "When I devised this story," explains the 'Postscript' to *Our Mutual Friend*, "I foresaw the likelihood that a class of readers and commentators would suppose that I was at great pains to conceal exactly what I was at great pains to suggest – namely, that Mr. John Harmon was not slain, and that Mr. John Rokesmith was he ...."
>
> "To keep for a long time unsuspected, yet always working itself out, another purpose originating in that leading incident, and turning it to a pleasant and useful account at last, was at once the most interesting and the most difficult part my design."[53]

Dickens' rhetoric of 'suspicion' and 'concealment' inserts the author himself into the play of doublings and dissemblances, disguises and deceptions, which his characters inflict upon each other – Rogue Riderhood upon Gaffer Hexam, Eugene Wrayburn on Bradley Headstone, and, paradigmatically, John Harmon on Bella Wilfer. As the orchestrator of all these machinations, however, Dickens emerges from behind his narrative curtain as the supreme victor in the plot of literacy. Significantly, his final ruse depends upon his reader's overhasty equation of the "Characters" in *Merryweather's Lives and Anecdotes of Misers* with Noddy Boffin himself[54]; upon a premature presumption of mastery over the text; upon a too-*literal* understanding, that is, of the link between word and world. Such misreaders share an unwillingness to recognise the propensity of language to curve around upon itself, to resist that collaring and throwing which Podsnappery purports to exact upon the unaspirated Orse – and in inscribing a work so blatantly untameable, Dickens re-educates his audience in the art of reading. It is appropriate, therefore, that *Our Mutual Friend*'s final quarter bears the title "A Turning," completing the proverbial fragment "A Long Lane" which denominates Book Three, since a *turn* is precisely what it works upon its public. The novel performs a tropological about-face – from the Greek *tropos*; a swerve, a deviation, a dodging[55] – and in doing so it demands a new kind of literacy, loosened from the strictures of the literal. Just as the work's opening pages blur the bounds between realism and allegory, and just as Twemlow might prove a "mild little elderly gentleman"[56] and yet remains, till the last, "an innocent piece of dinner-furniture,"[57] even reading itself, Dickens suggests, must ultimately become its own metaphor:

> You charm me, Mortimer, with your reading of my weaknesses. (By-the-bye, that very word, Reading, in its critical use, always charms me. An actress's Reading of

a chambermaid, a dancer's Reading of a hornpipe, a singer's Reading of a song, a marine painter's Reading of the sea, the kettle-drum's Reading of an instrumental passage, are phrases ever youthful and delightful.)[58]

Equally, though, Eugene might have added – *a writer's Reading of his public*. So youthful and delightful a practice, at least, runs unspokenly – though steadily, and urgently – throughout *Our Mutual Friend*.

Sylvia's Lovers, by contrast, reflects no such agonistic anxiety regarding textual control. Gaskell's concerns, rather, relate to language's dependence upon the pre-scriptions and proscriptions of society, and to the belatedness, consequently, of any form of writing. Having adopted a historical viewpoint, Gaskell nevertheless writes a narrative about the impossibility of history. The very concept, as one commentator notes, is divided, denoting both that which is *done* and that which is *written*[59]; and *Sylvia's Lovers* locates itself within the great gulf between these two poles. Most of the novel's protagonists, as noted, cannot read or write, and accordingly fall beyond Collins' "pale of literary civilization" – within a vast preliterate, prehistoric diaspora. Thus, whilst in Dickens' London various "voices of society" spill over their quotation marks into the third-person narration, churning together the ostensibly oral with the literate, Gaskell's characters speak in a dialect which marks itself as alien to the written word, as an overt departure from orthography. Whilst Dickens' plots converge into a single narrative strain, making it possible to refer to "persons and things *in general*,"[60] *Sylvia's Lovers* describes a process of distancing, as characters grow "veiled" even from each other[61]: when Kinraid returns to Sylvia, he sees "a terrible story in her eyes, *if he could but have read it*."[62] Of all such instances of estrangement, however, the most striking of all, perhaps, is that which opens within the texture of Gaskell's own story, as Sylvia's own narrative finally vanishes beneath the more powerful impress of posterity:

> Far away, over sea and land, over sunny sea again, great guns were booming on that 7th of May, 1799. The Mediterranean came up with a long roar on a beach glittering white with snowy sand, and the fragments of innumerable sea-shells, delicate and shining as porcelain. … One man left his fellows, and came running forwards, forwards in among the enemy's wounded, within range of their guns; he bent down over Kinraid; he seemed to understand without a word; he lifted him up, carrying him like a child; and with the vehement energy that is more from the force of will than the strength of body, he bore him back to within the shelter of the ravelin.[63]

Opening with a series of artificial images – of sand which is "snowy" and shells like fine china – the passage flouts its own literariness. The past which it portrays belongs no longer to that of living memory – that which Bakhtin terms "a *transi-*

tory past" – but rather to an epic totality, a Mediterranean temporality "far away" from Sylvia's own life: "distanced, finished and closed like a circle."[64] The press of the written and the authoritative, Gaskell seems to be arguing, has become too much for the real. Throughout the novel, a motif of learned and literate citation – the Monkshaven crowd as a "Greek chorus,"[65] flax-spinning as harp-playing[66] – has defined a perplexing gap between narrating subject and narrated object; and this final modulation into crashing biblical cadences, therefore – the Levantine landscape, the Passion-and-Ascension of Philip – merely completes the erasure of an unlettered Sylvia from her own story:

> But the memory of man fades away. A few old people can still tell you the tradition of the man who died in a cottage somewhere about this spot, – died of starvation while his wife lived in hard-hearted plenty not two good stone-throws away. This is the form into which popular feeling, and ignorance of the real facts, have moulded the story.[67]

But "facts," in the 1860s, depend upon testimony – sensation novels like Collins' *The Woman In White* have taught as much, at least[68] – and testimony depends upon writing. Shaping his actions around the story of Guy of Warwick from *Seven Champions of Christendom*, Philip steers the novel away from realism into the realm of the chivalric romance[69]; but equally, though, in his transformation into the horribly disfigured "bedesman of St Sepulchre," he might slip quite easily into the pages of Mrs. Henry Wood's contemporary sensation, *East Lynne*. Ultimately, therefore, the work garners narrative authority from an array of generic "pretexts,"[70] and these offer no language within which Sylvia's own story can be written. She might exist *historically* in its secondary sense, as an object of the past, but she cannot enter the literate world of historical testimony, and accordingly it is the narrative of 'Sylvia's lovers' – not that of the woman herself – which is inscribed into the collective memory. Perhaps, however, it should come as no surprise that it is the "memory of P.H" which the novel finally engraves into the Monkshaven landscape, since even in her first scene, the words of Gaskell's protagonist more resemble "a deal o'rubble" than "hewn stone."[71] Sylvia, unimpressed by "book-learning,"[72] seems fated to remain eternally buried. As the simple, prescient Kester puts it, "niver's a long word."[73]

For Gaskell, therefore, 'literature' denotes a haunted concept, always resting upon a shifting mass of the unread, the unwritten, the unremembered. Literacy encodes fact, rationality, history; beneath that, there is only the deep time of myth and hearsay; and beneath that, oblivion. But Dickens is somewhat less fatalistic. Whilst 'literacy,' he shows, constitutes little more than a synonym for pedantry and triviality, *literature* as a totality proves greater than the sum of its niggardly parts. Having demonstrated the pitfalls of an excessively zealous adherence to the *letter*, he simultaneously describes an alternative ethics of reading – a practice of reading as resurrection, as an animation of dead letters into something *inspired*, and alive. "No one who can read ever looks at a book, even unopened on a shelf, like one who cannot."[74] At its best, literature works a kind of re-enchantment upon the Veneering world of material things, just as the *articulation* of bones – with a significant homonymy[75] – reassembles waste matter into something which resembles life. "It's too late for me to begin shovelling and sifting at alphabeds and grammar-books," Mr. Boffin explains apologetically in an early chapter[76]; that's why, after all, he must engage his "literary man." But even in his act of enuncia-tion, however, Boffin already exemplifies this new process of creative confection, this new kind of literacy which has nothing at all to do with letters, and in his phonemic transformation of grammar into gardening he germinates a metaphor which will continue to bloom until the book's close.

"I wonder how it happens," muses Jenny Wren in her decidedly un-florid neighbourhood "that when I am work, work, working here, all alone in the sum-mer-time, I smell flowers."[77] Wonderful, yes, Dickens suggests; but inevitable, since nearly every bastion of goodness and imagination amidst the refuse of indus-trial London – the Boffin's "bower," Riah's "evergreens" between the chimneys, Bella's dream of a garlanded staircase[78] – makes its appearance in the pastoral mode. Literature, *Our Mutual Friend* suggests, is a kind of ecology, and language is always growing as it circulates, even when its self-proclaimed masters want it to hold still – Georgiana Podsnap becomes "Georgeute,"[79] an affidavit twists into an "Alfred David,"[80] and the metaphysical membrane between the "deceased" and the merely "diseased" proves unexpectedly permeable.[81] Whilst literacy kills, the novel affirms, *literature*, on the other hand, gives life: it is *mutual* in the word's root sense, as something shared; but also protean, changing, and therefore always liable to slip from its reader's grasp.[82] In the flagrantly ritualistic ending to the novel – Eugene's "baptism,"[83] the symbolic engagement of Jenny and Sloppy, the reader's own moral re-education – this mutual literariness finally loosens itself from the collar of literacy, proving, in line with Romantic orthodoxy,[84] some-thing more vivid and more profound than letters can spell out: a kind of house-hold Word.

But Gaskell salvages no such redemption from the sociolinguistic lexicon. Lit-erature, being tethered to literacy, can never really tell a full story, and so for Syl-via, language must remain a force which only obliterates, as the press of genre, authority and pre-text overwhelms the impulse to testify. This reading lesson, like that of *Our Mutual Friend*, is one which every reader of *Sylvia's Lovers* finds them-selves compelled to learn. Contemporary sensation novels marketed themselves upon their thrilling impressions on the reader – to some extent the terms 'impres-sion' and 'sensation' were interchangeable[85] – and by adopting the genre's narrative conventions, *Sylvia's Lovers* raises some insistently uncomfortable questions, since the very act of *impress*, as Gaskell has been at pains to demonstrate, is all about the restriction of liberty. "I could na stomach the thought o'being murdered i' my own language," says Daniel Robson at one point,[86] but his words assume an additional import by the end of the novel, which has shown how language contains an energy which cannot be possessed or coerced. Like Dickens' readers, therefore, Gaskell's audience is left wondering who, exactly, or rather *what*, is in control of the text. Literature, for both writers, and with varying degrees of success, strains to break through the barrier of the page, to shake off the quiescence of thousands of drawing rooms and hearths and salons, and come crashing from literacy into *life*:

> On Friday the Ninth of June in the present year, Mr. and Mrs. Boffin (in their manuscript dress of receiving Mr. and Mrs. Lammle at breakfast) were on the South-Eastern Railway with me, in a terribly destructive accident. When I had done what I could to help others, I climbed back into my carriage – nearly turned over a viaduct, and caught aslant upon the turn – to extricate the worthy couple. They were much soiled, but otherwise unhurt. The same happy result attended Miss Bella Wilfer on her wedding day, and Mr. Riderhood inspecting Bradley Headstone's red neckerchief as he lay asleep. I remember with devout thankfulness that I can never be much nearer parting company with my readers for ever than I was then, until there shall be written against my life, the two words with which I have this day closed this book: – THE END.[87]

If books can exist within books – if a work of literature can contain both the literate and the literary, and if it can school its audience in its own mode of discourse – then perhaps there are also books beyond books, greater books which both enclose and are enclosed by their own act of narration, and so *ad infinitum*: literature might be understood, then, as a kind of dressmaking, perhaps, for Rooshan dolls. For Dickens and Gaskell, this is the kind of giddy liberation which literature, as an ideal, can offer – a spiralling together of multiple planes of reality – and this is why a conception of literacy in purely social or instrumental terms must always, necessarily, miss the point. Though semantic kin, *literature* and *literacy* prove nonetheless imaginatively alien. That is why Sylvia's 'history,' lacking a language commensurate with its subject, must ultimately describe its own failure. That is why Dickens, equally, must jettison the literal in order to salvage the possibility of the meaningful. And that is why, of course, the most profound lesson of both novels inheres, quite simply, in the mutual, mutating, and endlessly mutable act of reading.

Notes

1. Raymond Williams, *Keywords: A Vocabulary of Culture and Society* (London: Fontana, 1976), 150-54.

2. See David Vincent, "Dickens's Reading Public," *Palgrave Advances in Charles Dickens Studies*, ed. John Bowen and Robert L. Patten (Basingstoke: Palgrave Macmillan, 2006), 177-78.

3. Hence, "hes nocht sufficient literatur to vndirstand the scripture" (1581); "He had probably more than common literature" (1780); "In many things he was grotesquely ignorant; he was a man of very small literature" (1880). All from "Oxford English Dictionary," in *OED Online*, ed. John Simpson and Edmund Weiner (Oxford Univ. Press, 1989).

4. Kathleen Tillotson, *Novels of the Eighteen-Forties* (Oxford: Oxford Univ. Press, 1956), 13-21.

5. Patrick Brantlinger, *The Reading Lesson: The Threat of Mass Literacy in Nineteenth-Century British Fiction* (Bloomington: Indiana Univ. Press, 1998), 3.

6. David Vincent, "The Progress of Literacy," *Victorian Studies*, 45 (2003): 413-14.

7. Vincent, "Dickens's Reading Public," 188.

8. Charles Dickens, *Our Mutual Friend*, ed. Michael Cotsell (Oxford: Oxford Univ. Press, 1998), 53.

9. John Hollingshead, "Mr. Charles Dickens as a Reader," *The Critic* (4 September 1874): 537, quoted in Malcolm Andrews, "Performing Character," in *Palgrave Advances in Charles Dickens Studies*, ed. John Bowen and Robert L. Patten (Basingstoke: Palgrave Macmillan, 2006), 83.

10. See Bradley Deane, *The Making of the Victorian Novelist: Anxieties of Authorship in the Mass Market* (New York: Routledge, 2003), 51-57.

11. On *Pickwick Papers*. Critic in *North American Review*, quoted in Deane, *The Making of the Victorian Novelist*, 28.

12. Dickens, *Our Mutual Friend*, 49-50.

13. Nancy Armstrong, *Desire and Domestic Fiction: A Political History of the Novel* (New York: Oxford Univ. Press, 1987), 8-9.

14. Elizabeth Gaskell, *Sylvia's Lovers*, ed. Andrew Sanders (Oxford: Oxford Univ. Press, 1982), 128.

15. Gaskell, *Sylvia's Lovers*, 92.

16. Gaskell, *Sylvia's Lovers*, 1.

17. Gaskell, *Sylvia's Lovers*, 68.

18. Gaskell, *Sylvia's Lovers*, 68.

19. Gaskell, *Sylvia's Lovers*, 1.

20. "Forms of Time and Chronotope in the Novel," in M M Bakhtin, *The Dialogic Imagination: Four Essays*, ed. Michael Holquist, trans. Michael Holquist and Caryl Emerson (Austin: Univ. of Texas Press, 1981), 250.

21. Gaskell, *Sylvia's Lovers*, 4-7.

22. Dickens, *Our Mutual Friend*, 1.

23. Dickens, *Our Mutual Friend*, 1. See Howard W. Fulweiler, "'A Dismal Swamp': Darwin, Design and Evolution in *Our Mutual Friend*," *Nineteenth-Century Literature*, 49 (1994): 50-74.

24. Dickens, *Our Mutual Friend*, 767.

25. For example, Richard D Altick, "Education, Print and Paper in *Our Mutual Friend*," in *Nineteenth-Century Literary Perspectives: Essays in Honor of Lionel Stevenson*, ed. Clyde de Ryals (Durham, NC: Duke Univ. Press, 1974): 237-54; Robert S Baker, "Imagination and Literacy in Dickens' *Our Mutual Friend*," *Criticism*, 18 (1976): 57-72; Stanley Friedman, "The Motif of Reading in *Our Mutual Friend*," *Nineteenth-Century Fiction*, 28 (1973): 38-61; Sharon Kubasak, "Reflexive Delight," *The Dickensian*, 90 (1994): 25-35; Patricia Marks, "Storytelling as Mimesis in *Our Mutual Friend*," *Dickens Quarterly*, 5 (1988): 23-30; Ruth Tross, "Dickens and the Crime of Literacy," *Dickens Quarterly*, 21 (2004): 235-45.

26. Dickens, *Our Mutual Friend*, 228.

27. Dickens, *Our Mutual Friend*, 198.

28. Dickens, *Our Mutual Friend*, 281.

29. Dickens, *Our Mutual Friend*, 811.

30. See, for example, Baker, "Imagination and Literacy in Dickens' 'Our Mutual Friend'"; Friedman, "The Motif of Reading in *Our Mutual Friend*," 60-61.

31. Robert L. Patten, "The Composition, Publication and Reception of *Our Mutual Friend*," (1998). Online at *Our Mutual Friend: The Scholarly Pages*, accessed 17 October 2006 <http://humwww.ucsc.edu/dickens/OMF/index.html>.

32. First published in *Household Words* (21 August 1858): 217-22. Wilkie Collins, *The Unknown Public*, accessed 20 October 2006 <http://www.web40571.clarahost.co.uk/wilkie/etext/sites.htm#Household%20Words>.

33. Gaskell, *Sylvia's Lovers*, 261.

34. George Eliot, *Felix Holt, the Radical*, ed. Lynda Mugglestone (London: Penguin, 1995), 311.

35. See generally Brantlinger, *The Reading Lesson: The Threat of Mass Literacy in Nineteenth-Century British Fiction*; Deane, *The Making of the Victorian Novelist*.

36. Lorna Huett, "Among the Unknown Public: *Household Words, All the Year Round*, and the Mass-Market Weekly Periodical in the Mid-Nineteenth Century," *Victorian Periodicals Review*, 38 (2005): 65.

37. Huett, "Among the Unknown Public," 71.

38. Dickens, *Our Mutual Friend*.

39. From *The Life of Charlotte Brontë*. Quoted in Deane, *The Making of the Victorian Novelist*, 115. Cf, however, the interpretation in Linda K. Hughes and Michael Lund, *Victorian Publishing and Mrs. Gaskell's Work* (Charlottesville, VA: Univ. Press of Virginia, 1999), 148.

40. See, for example, Deane, *The Making of the Victorian Novelist*, 113-16.

41. Gaskell, *Sylvia's Lovers*, 94.

42. Gaskell, *Sylvia's Lovers*, 40.

43. Gaskell, *Sylvia's Lovers*, 309.

44. Gaskell, *Sylvia's Lovers*, 421-22.

45. Gaskell, *Sylvia's Lovers*, 41-43.

46. Gaskell, *Sylvia's Lovers*, 6-7.

47. Elizabeth Gaskell to Charles Eliot Norton, c.1858, quoted in Tillotson, *Novels of the Eighteen-Forties*, 222-23.

48. Gaskell, *Sylvia's Lovers*, 94.

49. The title of Book 3, Chapter 12.

50. Dickens, *Our Mutual Friend*, 388.

51. Dickens, *Our Mutual Friend*, 128.

52. Dickens, *Our Mutual Friend*, 132-33.

53. Dickens, *Our Mutual Friend*, "Postscript: In lieu of Preface," 821.

54. Dickens, *Our Mutual Friend*, 479-85.

55. "Figure, Scheme, Trope" in Alex Preminger and T.V.F. Brogan, eds., *The New Princeton Encyclopedia of Poetry and Poetics* (Princeton, NJ: Princeton Univ. Press, 1993), 409-12.

56. Dickens, *Our Mutual Friend*, 567.

57. Dickens, *Our Mutual Friend*, 6.

58. Dickens, Our Mutual Friend, 542.

59. J. M. Rignall, "The Historical Double: *Waverly, Sylvia's Lovers, the Trumpet-Major*," *Essays in Criticism*, 34 (1984): 15.

60. The title of Book 4, Chapter 16, Dickens, *Our Mutual Friend* (Emphasis added).

61. See Gaskell's epigraph, from *In Memoriam*: "Oh for thy voice to soothe and bless! / What hope of answer, or redress? / Behind the veil! Behind the veil!"

62. Gaskell, *Sylvia's Lovers*, 377 (Emphasis added).

63. Gaskell, *Sylvia's Lovers*, 424-31.

64. "Epic and Novel," in Bakhtin, *The Dialogic Imagination*, 19. See also Rignall, "The Historical Double: *Waverly, Sylvia's Lovers, the Trumpet-Major*," 23.

65. Gaskell, *Sylvia's Lovers*, 29.

66. Gaskell, *Sylvia's Lovers*, 41.

67. Gaskell, *Sylvia's Lovers*, 502.

68. Brantlinger, *The Reading Lesson: The Threat of Mass Literacy in Nineteenth-Century British Fiction*, 146-47.

69. Gaskell, *Sylvia's Lovers*, 465. See Christine L. Krueger, "'Speaking Like a Woman': How to Have the Last Word on *Sylvia's Lovers*," in *Famous Last Words: Changes in Gender and Narrative Closure*, ed. Alison Booth (Charlottesville: Univ. Press of Virginia, 1993), 147-48.

70. See Hughes and Lund, *Victorian Publishing and Mrs. Gaskell's Work*, 51.

71. Gaskell, *Sylvia's Lovers*, 12.

72. Gaskell, *Sylvia's Lovers*, 94.

73. Gaskell, *Sylvia's Lovers*, 319.

74. Dickens, *Our Mutual Friend*, 18.

75. See Albert D. Hutter, "Dismemberment and Articulation in *Our Mutual Friend*," *Dickens Studies Annual*, 11 (1983): 135-75.

76. Dickens, *Our Mutual Friend*, 50.

77. Dickens, *Our Mutual Friend*, 239.

78. Other examples might include the "Judaical" garden planted by the owners of the paper-mill (522), Miss Peecher's wall-flowers (219) and Jenny's own "golden bower," loosened from her bonnet (438-39). See Garrett Stewart, "The 'Golden Bower' Of *Our Mutual Friend*," *ELH*, 40 (1973): 105-30.

79. Dickens, *Our Mutual Friend*, 279.

80. Dickens, *Our Mutual Friend*, 152.

81. Dickens, *Our Mutual Friend*, 50.

82. Nicholas Royle, "Our Mutual Friend," in *Dickens Refigured: Bodies, Desires and Other Histories*, ed. John Schad (Manchester: Manchester Univ. Press, 1996), 41.

83. Michael Peled Ginsburg, "The Case against Plot in *Bleak House* and *Our Mutual Friend*," *ELH*, 59 (1992): 190.

84. See Stewart, "The 'Golden Bower' Of *Our Mutual Friend*," 118.

85. Brantlinger, *The Reading Lesson: The Threat of Mass Literacy in Nineteenth-Century British Fiction*, 144.

86. Gaskell, *Sylvia's Lovers*, 38.

87. Dickens, "Postscript: In lieu of Preface," 822.

Popular Evolutionism:
Scientific, Legal, and Literary Discourse in Gaskell's *Wives and Daughters*

Phoebe Poon

Since the publication of Gillian Beer's *Darwin's Plots* in 1983, the discursive influence of Darwinian theory on nineteenth-century narrative has been "fertile ground for scholars of Victorian literature."[1] As Beer has argued, "In its imaginative consequences for science, literature, society and feeling, *The Origin of Species* is one of the most extraordinary examples of a work which included more than the maker of it at the time knew, despite all that he *did* know."[2] Once evolution became a popular discourse, it seemed to develop a life of its own, independent of its "maker's" control. To consider Darwin as the maker or "founding father" of evolution is inherently problematic because, although his work was largely responsible for embedding evolutionism in the Victorian consciousness, *Origin* itself was preceded by, and evolved conceptually from, the work of earlier theorists such as Charles Lyell, Jean-Baptiste Lamarck, and Robert Chambers.[3] More recently, Karen Boiko, and Leon Litvack's studies of Elizabeth Gaskell's *Wives and Daughters* (1866) have drawn attention to the methodological influence on Darwin of Georges Cuvier (1769-1832) and Geoffroy St.-Hilaire (1772-1844), two French naturalists who led scientific debate in the 1820s and 1830s on the comparative anatomy of species.[4] Evolution therefore had pre-Darwinian "origins," but its discursive "after-life" in the post-Darwinian context (from 1859 on) is particularly interesting because it allows not only Darwin, but also other writers from various fields of inquiry to be acknowledged as contributors to the development of a shared discourse.

In conventional methodology, the exchange of ideas between two fields of inquiry tends to be regarded as a kind of interdisciplinary cross-fertilisation, whereby a writer from one field is proven to have read the work of a writer from another field and vice versa, thus allowing a shared discourse to be deduced. For example, Darwin's reading of literary texts is complemented by novelists like Kingsley, Eliot, and Hardy reading Darwin's work. Yet both groups of writers were responding not only to each other's ideas, but also to a mainstream evolutionary discourse, which may have exerted a more powerful influence on their collective thinking than the act of reading itself, particularly after the publication of *Origin*. In order to illustrate the power of popular evolutionism, this essay considers Gaskell's *Wives and Daughters* not only as a response to Darwin's first book, but also suggests how her last novel can be seen to anticipate certain aspects of evolutionary theory that Darwin does not fully expound until he writes his second major work, *The Descent of Man, and Selection in Relation to Sex* (1871). Whereas Darwin privileges the concept of individual struggle in his early arguments about natural selection, his later arguments in *Descent* qualify the materialistic emphasis of *Origin* by considering social instincts and morality (highly evolved social instinct) as inheritable qualities that facilitate individual survival more readily than anti-social self-interest. Similarly, *Wives and Daughters* suggests that altruism – the virtue of acting for the good of others rather than self – is a more rewarding human quality than egotism. The conflict between egotism and altruism has attracted some critical attention in assessments of *Wives and Daughters*, and indeed, one might say that this conflict extends beyond the psychological experience of Gaskell's characters to encompass the experience of numerous protagonists in Victorian fiction.[5] As a post-Darwinian writer in relation to *Origin* but a pre-Darwinian in relation to *Descent*, Gaskell is uniquely positioned to promote self-sacrifice as an alternative form of behaviour to self-interest.

This essay also extends beyond a discussion of the "two-way" creative interaction between Gaskell and Darwin by considering the relevance of a *third* evolutionary thinker, Sir Henry Sumner Maine (1822-88), who was renowned in his lifetime as a jurist and legal historian, but was later recognised also for his contribution to the social sciences, particularly in the disciplines of sociology and anthropology. In his first and most famous book, *Ancient Law: Its Connection with the Early History of Society and its Relation to Modern Ideas* (1861), Maine presents his celebrated dictum that the "movement of progressive societies has hitherto been a movement *from Status to Contract.*"[6] Victorian readers interpreted Maine's status–contract thesis as a post-Darwinian theory of legal and social progress. Leslie Stephen writes: "Coming soon after the publication of Darwin's great book, which had made the theory of evolution a great force in natural philosophy, [*Ancient Law*] introduced a correlative method into the philosophy of institutions."[7] According to Frederick Pollock, one of Maine's greatest admirers, *Ancient Law* did "nothing less than create the natural history of law."[8] However, critics now agree that, although Maine integrated "popular" evolutionism into his arguments in order to appeal to a broad audience, he formulated the themes and ideas in *Ancient Law* long before the publication of *The Origin of Species*.[9] Like Gaskell's *Wives and Daughters*, Maine's work deserves to be read both as a pre-Darwinian *and* post-Darwinian text. The purpose of this essay is therefore to shift from a narrow conception of evolutionism as an exclusively Darwinian theory to a conception of it as a broad cultural discourse that crossed disciplinary boundaries, and shaped the thinking of Darwin, Gaskell, and Maine more profoundly than they or their contemporaries may have realised.

Science and Literature

Critical studies of *Wives and Daughters* tend to focus narrowly on Gaskell's exploration of Darwinian themes in *The Origin of Species*, neglecting Gaskell's contribution to the further development of those themes in literature before they received similar treatment in scientific analysis. In her chapter on *Wives and Daughters*, Hilary Schor suggests that the "scientific structure" of Darwin's "characteristically male system of thought … echoes and expands the 'fictional' structure of the novel, for it includes both history … and, in its widest form, the 'origin of species,' the entire evolutionary model."[10] Deirdre D'Albertis writes that "science and classification provide Gaskell with an ominously totalizing vision of social order that directly affects the shape and direction of her own narrative."[11] However, the science, the structure, or classificatory system that Gaskell presumably adopts from *The Origin of Species* is not the *only* science to be found in the novel. There is in fact only tentative evidence to suggest that Gaskell read *Origin*, and, as her knowledge of the "Cuvier–Geoffroy debates" suggests, it is more likely that she reached her own conclusions about evolution from reading books and periodical reviews of Darwinian theory than from any direct reading of Darwin's book itself.[12] From analysis of William Gaskell's borrowing record at Manchester's Portico Library (1850-65), Litvack concludes that Gaskell would have been "able to draw on a recognizable framework of scientific debate spanning the previous thirty years" by reading her husband's acquisitions of journals, "including the *Westminster*, *Quarterly*, and *Edinburgh*, along with *Blackwood's Edinburgh Magazine*, *Fraser's*, the *National Review*, the *Fortnightly Review*, the *British Quarterly Review*, and *Revue des Deux Mondes*."[13] Gaskell's encounter with Darwin's ideas through the writings of his supporters and detractors would have immersed her in a public discourse on evolution, which developed beyond Darwin's initiating work in *Origin*. The fact that Gaskell may never have read *Origin* has not stopped critics from saying that she expanded upon Darwinian themes in *Wives and Daughters*. Similarly, the fact that Gaskell was never able to read *The Descent of Man*, because she died before its publication, does not conceal her concern about the materialistic implications of natural selection (as theorised in *Origin*), which threatened "the concept of the [divinely implanted] immortal soul and hence the traditional foundations of morality."[14] As Mary Debrabant writes, "More than in previous works, Gaskell [in *Wives and Daughters*] poses complex moral and emotional problems, without the support of religious precepts. Instinctive selfishness is opposed to rational altruism, the latter often acquired with difficulty by fighting against one's true nature."[15] Before exploring the inner conflict between selfishness and altruism faced by the characters of *Wives and Daughters*, I shall first discuss the differences between the two Darwinian texts, *Origin* and *Descent*.

The Descent of Man is both a departure from and a sequel to *The Origin of Species*. Whereas "man is the determining absence in the argument of *The Origin of Species*," he is central to the argument of *The Descent of Man*, which, as the title suggests, traces man's kinship with lower forms of life and his gradual development into "the most dominant animal that has ever appeared on this earth."[16] However, the underlying theme of both Darwinian texts is the concept of natural selection, the process by which certain variations in the corporeal structure or behavioural instincts of an individual organism (human or non-human) are preserved as a means of increasing its ability to compete and adapt to changing environmental conditions. In *Origin*, Darwin emphasises the idea that only variations favourable to an organism's survival capability are inherited by its offspring and thus preserved. Natural selection therefore works for the welfare of the modified organism and its species, but not for the good of other species: "Natural selection cannot possibly produce any modification in any one species exclusively for the good of another species; though throughout nature one species incessantly takes advantage of, and profits by, the structures of another."[17] This statement is consistent with the notion that natural selection is essentially a "struggle for existence," which privileges the "survival of the fittest," while recognising that the extinction of weaker creatures is an unavoidable part of the evolutionary process. By focusing on the competition between individuals, Darwinian theory in *Origin* aligns itself with existing social discourses, such as *laissez faire* economics and Benthamite utilitarianism, which stress the pursuit of self-interest as the surest way to success in an industrial world, and which premises survival on individual competitiveness and adaptability, not on such qualities as sympathy and altruism.

However, Darwin defines natural selection as a "struggle" only in qualified terms, suggesting that it cannot "produce any modification in a species exclusively for the good of another species" and that species often depend on each other for their survival ("one species incessantly takes advantage of, and profits by, the structures of others"). He describes co-dependency as examples of "exquisite" and "beautiful co-adaptations," which can be seen "most plainly in the woodpecker and the mistletoe; and only a little less plainly in the humblest parasite which clings to the hairs of a quadruped or features of a bird; in the structure of the beetle which dives through the water; in the plumed seed which is wafted by the gentlest breeze" (*Origin*, 51). In his chapter on "Instinct," Darwin describes his observation of "aphides voluntarily yielding their sweet excretion to ants." Although he reiterates the belief that no "animal in the world performs an action for the exclusive good of another … species," he is clearly fascinated by the sight of two species cooperating with each other for mutual benefit – the aphid allowing its "extremely viscid" excretions to be removed conveniently by the ant, and the ant taking advantage of the aphid's sweet juice as food (*Origin*, 172).

In *Descent*, Darwin develops his study of co-dependency in his exploration of "social instincts" as the precursor to the development of "a moral sense or conscience."[18] Man is endowed with the strongest moral sense in the animal kingdom, a quality that Darwin admires as "the most noble of all the attributes of man, leading him without a moment's hesitation to risk his life for that of a fellow-creature" (*Descent*, 70). The concept of "sympathy," which is noticeably absent from *Origin*, is a term which recurs constantly in *Descent* and forms an integral part of the author's more expansive treatment of natural selection. In contrast to feelings of self-interest, sympathy describes the affinity between animals which induces them to aid and defend each other for the good of the whole community. Although acts of sympathy may be performed in order to gain approval or avoid disapproval of one's peers, such radical extension of sympathy as the risking of one's life to protect another is an act of altruism which would appear to contradict the principle of struggle, detailed in *Origin*. However, in *Descent*, Darwin believes that an individual's altruistic conduct results in the growth rather than the decline of the community to which that individual belonged, "for those communities, which included the greatest number of the most sympathetic members, would flourish best, and rear the greatest number of offspring" (*Descent*, 82). *Origin* is a work primarily of corporeality – the evolving body structure of organisms – but *Descent* considers morality to be as important to the survival of species.

Whereas "morality" is largely absent from Darwin's early evolutionary theory, it is central to Gaskell's narrative in *Wives and Daughters*. Like *The Descent of Man*, her novel is not narrowly focused on the display of self-interested, egotistical behaviour, but recognises that altruism plays a key role in natural selection, particularly in the family context when the interests of a community connected by blood ties may often overrule the interests of its individual members. Focusing on the figure of Roger Hamley, I shall consider him not primarily as the stereotypical Darwinian hero, whose survival is contingent on his "fitness" and competitive energy, but a caring son and brother, who embraces his familial responsibilities as much as his individual ambitions to succeed in a scientific career.

Roger's physical and intellectual vigour allows him to compete more readily in the Darwinian world than his languid, elder brother Osborne, who dies of a weak heart, or, as Debrabant suggests, is "weeded out" from society to make way for stronger, more self-reliant types like Roger.[19] Although he is privileged in terms of natural selection, Roger's domestic position is inferior to that of Osborne, who is given preferential treatment by their parents as the heir to the family estate. From boyhood, both Squire and Mrs. Hamley have admired Osborne for his gentlemanly beauty and poetic taste, qualities which are seen as superior to their younger son Roger's more awkward physique and fondness for "natural history." "He is a good, steady fellow, though, and gives us great satisfaction, but he is not likely to have such a brilliant career as Osborne," says Mr. Hamley, speaking for himself and his wife.[20] Although both parents prefer Osborne to Roger, they value their elder son for different reasons:

> In his father's eyes, Osborne was the representative of the ancient house of Hamley of Hamley, the future owner of the land which had been theirs for a thousand years. His mother clung to him because they two were cast in the same mould, both physically and mentally – because he bore her maiden name. (*WD*, 82-83)

The squire indulges Osborne because it is ancestral custom to show "feudal loyalty to the heir," but Mrs. Hamley worships her son simply because he has inherited all the qualities of his mother that she values in herself. However, parental expectations that Osborne's future will be brighter than that of his slower but steadier brother are unfulfilled, as Osborne almost fails to gain a degree in Classics, while Roger distinguishes himself by becoming Senior Wrangler and taking a Cambridge fellowship. Nevertheless Osborne retains his privileged status, particularly in the eyes of his mother, whose dying wish is to know news about Osborne, estranged from his father and banished from the house for the financial debts he accumulated at university. Despite his immense disappointment with Osborne, Mr. Hamley continues to view his elder son as the heir to his estate and never considers installing Roger in place of his first-born.

Whereas natural selection appears to favour Roger over Osborne, the prevailing system of inheritance places Osborne above Roger in the domestic and social hierarchy. Mr. Hamley may revere the practice of male primogeniture more than his wife, but the privileging of Osborne, particularly after his failures at university, is mainly due to the family's continued adherence to the legal custom of settling the family property exclusively on the eldest son.[21] According to D'Albertis, this inheritance system is a form of "institutional" selection, which is in "perpetual tension" with natural selection.[22] However, it can also be seen as a form of non-natural selection because primogeniture is not a matter of parental choice, but a rule that prescribes a fixed order of succession from male to female, and eldest to youngest, without considering which child might be best qualified to shoulder the responsibility of inheritance. Like the law of natural selection, the law of non-natural selection "is subject to randomness and chance," but also privileges individuals on the basis of their family status, not on their ability to compete or adapt in the world of evolutionary struggle.[23]

In the second edition of *The Descent of Man*, Darwin acknowledges that the inheritance of property interferes with natural selection, as it gives "the children of the rich ... an advantage over the poor in the race for success, independently of bodily or mental superiority" (*Descent*, 502).[24] He suggests that, although "the inheritance of property by itself is very far from an evil ..., primogeniture with entailed estates is a more direct evil" because it results in "the continued preservation of the same line of descent, without any selection" (*Descent*, 502-503). According to Darwin, the establishment of a single lineage for an indefinite period of time would be detrimental to the long-term biological survival of landed families like the Hamleys, who are especially vulnerable to extinction because of Mr. Hamley's inferior ability to adapt to an industrial economy.

Wives and Daughters is therefore a novel about both biological inheritance and legal inheritance. From an evolutionary point of view, Roger's ability to bring revitalised bourgeois energy to the family line would make him a better heir than Osborne, but from a legal perspective, he is unable to compete against his elder brother for inheritance of the patrimonial estate. Instead of challenging the system of non-natural selection that excludes him from landed society, Roger accepts that he will have to find a means of earning his own living without relying on support from his family. His response to the conditions of his birth is to negotiate a social status for himself outside the inheritance system through his scientific research. By contributing an article on the latest evolutionist debates, he draws the notice of the local peer, which leads to his invitation by Lord Hollingford to the Towers for a meeting with the French naturalist Geoffroy St-Hilaire, an actual historical figure. Thus Roger acquires opportunities denied Osborne to mix with the social elite, a situation that angers his father, who feels that his elder son as "the representative of the Hamleys" (*WD*, 302) ought to have been invited.

Although he is disadvantaged by his family's inheritance practices, Roger is instrumental to the perpetuation of primogeniture and entailment. Before embarking on his scientific voyage to collect specimens in Africa, he insists that Osborne marry his wife again in order to ensure the legality of the marriage and the lawful birth of his child in wedlock. By safeguarding the family patrimony for his brother's child, Roger not only prevents the estate from passing to their distant relations, "the Irish Hamleys" (*WD*, 352), but he also prevents the estate from passing to himself by acting "as conservative steward of family property."[25] His sense of responsibility for the family continues after Osborne's death, as he immediately returns home "to put his brother's child at once into his rightful and legal place" as the next heir of Hamley (*WD*, 590). Roger's acts in facilitating the law of primogeniture and allowing himself to be supplanted appear contradictory to the Darwinian laws of competition, and certainly to the conduct Mrs. Gibson expects of a person with any regard for the importance of social rank and material interest. "I should have thought that it was a little mortifying to Roger – who must naturally have looked upon himself as his brother's heir – to find a little interloping child, half French, half English, stepping in his shoes!" (*WD*, 638), she says. But while Roger may appear generous and more responsible than necessary to a family which has undervalued his merits, he may also be acting in his own interest by avoiding the burden of inheritance.

Roger's ability to acknowledge the needs of his family whilst pursuing his own career suggests that a careful balance needs to be struck between self-interest and self-sacrifice for individuals to achieve their personal ambitions without being unduly tied to family obligations. While reserving enough money for himself to pursue his career, Roger gives "the rest of his income" (*WD*, 347) to Osborne, who depends on his father for income until he can inherit the estate, a difficult financial situation for a man secretly married to a wife whom he needs to support. Roger's concern for Osborne's welfare has a paternal character, and Osborne's reliance on his brother reverses the family situation that primogeniture was meant to create, that is, the eldest son's provision for his younger siblings. Although Roger never complains about his financial sacrifices, Osborne, whom the narrator suggests is "too indolent to keep an unassisted conscience" (*WD*, 353), has few qualms about spending his brother's money on expensive trips to visit his wife, Aimée. Roger's generosity also extends to his father, to whom he promises money to finance the drainage works on the estate through money left to him by his maternal grandfather. In all his deeds, Roger shows that he is noble, but not self-abasing, as he never sacrifices his own ambitions for the sake of Osborne and Squire Hamley. In fact, he resolves to leave Hamley Hall and live in London with Molly Gibson, his wife-to-be, after completing the second leg of his scientific travels, determined to seek independence from the archaic ties which have bound generations of Hamleys to their land. Roger's instinct for self-preservation is clearly as strong as his altruistic tendencies.

Another character who shares Roger's family position is Lady Harriet, the youngest daughter of the earl and countess of Cumnor, who is also excluded from inheriting the family estate due to its entailment to her elder brother Lord Hollingford. In fact Harriet is excluded not only on the basis of age, but also of gender. However, like Roger, she does not allow the circumstances of her birth to dictate her future. Other characters attribute her disinclination to marriage to unhappy past experiences with men like the land-agent Robert Preston, but Harriet's indifference also suggests that she deliberately refuses to marry a wealthy peer as a means of maintaining her status and independence. Since Harriet is an aristocrat's daughter and not the son of a declining squire, she is more financially secure than Roger, but still faces significant pressure from her family in which she remains a dependant. This situation does not discourage her from applying the limited resources and social influence she possesses to help others. On discovering false rumours about Molly Gibson's involvement in a clandestine affair with Mr. Preston, Harriet takes her friend around the town and leaves her card (with Molly's name attached to her own) under the door of the Misses Browning, using her aristocratic prestige to silence Hollingford's gossips. Although this act of kindness is unappreciated by the uncomprehending Molly, Harriet's determination to see her young charge avoid the social stigma that she experienced (and indeed, continues to experience) as a consequence of being associated with Preston reveals a maternal concern for Molly's reputation which resembles Roger's nurturing attitude to his father and brother.

Thus years before Darwin addressed the criticism of his detractors in *The Descent of Man* that his evolutionary theory was based entirely on a materialistic model of human behaviour, Gaskell in *Wives and Daughters* demonstrated that the moral virtues of individuals like Roger and Harriet may be as active as their instincts of self-preservation. While her novel can be read as a literary precursor to Darwin's *Descent*, the notion that Gaskell simply "imitat[es] Darwinian investigative methodology in the fashioning of its plots" understates her achievement of pushing "Darwin's plots" into uncharted territory.[26] Darwin may have provided new biological inflections to words and concepts such as "kinship," "inheritance," and "succession," but Gaskell's novel is also attuned to the meaning of those concepts in legal terms, as her sophisticated awareness of English land law suggests. In *Wives and Daughters*, she reveals not only the shared qualities of scientific and literary discourse, but also the similarities between scientific and legal discourse.

Science, Literature, and Law

The 1860s is renowned as a post-Darwinian era, but the decade was also the "golden age" of Victorian jurisprudence, marked by the publication of a wide variety of works, including John Austin's *The Province of Jurisprudence Determined* (second edn., 1861), Henry Sumner Maine's *Ancient Law* (1861), James Fitzjames Stephen's *General View of the Criminal Law* (1863) and Walter Bagehot's *The English Constitution* (1867). Compared with Darwin, these writers may appear relatively obscure, but they were widely read in their day by academics, lawyers, informed laymen, and other non-legal writers, and were responsible for "elevating the profile of legal ideas" in their culture.[27] Unlike his predecessor Austin, whose *The Province of Jurisprudence Determined* took almost thirty years after its first publication to receive posthumous acclaim, Maine's *Ancient Law* was an immediate success, and although it may not have achieved the same popularity as *The Origin of Species*, its subsequent publication in ten editions from 1861 to 1884 underscores its appeal to a broad audience.

The reason for Maine's appeal is attributed by both contemporary and modern critics to the clarity, wit, and attractiveness of the writer's prose, a quality which may be related to the fact that *Ancient Law* began as a series of Middle Temple lectures delivered in the 1850s. Like Darwin who appeals to scientists and non-scientists, Maine makes complex legal principles accessible to non-lawyers. In his review of "English Jurisprudence" in the *Edinburgh*, Fitzjames Stephen draws attention to Maine's "extreme condensation of ... style, and the profusion of matter brought in by way of illustration, always in a thoroughly pertinent and most interesting manner."[28] A similar observation might be made with respect to Darwin's style. Maine and Darwin also resemble each other in theoretical terms. In *Ancient Law*, Maine advocates the idea that jurisprudence is not simply an abstract philosophy or science of law, but an evolutionary discourse which has to be understood with reference to its social and historical context. Early reviewers did not consider Maine an evolutionist; in their opinion, he was a legal theorist who developed the so-called "Historical Method" or the study of "the simplest social forms in a state as near as possible to their rudimentary condition."[29] Only after his death did his contemporaries suggest retrospectively that he applied evolutionary theory to the study of law.[30] Some modern commentators now qualify Pollock's claim that Maine did "nothing less than create the natural history of law" by arguing that, although "the author of Ancient Law [is] an evolutionist of a general sort ... there is not much direct evidence of any contribution of evolutionary biology to [Maine's] innovative and individualistic approach."[31] The debate about whether Maine is an evolutionist turns upon his most influential statement that "the movement of progressive societies has hitherto been a movement from Status to Contract" (*AL*, 165). "Unquestionably Maine's most famous dictum, it is also arguably one of his more ambiguous ones," writes John Burrow.[32]

Before arriving at this dictum, Maine provides the following analysis:

> The movement of progressive societies has been uniform in one respect. Through all its course it has been distinguished by the gradual dissolution of family depend-

ency and the growth of individual obligation in its place. The individual is steadily substituted for the Family, as the unit of which civil laws take account. ... Nor is it difficult to see what is the tie between man and man which replaces by degrees those forms of reciprocity in rights and duties which have their origin in the Family. It is Contract. Starting, as from one terminus of history, from a condition of society in which all the relations of Persons are summed up in the relations of Family, we seem to have steadily moved towards a phase of social order in which all these relations arise from the free agreement of Individuals. (*AL* 163)

By "Status," Maine describes a primitive conception of rights and duties as governed prescriptively by the status of individuals in their family, and by "Contract," a modern arrangement giving legal recognition to rights and duties that "arise from the free agreement of Individuals." Read in the context of the 1860s, Maine seems to propose a genuine theory of legal or social evolution. He refers to the "movement" from status to contract as a "law of progress," and uses gradualist language reminiscent of Darwin to describe the nature of progress (*AL*, 164). From a present perspective, his status-contract thesis is difficult to justify as an accurate prediction of future social relations. While "contract" was becoming an increasingly important part of relationships formed at arm's length in the Victorian era, family-based status has not been replaced universally by contract even today. Maine's inaccuracy, however, does not diminish the impact of his thesis, just as the discrediting of some Darwinian generalisations by later scientific discovery fails to diminish the suggestive brilliance of *The Origin of Species* or *The Descent of Man*. In the following analysis, I shall consider Gaskell's *Wives and Daughters* as a novel that explores the transition of Victorian society from a fixed hierarchical system of rank or *status* to a more flexible system of *contract*, where individuals freely negotiate, rather than inherit, their rights and duties. Although there is no evidence that Gaskell read Maine, it is likely that she read reviews of *Ancient Law* in the *Westminster*, the *Edinburgh*, the *Quarterly*, or the *Saturday Reviews*.[33] And as in the case of Darwin, the act of reading does not impose limits on an investigation into how Maine may have exerted an indirect but still potent influence on a literary author such as Gaskell.

The character in *Wives and Daughters* who exemplifies the movement from status to contract is Roger Hamley. Through his Cambridge fellowship money and his contract with the board of trustees that pays the expenses of his scientific travels, Roger is able to perform his duty to the family, whilst pursuing a profession that will grant him freedom from future family obligations. After ensuring the safety of his brother's patrimony, Roger's decision to leave Hamley Hall is an announcement of his intention to keep his family at arm's length in order to determine his own rights and duties. In contrast, Osborne, restricted by his status as the eldest son, is unable to negotiate a place for himself outside the realm of his "status"-based duties. The entail on the Hamley property makes Osborne's relationship with his father a contractual one, but it does not grant him or the squire any individual freedom of contract. Paradoxically, the entail, which seems to be a contract conferring exclusive rights of succession to Osborne, is in fact a mode of inheritance that regresses to the practice of joint ownership between father and son that Maine identified as a primitive custom (*AL*, 221). By giving a mere life interest to the father and an income charged on the land to the son, the entail operates against the modern principle of absolute private ownership: Mr. Hamley is not a real "owner" as such, but a "tenant for life", and Osborne is his "tenant in tail," both holding the land jointly as "trustee[s] for the transmission of the patrimony to ensuing generations."[34] Bound by his status as a life tenant, Hamley is unwilling to sell "any part of the estate which he inherited from his father," and also hindered from selling it even if he wished to do so (*WD*, 248).[35] "By continuing the primitive manners and customs of his forefathers" (*WD*, 41), Mr. Hamley struggles to find adequate income to drain and make improvements on the land, and despite his pride in ancient family lineage, he is clearly annoyed by the ancestral restrictions on his ability to exploit the full value of his property. "I'm so tied up I can't cut down a stick more [of timber], and that's a 'consequence' of having the property so deucedly well settled," he complains to Roger (*WD*, 348).Instead of facilitating a movement from status to contract, the English land laws are a disincentive to progress.

In contrast to Maine's rather utilitarian view that the substitution of familial by contractual obligations is progressive and therefore desirable, Gaskell demonstrates that entailment is a regressive practice, which weakens and even prevents, familial relations. The squire's treatment of Osborne more as an heir than a son represses the parental and filial affection that otherwise would have been the basis of their relationship. On several occasions, the narrator intimates that reconciliation between the squire and his son may have been possible if one of them willingly put aside his acrimony towards the other and made an attempt at reconciliation. Osborne's return from exile to Hamley Hall after his mother's death marks one of these occasions:

> Osborne did not stand up when his father entered. He was too much exhausted, too much oppressed by his feelings, and also too much estranged by his father's angry, suspicious letters. If he had come forwards with any manifestation of feeling at this moment, everything might have been different. But he waited for his father to see him before he uttered a word. All that the squire said when his eye fell upon him at last was, –
> 'You here, sir!'

And, breaking off in the directions he was giving to Molly, he abruptly left the room. All the time his heart was yearning after his first-born; but mutual pride kept them asunder. (*WD*, 205)

Waiting for his son to make the first move, the squire makes reconciliation difficult because he blames Osborne for bringing on Mrs. Hamley's illness and death, accuses him of speculating on his future inheritance, and tries to force him to marry according to paternal dictate. While Osborne may be judged too harshly, the narrator suggests that if he "had met [his father] half-way, it is probable that the old bond between father and son might have been renewed" (*WD*, 429). Instead Osborne invalid habits, indifference to the management of the estate, and secret marriage to a woman below his rank (without parental knowledge or consent), reveal a lack of responsibility to filial obligations that further estranges him from Mr. Hamley. However, Osborne's behaviour is not surprising for a young man, struggling to fulfil the demands of his status, and whose only proven act of disobedience is to "claim the right of choosing [a] wife for [him]self, subject to no man's interference" (*WD*, 432). Unlike Roger, whose inferior status grants him a certain degree of autonomy, Osborne is held to account for his actions more strictly than his younger brother, and is further restricted by his duty as an heir from determining his own personal, professional and marital rights.

Roger is, of course, not the only character who enjoys the benefits of contractual freedom in the novel. Mr. Gibson's work as a country doctor gives him greater financial independence than his neighbour Squire Hamley, who has a higher status than Gibson but less self-sufficiency. The relationship between doctor and patient is a contractual one: Gibson has a professional duty to visit his patients whenever they call on him, regardless of the inconvenience; his patients in turn are obligated to pay for his services. However, Gibson's experience also demonstrates that "status" is often as important as "contract," even in professional circumstances. Initially brought in to Hollingford as a partner of the established local doctor Mr. Hall, Gibson has to gain gradually the trust of the local townspeople, who need to be assured by Mr. Hall that the newcomer's "professional qualifications were as high as his moral character, and that both were far above the average" (*WD*, 30). Even the assurances of his partner do not secure Gibson's position in the mind of the community until he is invited to dine with the Cumnor family at the Towers. As his practice grows, the doctor interprets this as evidence of the community's trust in "his greater skill and experience," and is unaware that his increased business is largely due to Hollingford's knowledge of his connection with the Cumnors. Gibson realises, however, that the Cumnors exploit their aristocratic position by deliberately neglecting to pay his fees fully because they consider the honour of attending at their house as sufficient payment for the doctor's services. "So the prestige was tacitly sold and paid for; but neither buyer nor seller defined the nature of the bargain," says the narrator (*WD*, 321). Gibson therefore relies more on his status *vis-à-vis* the local peerage than his explicit contractual relations with the non-aristocratic patients who supply him with regular income to support Molly and himself.

Gibson faithfully discharges his duty by going on his daily rounds, but he is also anxious to fulfil a broader social responsibility to transfer his medical knowledge to the next generation. He develops the habit of taking "two 'pupils' ... to learn [the] business," despite the fact that he finds them "terribly in the way" (*WD*, 33). The presence of these male students in his home becomes increasingly awkward, particularly when Gibson becomes aware of Molly's attractiveness to one of his apprentices, Mr. Coxe. In order to find a chaperone for his daughter, Gibson decides to remarry, but he views his second marriage with Mrs. Hyacinth Clare Kirkpatrick in the same way as he views his professional relationships, that is, as a contract. Thus Maine's status-contract thesis is relevant not only to Gibson's public life, but also to his personal, marital affairs.

The most significant feature of Gibson and Clare's spousal relationship is that they marry with separate agendas, but implicitly reach a mutual agreement. Clare's main motive for marrying the doctor is to avoid having to earn her living as a governess. Her immediate reaction to his proposal is "a wonderful relief ... that she need not struggle any more for a livelihood" (*WD*, 106). According to D'Albertis, she "regards her second marriage strictly as an economic proposition," or in other words, as a contract, made on the terms that Mr. Gibson will provide her with a home and financial security in exchange for her guardianship of Molly.[36] However, while she readily accepts the idea of becoming a wife cared for by her husband, she is uncommitted to discharging the concomitant duties of a stepmother that Gibson expects her to perform as part of the bargain. In his proposal of marriage, Gibson makes it clear that his marital agenda is not so much to find a second wife as it is to find a new mother for Molly. "Could you love [Molly] as your daughter? Will you try?" he asks Clare. "Will you give me the right of introducing you to her as her future mother; as my wife?" (*WD*, 106). By accepting him, Clare deceptively misleads Gibson into believing that she agrees to follow his agenda, concealing her real intention, which is to gain only spousal privileges, not maternal duties.

As soon as they are married, Clare takes advantage of her new status as mistress of the household by misusing her authority over the servants, thus forcing Molly's beloved nurse Betty and the cook to give notice. She plays the part of an impartial stepmother by refurnishing Molly's room, consigning her stepdaughter's "cherished relics of her mother's maiden-days" ... to the lumber room (*WD*, 183), but disparages Molly in front of the Hamley brothers in order to give her own daughter Cynthia a better chance than her stepsister of snaring one of them in the marriage market. Wilfully unaware of his wife's activities, Gibson congratulates himself on having "obtained an unexceptionable chaperone, if not a tender mother, for his little girl; a skilful manager of his formerly disorderly household; a woman who was graceful and pleasant to look at for the head of his table" (*WD*, 321), ignoring the fact that he makes concessions to his wife in the interest of fostering kinship and family harmony, while Clare serves only her own interest in usurping her husband's domestic authority.

Whereas Gibson honours his side of the bargain, Clare not only fails to fulfil her obligations, but breaks the sanctity of the marriage contract by engaging in dishonourable behaviour that poses a threat to her husband's personal and professional integrity. Eavesdropping on a private conversation between her husband and Dr Nicholls, she learns about Osborne's potentially fatal heart condition, and acts on this knowledge by changing her attitude to Roger, whom she perceives would inherit his father's estate on Osborne's death, and manoeuvring him into an engagement with her daughter Cynthia. Clare's behaviour confronts Gibson with "the fact that the wife he had chosen had a very different standard of conduct to that which he had upheld all his life, and had hoped to have seen inculcated in his daughter" (*WD*, 386). Gibson's reaction to Clare (a nervous sensitivity "to his wife's failings," a "dry and sarcastic" manner and a refusal to reinstate her "in his good graces") suggests that her behaviour towards Roger is considered a breach of their marriage contract (*WD*, 410-401). Although Gibson's moral position is understandable, his marital disappointments stem from an early misconception that his wife had considered herself bound to a contract when the reality is that Clare simply moves from one status to another, from governess to wife.

Conclusion

By considering *Wives and Daughters* in light of both scientific and legal discourse, we can appreciate the extent to which discursive interaction is not simply a two-way exchange of ideas, but a multi-disciplinary creative process in Gaskell, Darwin and Maine are as much the products of popular evolutionism as they are the creators. *Wives and Daughters* has long been regarded as a post-Darwinian text, and its author portrayed as reaching the most "pro-Darwinian" stage in her career. But Gaskell's views on mid-nineteenth-century science may be more complex than we may think, and her ability to broaden the discourse of natural selection to consider not only egotistical, but also the virtue of altruistic behaviour suggests that she was, in many ways, ahead of her time. That she wrote during a time when the extrapolation and application of Darwin's evolutionary biology to the social realm was common practice does not diminish our sense of her achievement. If Gaskell's contribution to scientific discourse has not been fully appreciated, then her contribution to legal discourse has been undervalued even more profoundly. The novel features an "inheritance plot" and a "marriage plot" that incorporates two evolutionary narratives, one biological, and the other legal.

Notes

1. Karen Boiko, "Reading and (Re)writing Class: Elizabeth Gaskell's *Wives and Daughters*," *Victorian Literature and Culture,* 33 (2005): 88.

2. Gillian Beer, *Darwin's Plots: Evolutionary Narrative in Darwin, George Eliot and Nineteenth-Century Fiction* (London: Routledge, 1983), 4.

3. Beer, *Darwin's Plots*, 5, 14. From the third edition on (1861), Darwin prefaced *Origin* with "An Historical Sketch of the Progress of Opinion on the Origin of Species." Responding to criticism that he had insufficiently acknowledged the work of his predecessors, he added the phrase "Previously to the Publication of the First Edition of this Work" to the sixth edition (1872). See Beer, Introduction, *The Origin of Species (1859), by Charles Darwin* (Oxford: Oxford Univ. Press, 1996), ix.

4. Boiko, 85-106; Leon Litvack, "Outposts of Empire: Scientific Discovery and Colonial Displacement in Gaskell's *Wives and Daughters*," *The Review of English Studies*, n.s., 55.222 (2004): 727-58.

5. My analysis of "egotism" and "altruism" is partly inspired by brief allusions to these terms in Mary Debrabant, "Birds, Bees and Darwinian Survival Strategies," *Gaskell Society Journal*, 16 (2002): 17, 26; and Jenny Uglow, *Elizabeth Gaskell: A Habit of Stories* (London: Faber, 1993), 586-87. More detailed discussion is provided by Julia M. Wright, "'Growing Pains': Representing the Romantic in Gaskell's *Wives and Daughters*," *Nervous Reactions: Victorian Recollections of Romanticism*, ed. Joel Faflak and Julia M. Wright (Albany, NY: SUNY Press, 2004), 163-85. However, only Debrabant reads egotism and altruism with reference to Darwinian discourse. Uglow focuses on the "conflict of self-interest and altruism in relation to money" (587). Wright identifies egotism as a Romantic "discourse of sensibility" that opposes self-sacrifice, a Victorian discourse stressing the importance of individual duty to society.

6. Henry Sumner Maine, *Ancient Law: Its Connection with the Early History of Society and its Relation to Modern Ideas* (1861), Introduction and notes by Sir Frederick Pollock (Gloucester, Mass.: Peter Smith, 1970), 165.

7. Leslie Stephen, "Sir Henry James Sumner Maine (1822-88)," *Dictionary of National Biography*, volume 35, ed. Sidney Lee (London: Smith, Elder & Co., 1893), 346.

8. Frederick Pollock, "Sir Henry Maine as a Jurist," *Edinburgh Review,* 178 (July 1893): 104.

9. According to J. W. Burrow, "the substance of *Ancient Law* had existed in the form of lectures since 1853 and probably earlier." Burrow, *Evolution and Society: A Study in Victorian Social Theory* (Cambridge: Cambridge Univ. Press, 1968), 142-43. R. C. J. Cocks suggests that "the ideas which appear in *Ancient Law* may ... have been in his mind by the late 1840s and have been subject to further development in the course of the lectures he gave in London during the next decade." Cocks, *Sir Henry Maine: A Study of Victorian Jurisprudence* (Cambridge: Cambridge Univ. Press, 1988), 29. See also Cocks, *Biography*, eds. H. C. G. Matthew and Brian Harrison (Oxford: Oxford Univ. Press, 2004), par. 3, 6. Accessed 7 Dec. 2006 <http://www.oxforddnb.com/view/article/17808>. Cf. George Feaver, *From Status to Contract: A Biography of Sir Henry Maine, 1822-1888* (London: Longmans, 1969).

10. Hilary Schor, *Scheherezade in the Marketplace: Elizabeth Gaskell and the Victorian Novel* (New York: Oxford Univ. Press, 1992), 183-84.

11. Deirdre D'Albertis, *Dissembling Fictions: Elizabeth Gaskell and the Victorian Social Text* (New York: St. Martin's Press, 1997), 140.

12. Charles Eliot Norton wrote to Gaskell in 1859: "At any rate I wait to be convinced that I am nothing but a modified fish. You I fancy have not read the book." (Jane Whitehill, ed. *Letters of Mrs. Gaskell and Charles Eliot Norton 1855-65* [London: Oxford Univ. Press, 1932], 43). "Norton's conjecture," as Debrabant suggests, "remains open to discussion" (14).

13. Litvack, 741.

14. Peter J. Bowler, *Charles Darwin: The Man and His Influence* (Cambridge: Cambridge Univ. Press, 1996), 177.

15. Debrabant, 26.

16. Beer, *Darwin's Plots*, 58; Charles Darwin, *The Descent of Man, and Selection in Relation to Sex* (1871), second edn., *The Works of Charles Darwin*, volume 21, eds. Paul H. Barrett and R. B. Freeman (London: Pickering, 1989), 136. Subsequent references to this book will be placed in parentheses in the main text. They will take the following form: *Descent*, 136.

17. Charles Darwin, *The Origin of Species* (1859), second edn, ed. Gillian Beer (Oxford: Oxford Univ. Press, 1996), 163. Subsequent references to this book will be placed in parentheses in the main text. They will take the following form: *Origin*, 163.

18. Charles Darwin, *The Descent of Man, and Selection in Relation to Sex* (1871), second edn, *The Works of Charles Darwin*, volume 21, eds. Paul H. Barrett and R. B. Freeman (London: Pickering, 1989), 71.

19. Debrabant, 17.

20. Elizabeth Gaskell, *Wives and Daughters* (1866), introduction and notes by Pam Morris (London: Penguin,2003), 66. Subsequent references will be placed in the main text in the following form: *WD*, 66.

21. According to the legal historian A.W.B. Simpson, "Since the abolition of military tenure in 1660, primogeniture was purely optional, applying only in the event of intestacy." Simpson, *A History of the Land Law*, second edn (Oxford: Clarendon Press, 1986), 284. However, the practice of primogeniture continued to be adopted in the mid- to late-nineteenth century, especially by the English peerage and gentry as a means of keeping their estates intact and undivided. Primogeniture was not abolished until 1925.

22. D'Albertis, 142.

23. D'Albertis 143.

24. In the first edition, Darwin's perspective on the issue of inheritance focuses more on racial than biological implications, as he writes: "In all civilised countries man accumulates property and bequeaths it to his children. So that the children in the same country do not by any means start fair in the race for success. But this is far from an unmixed evil" (*The Descent of Man, and Selection in Relation to Sex*, first edn [London: John Murray, 1871], 169).

25. D'Albertis, 143.

26. D'Albertis, 138.

27. Kieran Dolin, *Fiction and the Law: Legal Discourse in Victorian and Modernist Literature* (Cambridge: Cambridge Univ. Press, 1999), 37.

28. James Fitzjames Stephen, "English jurisprudence," *Edinburgh Review*, 114 (Oct. 1861): 478.

29. *Ancient Law*, 115. Subsequent references to Maine's *Ancient Law* will be placed in parentheses in the main text. They will take the following form: *AL*, 115.

30. Pollock, 104.

31.   Pollock, 104; George Feaver, "The Victorian Values of Sir Henry Maine," *The Victorian Achievement of Sir Henry Maine: A Centennial Reappraisal*, ed. Alan Diamond (Cambridge: Cambridge Univ. Press, 1991), 42.

32.   John Burrow, "Henry Maine and mid-Victorian Ideas of Progress," *The Victorian Achievement of Sir Henry Maine*, ed. Diamond, 55.

33.   See Frederic Harrison's review of *Ancient Law* in the *Westminster Review*, 19 (19 April 1861): 457-77; see also Fitzjames Stephen's above-mentioned article, "English Jurisprudence," in the *Edinburgh Review*, and M. Bernard's "Maine's *Ancient Law*," *Quarterly Review*, 110 (July 1861): 114-38.

34.   Lawrence Stone and Jeanne C. Fawtier Stone, *An Open Elite? England, 1540-1880* (Oxford: Clarendon Press, 1984), 73.

35.   Before the passage of the Settled Land Act 1882, a life tenant could not alter the terms of entailment except by Private Act of Parliament. The process of making a petition to parliament was difficult and expensive, which explains why Mr. Hamley does not even contemplate the idea of breaking the entail. See Simpson, 285.

36.   D'Albertis, 149.

213

Index